D1617065

The
Swedish
Texans

THE TEXIANS AND THE TEXANS

A series dealing with the many peoples who have contributed to the history and heritage of Texas. Now in print:

Pamphlets—*The Afro-American Texans, The Anglo-American Texans, The Belgian Texans, The Chinese Texans, The Czech Texans, The German Texans, The Greek Texans, The Indian Texans, The Italian Texans, The Jewish Texans, The Lebanese Texans and the Syrian Texans, The Mexican Texans, Los Tejanos Mexicanos* (in Spanish), *The Norwegian Texans, The Spanish Texans,* and *The Swiss Texans.*

Books—*The Danish Texans, The English Texans, The German Texans, The Irish Texans, The Japanese Texans, The Polish Texans, The Swedish Texans,* and *The Wendish Texans.*

The
Swedish
Texans

Larry E. Scott

Library of Congress Cataloging-in-Publication Data
Scott, Larry E., 1947-
 The Swedish Texans / Larry E. Scott. — 1st ed.
  p. cm. — (The Texians and the Texans)
 Includes bibliographical references.
 ISBN 0-86701-042-8. — ISBN 0-86701-044-4 (pbk.)
 1. Swedish Americans—Texas—History. 2. Texas—History.
 I. Title. II. Series.
 F395.S23S44 1990   89-16656
 976.4'004397—dc20   CIP

The Swedish Texans
by Larry E. Scott
First Edition

John R. McGiffert, Executive Director

Production Staff: Sandra Hodsdon Carr, Jim Cosgrove, Dwight
  Engstrom, David Haynes, Tom Shelton; Alice Sackett, indexer

This publication was made possible by grants from the
Texas Swedish Cultural Foundation, SVEA of Texas, Linnéas
of Texas, the Gulf Coast Scandinavian Club, and the Houston
Endowment, Inc.

Printed in the United States of America

Contents

Introduction

Swedish immigration to Texas began in 1848 as a result of the efforts of one man, Swen Magnus Swenson, who had himself emigrated from Sweden to the United States in 1836. Swenson had become a wealthy man in the ten years following his arrival in Texas, primarily from shrewd land purchases and revenue from his cotton plantation in Fort Bend County. In 1844 he had been joined by his uncle, Swante Palm, who helped him in his increasingly prosperous business ventures. Palm was the first Swede to immigrate to America with Texas as his specific goal.

Swenson was a friend of General Sam Houston, who encouraged the Swede to send back to his homeland for more Swedish immigrants to settle the vast and sparsely inhabited interior of Texas. Swenson did just as Houston had suggested, returning to Sweden in 1847 to recruit families from his home parish of Barkeryd in northern Småland. That first year only his sister accompanied him back to Texas, but the following year a group of 25 people, related to one another or to Swenson or Swante Palm either by birth or marriage, became the first group of Swedes to repeat the journey Palm had made a few years earlier.

Initially they joined Swenson in Fort Bend County, but he soon sold his plantation (and its attendant slaves) and moved to a large sheep and cattle ranch east of Austin, which he named "Govalle" after a dialectal Swedish phrase roughly translatable as "good grazing." Govalle became Swenson's home for over

Swen Magnus Swenson

a decade, during which time it was also the first home newly arriving Swedish immigrants would know in the New World. Swenson and his uncle arranged passage for the Swedish families from Småland, and they, in turn, worked for Swenson in Texas to pay off the price of the ticket. Most of the early immigrants also bought land from Swenson—he owned some 100,000 acres in and around the Austin area—and settled down to farm cotton.

The city of Austin thus became the home of the earliest and largest concentrations of Swedes in Texas. North of Austin, in Williamson County, some of the first settlers bought land from Swenson along Brushy Creek and formed the nucleus of what eventually became several contiguous rural colonies: Brushy Creek, Palm Valley, Hutto, Jonah, Taylor, and Round Rock. On the blackland prairie in northeast Travis County Swedes began to settle after the end of the Civil War, establishing the colonies of New Sweden, Manor, Kimbro, Manda, and Lund. All these areas were almost exclusively devoted to cotton production, a crop which was, of course, quite unfamiliar to Europeans but to which they quickly adapted.

Swedes settled in Central Texas for a variety of reasons. First, many of them had to work off their passage on the Swenson lands in and around Austin. Second, they tended to buy land in areas already settled by fellow Swedes whom they had known back home in Småland. Finally, many of them were given favorable prices for land by Swenson, who wanted to attract as many of his countrymen to Texas as possible. Even though only about 150 immigrants had made the voyage to Texas before the outbreak of the Civil War, they were located in key agricultural areas of Travis and Williamson counties. When immigration to Texas resumed on a larger scale in the late 1860's, these "target" or "magnet" colonies which could attract Swedish immigrants in larger numbers were already well established.

Swedes were neither the first nor the largest group of Europeans to settle in Texas in the years following the Texas Revolution. Indeed, even before 1836 Irish colonists had been granted land in Refugio and San Patricio counties. Germans—more than 3,000 of them—had bought enormous tracts of land in Gillespie, Comal, and Kendall counties before 1850. A tiny contingent of Norwegians had settled in Norse in Bosque County; several Wendish, Czech, and Italian families had moved into Fayette County; and there were French settlers in Medina and Dallas counties. There were also Englishmen in northeast Texas, creating the basis for some of the great cattle empires of the 1880's and 1890's. Thus the very modest Swedish immigration of the prewar period should not be seen in isolation. The experience of the Swedish Texans parallels that of almost every other ethnic group on the Texas frontier. Their efforts in America were expended on three fronts: to survive, adapt, and succeed. Survival meant the literal struggle for shelter, food, and safety, an ordeal that proved too daunting for more than a few. Adaptation meant the task of learning the language, mores, habits, and skills of the new country and incorporating them as quickly as possible into their European frames of reference. And success—real economic achievement, as landowners and ultimately as persons of quality, the equals of native-born Americans—was their dearest dream.

But survival, adaptation, and success were not to be perceived in wholly American terms. Preservation of ethnic identity became particularly important among the smaller groups such as the Norwegians, Swedes, or Wends. Maintenance of community identity was initially not as difficult in the tightly knit but far-flung colonies on the prairies: there, the ethnic tendency to cluster with fellow countrymen aided their sense of community identity. More difficult to preserve were the customs, rituals, traditions, and folk-ways of the European homeland and, most importantly, its language. To keep these alive, something more than just a community was needed—and so developed the unique institutions generated by each ethnic group. Supreme among them were the ethnic churches. No other institution secular or profane did more to create a sense of self and identity in America, nor did any other institution do as much to carry the values of the immigrants down through the generations. Finally, as the principal bearers of immigrant culture, the churches were also responsible for the maintenance and nurture of the ethnic languages until the day came that each group, now thoroughly assimilated or "Americanized," felt that it was quite capable of doing without that now-embarrassing relic of grandfather's and grandmother's European roots.

Picnic for members of the Philippi Swedish Evangelical Lutheran Church of El Campo, late 1890's

Churches, clubs, newspapers, athletic teams, fraternal lodges, pioneer societies, historical chapters, bands, choirs, and literary societies—these were part and parcel of ethnic life in Texas during the last hundred years. Swedes, like other Europeans, were forced to adjust to a new language, a new lifestyle, new crops, and a new climate. As their numbers increased, they founded new colonies the length and breadth of the state, from Stockholm near

Brownsville to Olivia on Matagorda Bay to Ericksdahl in North Texas. By the 1890's the sense of a Texas Swedish community had become statewide instead of being limited to Central Texas. At its peak in 1918, 80 years after S.M. Swenson's arrival in Texas, the population of the first- and second-generation Swedish Texans—the Swedish-born parents and their American-born off-spring—numbered more than 11,000. In absolute figures, Texas ranked 26 among the 48 states in numbers of Swedish inhabitants.

This is their story.

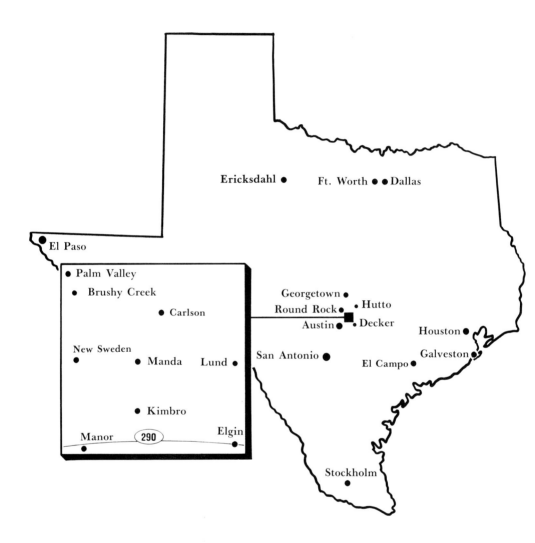

Ericksdahl ●   Ft. Worth ● ●Dallas

● El Paso

● Palm Valley

● Brushy Creek

● Carlson

Georgetown ●
Round Rock ● ● Hutto
Austin ● ■ ● Decker

Houston ●

New Sweden
● ● Manda Lund ●

San Antonio ●

El Campo ●

Galveston ●

● Kimbro

Manor ⬭290 Elgin
● ●

Stockholm
●

1

Texas in the 1850's

"A Land Most Suitable for Europeans"

The Republic of Texas, in which several thousand Swedes were eventually to settle, was a largely empty frontier territory where Indians were still a serious threat to settlement and where the discontent fostered by the revolution was still seething. The population had more than doubled between 1831 and 1836 (from 20,000 to 52,000), and it grew even more rapidly in the decade that preceded annexation. Europeans were arriving in ever-larger numbers, especially from Germany, and it was to the German colonies of Central Texas in 1853 that a Swedish writer of great distinction made his way.

He was impoverished and exhausted, and he desperately sought employment as a journalist among the Germans of New Braunfels. His name was Carl Jonas Love Almquist, and, until his hasty departure from Sweden under a cloud of ignominy and suspicion (he was accused of forgery and attempting to poison a moneylender), he was one of the most brilliant Swedish novelists, poets, essayists, and social theorists of his day. His early career had been decidedly "Romantic," but a few years before he was forced to flee Sweden, in a novel hailed as "the first novel of women's liberation ever written," he pursued a revolutionary new, realistic style.

But his abrupt flight from Sweden and subsequent wanderings in exile had sadly reduced him, and by the time he arrived in New Braunfels he was nearly a broken man. Almquist's

7

Carl Almquist

idea in fleeing to America had been to resume his literary career among Swedish Americans and to inform the reading public in Sweden about the cultural attainments of countrymen in the vanguard of the pioneers engaged in taming a new land.

Unfortunately for Almquist, he arrived too early to be able to write for Swedes in America — the first real "national" Swedish-American newspaper, *Hemlandet,* would not be founded until 1855 — so he sought out the German Americans. Writing pseudonymously for the *Neu-Braunfelser Zeitung,* he found in Texas the home he sought, even if it was only a temporary one.[1] His natural curiosity led him to explore the area of German settlement around New Braunfels and Fredericksburg, but he wandered far afield, traveling to the San Jacinto Battlefield, north into Comanche country, and south to Galveston.

Almquist was a careful and keen observer. Perhaps his own words serve best to describe the Texas that Swedes would soon be settling in larger and larger numbers. (The quaint English and its spelling are Almquist's own):[2]

The first view of the Texas coast affords nothing of interest, no picturesque and splendid Sceneries, no magnificent chain of Mountains, no remarkable point, which could attract the attention of the observer, or where he could repose his eye with joy, or immerge in the pleasure of delightful contemplation. The landscape all over is very low (scarcely 2-4 feet above the Waterline), the shore is bare; you will see no Wood, and very little marks of human industry. . . . The whole country . . . is a vast Prairie, with some small and sparse Groves of life-oak, chestnut, pine and willow. . . .[A]ll around [we saw] nothing but an immense plain of grass and all over us the vast firmament, adorned with millions of Stars, forming brilliant and for the most part in Europe unknown or unseen Constellations. The night was delightful, the air being refreshed and cooled by pleasant breezes. . . . The land on the other side of Victoria grows handsomer, the region seems by degrees to ascend, the fertile soil abound with flowers and trees of majestic size and often fantastical forms, being overgrown with spanish moss, and resembling Giants, with grey arms, dark faces, and threatening aspect. . . . in the first summer, before the herbs wither and fade by the hot burning Sunbeams [the land is very agreeable]. Texas is no Tabel-land in the proper sense of that word. It can geologically be divided in three Regions. The whole country along the Mexican Gulph seems formerly to have been overflowed, the Ocean in earlier times probably approaching the Rocky Mountains or at least the Sierra Guadalupe, on the eastern side of the Continent. In that period all Texas was the property of Neptune,

9

who afterwards withdrew his empires, removed his waves, and made the World a present of this new land.

The second or middle part of Texas commences by Austin, Bastrap and the old Nacogdoches-road. The country in that region is a kind of rolling land on alluvial bottom. The lower Texas, and some Countys of the south Boundary, and Sabine River, which divides Texas from Louisiana and Arkansas, you will find a great number of big Rivers, all discharging their currents in the Gulph, viz. Nueces, Guadalupe, Colorado, Brazos, Trinity and Neches. Their banks are settled and cultivated, they afford plenty of good water and abundance of woods, Cypress, Cedar, Walnut, Life-oak, Pine, Fig, Mulberry, Shadowtrees, etc.; but between them you will see nothing but immense Prairieland, almost bared from wood and without water excepting in some sparsed, artificial Wells. . . .

The third part of Upper Texas is mountaneous, hilly and woody, fertile in the Valleys and conceiling mineral, inexplored riches in abundance. The last year (1852) massy Gold was rumored to have been found by San Saba, Llano, Pedernales and elsewhere in Gillespie and Travis Counties; but the report was nothing but Humbug; and the disappointed Gold-diggers went home again, discontented, but glad to have saved themselves from the Indian Tomahawk and the arrows of the Comanches.

The Texas that Almquist saw, and to which more than 5,000 of his fellow Swedes would ultimately immigrate, was a land of enormous potential, waiting for enterprising hands to till the soil, tame the rivers, and build the cities. It is typical of Almquist's star-crossed life that he left Texas in 1855, after S.M. Swenson was comfortably established in Austin and where he surely would have been received with kindness by Swante Palm, who knew Almquist's early works well. But he left Texas without even hearing of the small Swedish colony that had been established in Travis County. Nor had he realized, on a trip through Småland just a year before his departure from Sweden in 1851, that people from one of the parishes he found most pleasant — Barkeryd Parish near Nässjö — would precede him to Texas, the land of his early exile. An unintentional immigrant, Almquist died in Bremen, Germany, in 1866, without ever seeing Sweden again.[3]

Another Swedish writer, a native of Småland, provided readers with a different view of Texas almost exactly contemporaneous with Almquist's. Unlike Almquist, however, Johan Bolin of Växjö had never seen the land he described in *En beskrifning öfver Nord-Amerikas Förenta staterna* (1853), nor did he want to. His guidebook was intended for potential emigrants, but he himself was never a victim of "America fever." The cruel ironies of Almquist's life were compounded by the fact that no one was ever to read Almquist's eyewitness account of the geography of Texas, while thousands read Bolin's, which was culled exclusively from secondary sources. Yet even though Bolin had never been to America, his descriptions of its topography, crops, climate, and customs were fairly accurate. His section on Texas must have sounded almost unbelievably exotic to a Swede reading of its flora for the first time:

> [In Texas one finds] melons, watermelons, pineapples, cucumbers, sweet potatoes, yams, potatoes, several kinds of cabbages, radishes, asparagus, peas, lettuce, parsley, spinach, artichokes, edible thistles, celery, purslane, wild strawberries, cayenne peppers, tomatoes, of which one wild variety, orchards of peach trees, figs, pomegranates, plums, mulberry trees, apricots, cherries, gooseberries, grapes, lemons, oranges, tamarinds, wild purslane, nut and almond trees, Spanish mulberry trees, black raspberries, wild cherries, wild plums, dwarf chestnuts, olive, hickory, black walnut, pecan, persimmon, cactus, cactus figs, magnolia, sassafras, Chinaberry, Seville oranges, wild vanilla, myrtle, laurel, locust, elderberry, sumac, many types of medicinal plants, many kinds of oak, cedar, cypress, ash, sugar maples, . . . linden, cottonwood, yew, balsam, wild stock, red

sage, purple thistle, begonias, clover, white anemones, as well as a myriad of other trees, bushes, flowers, plants, herbs, etc., both familiar and unknown.[4]

If readers found the plants of Texas unusual, how much more unusual must its fauna have seemed when they read Johan Bolin's account:

[There are] cattle, horses, sheep, goats, mules, donkeys, . . . turkeys, guinea-fowl, geese, ducks, black and gray bears, American hart, fallow, moose, mountain sheep, antelope, bison, wild boar, jaguars, leopards, wildcats, muskrat, weasel, beaver, river otter, rabbit, hare, raccoon, opossum, squirrel, jackrabbit, silver fox, prairie dog and wolf.[5]

Bolin points out that flocks of huge wild turkeys commonly numbered over 400 birds, in addition to flocks of ducks, swans, and pelicans. There were sandpipers, plovers, grouse, partridges, songbirds of all kinds "equal to the nightingale," goldfinches, birds of paradise, larks, hummingbirds, woodpeckers, kingfishers, eagles, falcons and hawks, owls, and many other species of birds. The streams and rivers teemed with turtles, alligators, chameleons, crayfish, oysters, mussels, redfish, trout, eel, carp, and catfish. Bolin does not mention tarantulas and scorpions, only wild bees, flies, and grasshoppers, but he does add, rather ominously, that Texas has "an abundance of snakes in all uninhabited areas." The deadliest of these was considered the water moccasin, followed by "two or three" species of rattlesnake, the corn snake, and the cottonmouth.

All in all, Texas was not going to be much like Småland!

12

2

The Great Migration
Swedish Immigration to the New World

Between 1840 and 1915 nearly 1,250,000 Swedes left their homeland to resettle in the New World, nearly a quarter of the entire population. Only Ireland and Norway sent a higher percentage of their sons and daughters to America than did Sweden.[1] These Swedes were part of the greatest mass movement in history; during the course of what came to be called the "Great Migration," more than 30 million Europeans left their ancestral homelands to start their lives over and raise families in America, families that would know the old homeland only through the eyes of their parents. They came, to fill a vast and empty continent and to seek their fortunes in the new American republic.

They came from every part of every country, every social class, and every occupation. They were young and old, rich and poor, men and women, young zealots and radical atheists, social reactionaries and outright anarchists, industrious skinflints and ne'er-do-wells. The tired, poor, huddled masses of whom Emma Lazarus wrote contained not a few scoundrels, thieves, cutthroats, and con artists, but they all added to the seething admixture that was becoming America. And certain patterns emerge if one examines the course of the Great Migration over more than a century.

For example, the early pioneers tended to emigrate as families: their children would be American, but the Old World would be forever in the hearts of those born there. And, while they represented every social class and profession, most of the emigrants belonged to the huge class of rural poor, created by the rapid increase in population after 1800. Young people were seldom married before coming to the U.S.—they came seeking spouses and usually found them. Young men initially outnumbered the women, but by the turn of the century an equilibrium was attained as young girls, too, rushed to reach America to find jobs as maids in the houses of the well-to-do, while their male counterparts found employment in the mines, forests, factories, and shops of the rapidly growing nation. They were all hungry, often land-hungry; they were clever and resourceful, flexible and open-minded, ready and eager to provide a full day's work for a day's pay.[2]

Swedes and Native Americans

The first groups to arrive in America came by sailing vessels to New York or Boston, the traditional ports of immigrant entry since colonial days. The voyage was long, dangerous, and very expensive; few could afford even the one-way journey unless and until they had sold virtually everything they owned in Europe. Return journeys, of course, were out of the question, except for the very few who made money soon after arriving in America.

With the end of the Civil War and the unprecedented Homestead Act of 1862, land in almost limitless amounts was made available to anyone hardworking enough to be willing to improve it. But even President Abraham Lincoln could not have foreseen how many millions of land-hungry Europeans would flock to American shores in search of their dreams, then embodied in 160 acres of virgin land, free to anyone who could settle, tame, and improve it. And after the farmers came the other folks: the watchmakers, carpenters, cobblers, cooks, farmhands, gamblers, ministers, editors, poets, boilermakers, hoopers, cartwrights, bartenders, wranglers, and hostlers. The dreamers, drifters, and entrepreneurs who raced to California in 1849 to search for gold (among them not a few Swedes) were but the vanguard of a vaster horde who took cheap passage on the fast new steamers of the 1870's, 1880's, and 1890's to seek a different (and stabler) kind of wealth in America's teeming new cities.

Failed Experiment:
New Sweden on the Delaware, 1638-1655

Actually, Swedish immigrants had been on American soil long before the Civil War, the Homestead Act, the California Gold Rush, or even the American Revolution. The first concerted effort to establish a Swedish presence in North America had been made in 1638. In March of that year two small Swedish merchant vessels, the *Fogel Grip* and the *Kalmar Nyckel,* dropped anchor in the Delaware River near the site of what is today Wilmington. The colonists on board—probably less than 100—quickly began to fortify the land which they bought from the Indians and which they named Nya Sverige, New Sweden. During the following decade and a half, with very little help from home, forts were erected along the Delaware River to protect the tiny colony from incursions by the Indians and the neighboring Dutch and English colonists. Eventually New Sweden claimed an area slightly larger than the present state of Delaware, but it was a very sparsely settled area, almost impossible to defend. Only a few resupply ships ever sailed from Sweden, and a critical shortage of manpower remained the colony's most pressing problem. Despite effective leadership by such colorful figures as the 300-pound governor, Johan Printz (called "Big Belly" by the Indians), and Johan Rising, encroachment from without and disease and disenchantment from within took their toll among the colonists. Finally, in 1654, the colony had to capitulate to the forces of New Holland under Peter Stuyvesant, and New Sweden ceased to exist as an independent entity.

But a few lasting accomplishments were achieved by the ill-fated venture. Swedish clergymen had accompanied the colonists in 1638, and there was never a time that the colony was completely without spiritual leadership, even when Sweden seemed determined to deny it all secular sustenance. For over a century after the colony's demise, moreover, the State Church of Sweden continued to send Lutheran pastors to the Delaware Valley to minister to the needs of their far-off flocks. These dispersed colonists in turn founded small Swedish Lutheran congregations which were served by the visiting clergy. Some of them, such as the so-called "Old Swedes' Churches," Gloria Dei in Philadelphia and Holy Trinity in Wilmington, are still alive and among the oldest Protestant churches in America. A few place-names and sites have also survived from the New Sweden period, such as Fort Christina on the Delaware (now a national park) and Johan Rising's stone house. But perhaps the most important thing that New Sweden accomplished was to bring word of America to Sweden for the first time. The glowing reports of Governors Printz and Rising were full of enthusiastic descriptions of the excellence of the American soil, the abundant game, and the immensity of the wilderness. It is not an exaggeration to say that the "America fever" which swept Sweden in the 19th century had its origins in the 17th: America had been described as the land of promise and opportunity, and that description lingered and did not go away.[3]

Swedish Settlements in the Early 19th Century

The factors that "pulled" emigrants toward America were as various as those which "pushed" them from their homeland. The golden promise of America as the land of opportunity, of virtually limitless free land, and of a new kind of classless society, proved to be a mighty magnet indeed, whose power increased with each glowing letter home describing the bounty of the New World. Relief from the cycle of drought and famine became especially important after major crop failures in southern Sweden in the late 1860's. The Homestead Act (1862) was the key to the vast prairie lands of the Midwest: a farmer intending to become a citizen could claim 160 acres and improve it by cultivation.

Though few in number, the earliest emigrants in the vanguard of the Great Migration of the 19th century—those of the 1830's and '40's—were extremely important. The colonies which they founded acted as focal points for subsequent in-migration, "pulling" the newly arrived Europeans to specific points on the advancing frontier. In the case of Swedish immigrants, early colonies were successfully established in Wisconsin (Pine Lake, 1841), Iowa (New Sweden, 1845), and Illinois (Bishop Hill, 1846). (Minnesota, that most Swedish of states, had, surprisingly, no substantial Swedish settlements until 1850.) At that time the frontier lay roughly along the Illinois-Indiana border and moved steadily westward year by year. Thus early Swedish settlement took place west of that imaginary line, and future settlement "leapfrogged" over the more established areas where available land had already become scarce and expensive. Finally, toward the end of the pioneering period, Swedish immigrants turned west and south in relatively large numbers to settle in the Dakotas, Nebraska, Kansas—and even Texas, though none of these states would ever be "Swedish" in the way that Illinois, Minnesota, Wisconsin, and Iowa were later to become.

Not all Swedish provinces (*landskap*) sent equal numbers of emigrants across the Atlantic—some, like Skåne or the northern provinces of Lappland, sent hardly any emigrants, either because the soil was rich enough to support all the people who cultivated it or because distances were too great and information about America too sparse. From others, such as Småland, Halland, and Värmland, disproportionately large numbers of emigrants set out for America, leaving behind poor soil, tiny farms, and deep forests for the promise of the New World.[4]

Politics and Economics in Sweden: The "Push" Factors behind Emigration

For some potential emigrants, the increasingly rigid class system at home pushed them over the sea to the democratic freedom promised and practiced in America. The turbulent era of the Napoleonic Wars in Scandinavia ended in 1809 when Sweden lost a disastrous war with Imperial Russia. The result was the loss of Finland, for more than 500 years the eastern half of the Swedish-Finnish empire. The political repercussions of Prince Metternich's despotic and reactionary imperialism were also felt in Sweden: King Gustaf IV Adolf was forced to abdicate in favor of his senile and childless uncle, who reigned briefly as Carl XIII.

A new dynasty began in 1810 with the election of Jean Baptiste Bernadotte, one of Napoleon's former field marshals, as crown prince and heir apparent to the Swedish throne. Shortly thereafter, through a series of energetic diplomatic maneuvers (including the threat of military intervention), Bernadotte forced Norway into an alliance with Sweden to compensate for the loss of Finland. Irksome as the union between Sweden and Norway was, it lasted for nearly 100 years before finally being dissolved in 1905. Bernadotte ascended the throne of Norway-Sweden as King Carl XIV Johan in 1818 and ruled, with increasing despotism, for nearly 30 years.

A liberal trend began in the Riksdag (Parliament) toward the end of the 1840's in reaction to worsening economic conditions, especially among the poorer rural classes. A generation of peace, intense cultivation of the potato, and improved hygiene had produced an unprecedented growth in the population. Certain sweeping reforms were initiated—compulsory universal education to be provided through the State Church (the first such law in the world) and a bill prohibiting the division of a farmstead (*hemman*) more than four times (i.e., into sixteenths) to prevent farms from becoming too small to support a family even at the subsistence level. But the first of these measures languished for years until it became practical to initiate it, and the second had the effect of creating a huge, landless rural proletariat almost overnight, since it prohibited the younger children of a farm-owner (*hemmansägare*) from inheriting any land at all. This large class of hired hands, maids, sharecroppers, and laborers provided the first and most willing volunteers for the voyage to the promised land of America.

A lesser but still disturbingly reactionary trend was that demonstrated by the Swedish Evangelical Lutheran Church, since 1542 the official (and only) Church of the Kingdom of Sweden. To maintain control over the doctrine of the faith and to ensure compliance with Luther's Catechism and other matters of dogma, the Church (the Second Estate of the Riksdag) promulgated the so-called Konventikelplakatet, or Conventicle Acts, in 1789 in the last years of the reign of King Gustaf III. This law was to prevent the gathering of any group with the intention of receiving the sacrament of Holy Communion from the hands of anyone not an ordained minister of the Church of Sweden.

In the early part of the 19th century, a number of dissenting groups had broken away from the State Church as a wave of pietism swept down across Scandinavia. In Norway the followers of H.N. Hauge and converts to Quakerism had left for America as early as 1825. In Sweden the pietistic movement found a natural leader in Erik Jansson, whose messianic visions of a perfectionist, evangelical Christianity led him to burn all books other than the Bible and to proclaim himself an incarnation of deity. Jansson was arrested on numerous occasions for violating the Conventicle Acts. Finally, in 1844, he proclaimed that he would found a New Jerusalem in America and, like Moses, would lead his people out of religious bondage to freedom in the New World. This was the beginning of Jansson's and his followers' ("Erikjansare" in Swedish, "Janssonists" in English) long and arduous journey across the Atlantic to their new homes in Bishop Hill, Illinois, the communistic religious colony on the prairie that marked the apex of emigration from Sweden for religious reasons.

But there were other religious winds blowing in Sweden as well. Both Baptists and Methodists had made inroads in Sweden in the 1840's, and more and more people were defying the Conventicle Acts to join them. At last, in 1858, the laws prohibiting adherence to any Christian religious group other

19

than the State Church were rescinded, and ministers of other faiths were free to preach and to convert—one of the last barriers to full participatory democracy in Sweden had fallen.

America was still largely unknown to the Swedish common people, but the first immigrants rapidly changed that. From Bishop Hill, Pine Lake, and New Sweden, the new colonists began sending letters filled with details about life in the New World to newspapers and friends in Sweden. These letters were often first passed from hand to hand; some of the published *Amerikabrev* ("America letters") were translated from French, German, or Norwegian. Guidebooks, specially written for the prospective emigrant, often by people who had never set foot in

Bild 69. Gata i San Antonio.

Commerce Street, San Antonio. From Nord-Amerika, *published in Stockholm, 1880.*

the New World, contained precise and occasionally even accurate descriptions of America— its geography, climate, transportation systems, crops, land prices, and sometimes even a glossary of English words with their Swedish equivalents and approximate pronunciations. One of these guidebooks was published in Christiania—now Oslo—Norway, by a Norwegian who had settled in Henderson County, Texas. Johan Reinert Reiersen's *Veiviser for Norske Emigranter til de forenede nordamerikanske Stater og Texas,* 1844, (Pathfinder for Norwegian Emigrants to the United North American States and Texas), was the first guidebook written *by* a Scandinavian *for* Scandinavians intending to immigrate to the Republic (soon to be State) of Texas. So popular were these guidebooks that by 1880 most rural Swedes knew more about Chicago (then the second-largest ''Swedish'' city in the world, with more Swedes than Göteborg) than about Stockholm, their national capital.[5]

These, then, were some of the reasons Swedes joined other Europeans in the search for a new home in a vast, new land in the West, where there was soil to be tilled and freedom from economic, political, and spiritual tyranny. Each emigrant, of course, had his or her own secret and personal reason for setting out on the long and dangerous voyage: a cuff from a sadistic master, perhaps, or escape from an unhappy love affair, or desire for fame and fortune in a new land where money was rumored to grow on trees, or the wish to raise children in a home that would never again know want. All of this America offered them, and they came, and they came, and they kept on coming.

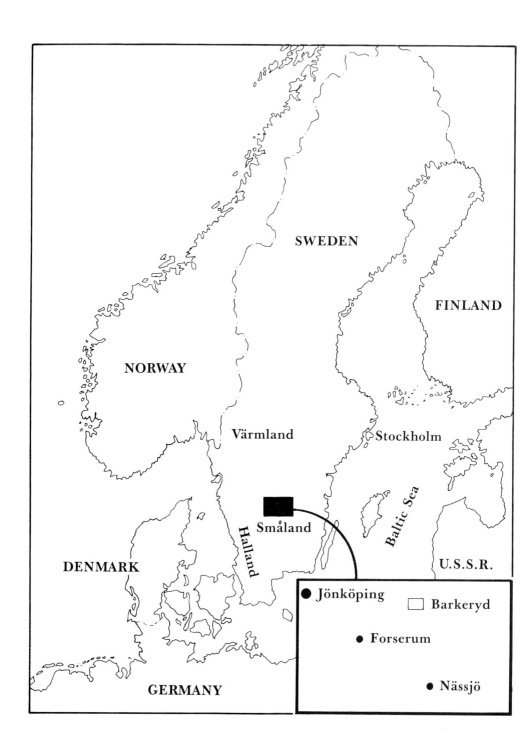

SWEDEN

FINLAND

NORWAY

Värmland

Stockholm

Baltic Sea

Småland

Halland

DENMARK

U.S.S.R.

● Jönköping   ☐ Barkeryd

● Forserum

● Nässjö

GERMANY

3

Småland to Govalle

No area in Sweden sent more of her sons and daughters to Texas than the parish of Barkeryd, Jönköpings *län*, or County, in the northern part of the province of Småland. What was this homeland like that so many left behind for the distant plains of Texas?

The area is not unlike the parts of southern Småland known to readers of Vilhelm Moberg's epic tetralogy, *The Emigrants.* [1] Thick forests of pine and fir conceal the rocky, thin soil on which countless generations toiled and planted. Numerous hills and small lakes — one-seventh of the land area — break up the forests, adding variety to the landscape but isolating the small farms from one another. The church was the single and central community gathering place, the heart and focal point for the whole community.

Barkeryd is first mentioned in surviving records dating back to 1301, indicating that the parish was even then well established. In the 16th century its church bells were hidden from the tax collectors of King Gustaf I Wasa (who wished to melt them down into cannon), and they have never been relocated. The medieval church — familiar to the early emigrants — was torn down in 1844, and a new church (designed along the lines suggested by Bishop Esaias Tegnér of Växjö and therefore commonly if somewhat irreverently known as a "Tegnérlada," or "Tegnér barn") was erected on the site. Its high spire, wide, bright nave,

Church and cemetery, Barkeryd, Sweden, 1980's

simple interior, and large, clear, arched windows make it an excellent house of worship but one sadly lacking in the irreplaceable quaintness that the ancient church must have possessed.[2]

The church in Barkeryd has been the center of parish life and culture for nearly 800 years. Long before 1674, when the church was rebuilt in stone, a wooden "stave" church had stood on the spot. Beginning in 1350, the Black Death ravaged the landscape like the scourge of God; in 1355, thankful for their deliverance, the local people rebuilt the old church on greater, grander lines. In its final form, it lasted nearly 400 years.

Under the floor still repose the bones of the finer folk of the parish — the Ribbings of Ribbingsnäs, the von Gertens of Boarp, the various families who have owned Långåsa over the centuries, the faithful Fovelins, for a hundred years the ministers and pastors of Barkeryd parish. Their gifts — chandeliers, candelabra, and crucifixes — were transferred to the new church and tended carefully over the years. Their coats-of-arms adorn the walls, symbolizing the class-structured society which the emigrants later rejected.[3]

In 1844 Barkeryd parish consisted of 32⅞ *mantal,* or taxble farmsteads. Of these, however, 15 (or nearly half) had already been reduced by at least one-half through inheritance; one or two were only one-eighth of a full farm. As the century wore on and the population proliferated, the number of divided farms also continued to increase. Below one-eighth mantal was considered to be below the level even of basic subsistence agriculture. But the continuing population growth, accelerated, as Bishop Tegnér put it so succinctly, by "peace, potatoes, and [smallpox] vaccination," soon made such small divisions among the area's younger sons inevitable. In 1850 forests covered nearly half the remaining land, as indeed they do again today. At that time Barkeryd parish consisted of some 1,400 people, the overwhelming number of whom lived by subsistence farming.[4] The crop failures of the early 1860's sent many a discouraged farmer off onto the paths of the pioneer settlers in the New World. And, when the railroad link came, not to Barkeryd but to its smaller neighbor to the east, Nässjö, in 1864, the parish quickly began to decline. Nässjö is now a bustling railhead city of 18,000, while Barkeryd is little more than a parish church, a community cemetery, and a tiny museum of local culture. Its population (1,200) is smaller now than it was in the mid-19th century.

Although the railroad was built a few fatal kilometers distant from Barkeryd, it was not difficult for villagers to get to Jönköping, for instance, or to the expanding metropolis of Nässjö and from there either north to Stockholm or south to Växjö, Kalmar, and the Continent. The nearest station was (and still is) Forserum, from whence 100 pioneers set out for Texas in 1867.[5]

Patterns of Migration and Settlement

Early Swedish emigration to Texas was of a special kind known as a "chain migration." This means simply that, because of several factors, individuals from one locale in the home country emigrate over time to a single area in the new country. In the case of the Swedish emigrants to Texas, the home locale was centered in Barkeryd parish in Småland. S.M. Swenson, the parish's most famous son, was the first to immigrate to Texas, and, on 16 return trips made over half a century, he personally kept the "Texas fever" alive in his home parish. A number of Swedes returned to Barkeryd from Texas to visit, but even more wrote

Relatives of a Swedish-Texan family, Barkeryd, c. 1900

home to their families about their increasing prosperity in the Lone Star State.

The migration proceeded almost exclusively through families: Swenson, then his three uncles Swante, Anders, and Gustaf Palm, the four Hörd brothers and their families, the five Forsgård brothers and their families, all moved directly from the Barkeryd area to Texas. Geographically, the number of emigrants decreased directly with the distance from Barkeryd.[6] And this point of origin held remarkably steady for over 40 years. From 1848 to 1861, for example, more than 75 percent of the immigrants to Texas came from Barkeryd and nearby Forserum parishes. And, even as late as the period 1895-1914, Barkeryd parish sent more Swedes to Texas than any other place in Jönköpings län.[7]

Later Swedish migrants came not from Sweden but from the northern United States. This pattern began rather suddenly in 1870 and ended equally suddenly about 1900. These Swedes were lured to Texas largely by promises of abundant cheap land made by land agents. By the time they migrated to Texas, most of these northern Swedes had been in America for some time and were more or less used to American agricultural methods. They had learned some English, and most had even saved a bit of money. Unlike the direct emigrants, these Swedes came from all over Sweden, although Småland was still the province providing the most emigrants to the New World and, on a smaller scale, to Texas as well.

Swedish migrants from the North came principally from Illinois and Iowa, from the regions settled earliest by Swedes. Henry County, Illinois, and Swedes Point (Madrid), Iowa, were two typical areas. There were relatively few Minnesota Swedes among those who moved south into Texas.[8]

Settlement patterns in Texas were related to the familial nature of the early immigration and the personal involvement of S.M. Swenson. Swedes in Texas settled near relatives on adjoining plots of land, to live much as they had done in Barkeryd.[9] In fact, the early Swedish colonies in Texas were all located within 20 miles of one another, centering on Austin (site of Govalle, S.M. Swenson's large ranch), north to Brushy Creek and Palm Valley, and east to Manor. Later Swedish in-migration spread to Round Rock, Decker, New Sweden, and Georgetown, but even in the 1880's (when migration from the northern states accelerated), 75 percent of the Swedes who had immigrated directly to Texas all lived in "a relatively small contiguous area in south central Williamson County and northeastern Travis County."[10] This "stock effect" pattern of settlement lasted until the ceasing of immigration in the 1920's.[11]

Initially, S.M. Swenson's ranch near Austin provided the first home in America for newly arriving Swedes. For most, if not all of them, Swenson had paid their passage and, in return, expected up to a year of labor to repay the ticket. He was, of course, also related to most of the early immigrants, either by blood or by marriage, and he usually gave them generous terms when they were ready to buy land of their own from him.

In addition to settling on Swenson's ranch (and without wishing to get too far ahead of the story), immigrants could also proceed north into Williamson County where Swenson's several uncles, nephews, and brothers-in-law had established themselves as early as 1852. The valley along Brushy Creek would become almost exclusively Swedish as arriving families settled down next to one another, much as they had lived in Sweden. They began to clear land, raise cotton and corn, and build homes, churches, and businesses. Barkeryd had arrived in Texas.[12]

Lutheran parsonage with church in background, Palm Valley, c. 1885

Everyday Life in Swedish Texas

Swedish Religious Diversity

The pattern of emigration from Småland to Texas paralleled the general pattern of Swedish emigration to the United States. But another factor that shaped the lives of Swedish Texans diverged somewhat from the norm. This was the unusual diversity of their religious affiliations, which, again, depended almost exclusively on where they came from in Sweden. Jönköpings län in the 19th century was one of the nation's centers of religious dissent and remains today one of the areas with the highest percentage of non-Lutherans in all of Sweden. Particularly active were the Missionsvännerna (Mission Covenant Church) and the various Baptist and Methodist organizations.

Because confirmation in the State Church of Sweden required competence in reading and writing, albeit at a simple level, virtually all Swedes—including potential emigrants—were literate.

It was, in fact, because of their literacy that the early religious dissidents were able to achieve their initial successes. The great wave of pietism that swept over Sweden in the 18th century was, thanks to the countereffects of rationalism, largely spent by 1750. But at that time, especially in Småland, a new interest in individual Biblical interpretation began, which earned its adherents the sobriquet *läsare*, or "readers," because of their insistence on the primacy of personal scriptural analysis.[1] One of the primary tenets of the läsare was strict temperance and a puritanical disavowal of secular celebrations, such as dancing at weddings, cardplaying, and "pagan" holidays like Midsummer. The Swedish "readers" and those affected by them, even if they remained in the state church, became a pious, stern, hard-working people.[2]

Thus it is not surprising that the habits of the homeland became even more ingrained when transferred to America, since such habits were not only admired by the American community but had strong "survival value." A hard-drinking immigrant was not only on the road to Hell but also to financial ruin, while a churchgoer, be he Lutheran, Methodist, or Baptist, remained on the proper path, in all senses of the word.

The high percentage of non-Lutherans (36.5 percent of the immigrants who came *directly* from Jönköpings län to Texas) perhaps exaggerates the basic religious orientation shared by virtually *all* the immigrants.[3] And the monopoly of Augustana Lutherans among the later immigrants from the northern United States simply reflects their common experience in an area where that church was predominant.[4]

The Swedish Family

The early immigrants who came to Texas directly from Sweden before 1880 and those who arrived after that date from the northern states differed somewhat from both the homeland societal makeup and from the average American social structure. The ratio of men to women, for example, was 94.3 to 100 on the whole in Sweden, while it was 149 to 100 among the Swedish immigrants to Texas, about the same imbalance found in Swedish immigrant communities elsewhere in the United States.[5] This meant, of course, that there were few single girls among the immigrants and that women had the luxury of delaying marriage and having a mate of their own choosing. Thus many of these women married rather older than they would have in Sweden. Because

Anders and Anna Larson with their 12 children, Carlson Community, c. 1914

of their scarcity on the frontier, women came to have greater independence and higher status than they had had at home. Families tended to be large—10 or 12 children were not uncommon—as they had been in Sweden, where many farmhands were needed and infant mortality had traditionally been high. Initially, then, because of tradition and because cotton cultivation (the standard crop in Central Texas) was so labor-intensive, Swedish families in Texas tended to remain large. But as Swedish farmers retired to the towns and villages, their urban-dwelling offspring were often fewer, and the size of Swedish-American families shrank to match that of the American—that is, four to five children in the 1920's.[6]

Traditional Swedish families were monogamous, stable, and patriarchal, with wives and children willingly deferring to the head of the family. The family was the center of social life; both in Sweden and in Texas the momentous events of family life—births, baptisms, confirmations, weddings, and funerals—were also the most important social events. Only in magnitude and intensity did wedding parties in Texas differ from similar festivities in Sweden. The austere life on the frontier prohibited the extravagant four- and five-day parties common in Småland, and religious temperance, of course, forbade any form of alcohol. Coffee, the ubiquitous, universal Swedish social pastime, quickly took its place.[7]

Divorce rates among the Texas Swedes were low, as they were in the homeland 100 years ago. The process was painful and shameful, although not prohibited by the clergy, and it remained equally shameful when translated to America. As late as 1930 Texas Swedes divorced at a lower rate than Americans—three to four per thousand marriages as compared to a national average of seven to eight per thousand.[8]

Equally uncommon, at least until the very close of immigration, were marriages between Americans and immigrants. Only in the early days, when there simply *weren't* any fellow immigrants to marry, and after 1930 or so, when it no longer made any difference, were intermarriages more common than marriage within

Wedding of Josephine Johnson and Walfred Morell, Swedish Methodist Episcopal Church, Manda, December 25, 1906

the ethnic group. This pattern held true throughout Swedish America, as it did for almost every immigrant group. English-speaking third- and fourth-generation Swedish Americans were as prone to marry outside their group as within it.[9]

Swedish Methodist Episcopal Church outing, Austin, 1890's

Attitudes

The unusually strong religious ties among Texas Swedes meant that virtually everyone had an identity outside the home and within a larger Swedish shelter organization. Indeed, so strong were the ties between church and community that it was rare to find a Swede in Texas who did not belong to a church.[10] This was in stark contrast to northern Swedish areas, such as Moline, Illinois, where sometimes less than half of the Swedish population had official church affiliations.

This meant, too, that the church was the center of social as well as spiritual life. The importance of the Swedish minister can scarcely be overemphasized. Not only was he usually the best-educated man in the community, but it was he who presided over virtually all the events in community life. No birthday surprise party, political rally, patriotic evening, young people's camp, anniversary, or ice cream social was conceivable without a clerical blessing, prayer, or speech. Much more than weddings, baptisms, and funerals thus came under the direct purview of the Swedish pastor, no matter to what denomination he belonged. And, while Swedish Baptists may have had little to do with Lutherans, Free Churchers, or Methodists socially (and vice versa), the patterns of behavior and the dominant role of the clergy was the same for each.

Patterns of life also followed religious dictates. All groups severely disapproved of any activities other than religious ones taking place on Sunday. This helps explain, for example, the dearth of Swedish baseball or basketball teams in Texas.[11] Games would necessarily have been played on Saturday, an important workday, or on Sunday, which was unthinkable.

Another moral precept shared by all the Swedish religious groups in Texas was the almost universal abhorrence of alcohol in any form. This was, again, a natural reaction considering the importance of temperance in Småland just prior to the emigration. But this was also a sentiment shared by migrating Swedes from the northern states. Indeed, next to his general opposition to slavery, no issue was as close to the average Scandinavian immigrant's heart as was his opposition to alcohol.[12]

Social Life and Holidays

Despite this somewhat puritanical façade—which also included taboos against all forms of tobacco, card-playing, and dancing—Swedish Texans were a sociable people. There being no proscriptions against eating, Swedish gatherings were characterized (as they still are today) by enormous amounts of food. Most often the menu was American or Texan; barbecues were especially popular. But the ubiquitous strong coffee—after some years, even imported directly from Europe—and the provincial varieties of *Wienerbröd* (coffee bread) and *småkakor,* (cookies) stamped these events as thoroughly Swedish.

Christmas gave Swedes a chance to indulge in religious and secular delights at the same time.[13] Traditions of the Christmas season were among the best-remembered and longest-lived

Afternoon coffee, El Campo, c. 1900

Old Country customs practiced by the immigrants—some are still honored today.

Hulda Anderson related to researcher Folke Hedblom how, as a young immigrant housewife in Brushy Creek in the 1870's, she prepared for Christmas. First, she *lutade* fish, that is, soaked salted, dried fish in lye to leach out the salt. Her father salted pork and boiled fish, including catfish. Other meats were smoked over oak bark or hung to dry. Calves were slaughtered to prepare for *kalvsylta,* a kind of Swedish head cheese. And Hulda's pride were her cheeses, for which she and her women friends were completely responsible. She milked and churned and baked *ostkaka* (the Småland specialty dessert made of curdled milk, quite unlike its American counterpart, cheesecake), week in and week out. At the Christmas service, everyone brought cheese as a *juloffer* (Christmas offering) to the minister, who stood behind the table on which the offerings were placed, taking note of who had contributed what![14]

In spite of the distance from other areas of Swedish settlement Christmas in Swedish Texas meant traditional Swedish foods. The great Christmas ham (*julskinka*), brown beans (*bruna bönor*), and rice pudding (*risgrynsgröt*) were served alongside American specialties such as sweet potatoes, tomatoes, and turkey. In many homes a cedar tree replaced the Swedish fir tree (*julgran*), but the evening reading of the Nativity story in Swedish by the head of the family remained the same as in the homeland, as did the custom of celebrating on Christmas Eve instead of the more American tradition of Christmas Day.

Julotta, the Swedish early morning worship service on Christmas Day, in which the church is lit only by candlelight, meant as much to Swedish Americans as it did to Swedes back home. Virtually every Swedish church in Texas once held some kind of special Swedish service early on Christmas morning, and many still do, often the only time during the year that the former ethnic origin of the congregation is emphasized. In addition to the exclusive use of lighted candles as the source of illumination, a Swedish sermon was (and is) preached, and the best-loved Swedish Christmas hymns were sung. Chief among these in popularity were "Var hälsad sköna morgonstund" ("Greetings, Lovely Morning Hour"), "Stilla natt" ("Silent Night"), "Betlehemsstjernan" ("The Star of Bethlehem"). Sometimes the congregation liked to sing the two most popular Swedish hymns, even though they had little to do with Christmas: "O store Gud" ("How Great Thou Art") and "Tryggare kan ingen vara" ("Children of the Heavenly Father"); almost any "Swedish" occasion was a good time to sing these old favorites.

Lucia program sponsored by SVEA of Texas, Houston, December 9, 1990

The present-day celebration of Sankta Lucia, while quite common in Swedish America, has only recently become equally popular in the homeland. (The tradition was once typical only of Värmland.) Most of the Swedish churches and clubs in Texas have some kind of Lucia celebration, often together with julotta or a *smörgåsbord,* the full-fledged Swedish hot and cold buffet. Generally, a young girl of the congregation is chosen to wear a crown of lighted candles and to preside over the singing of Swedish Christmas carols, the eating of *lussekatter* ("Lucia cats," special cookies), and the consumption of gallons of coffee. Originally a Catholic remembrance of the young Sicilian saint who, in the 4th century, chose martyrdom rather than abjure her faith, Lucia has come to represent the coming of Christian light to a benighted pagan Scandinavia as well as a harbinger of spring in the midst of the profound winter darkness. Sometimes she is accompanied by *stjärngossar,* or star boys, who carry star-tipped wands symbolizing the Christmas Star and wear tall, pointed "magicians'" hats harking back to the Wise Men of the Orient, the Magi. By moving the event from the home (where the eldest girl of the house traditionally served coffee and cakes before sunrise on December 13) to the church, it has become a public affirmation of ethnicity without denominational overtones in which all Swedish-American families can partake.

One last note of a more secular nature concerns the origins of the Texas version of Santa Claus. According to an article written for the next-to-the-last edition of *Texas-Posten,* Santa Claus was imported to Texas by none other than S.M. Swenson himself.[15] The idea is hard to credit, but the custom of honoring *jultomten,* the Swedish version of Father Christmas, literally, the "Christmas elf," seems to have entered Texas with the first Swedish immigrants of 1848, who were recruited by Swenson himself. At that time, jultomten, or *nissen,* was a tiny old man with a long white beard who lived in or around every peasant family's barn. To keep him happy (and to avoid such disasters as spoiled or spilt milk or open barn doors and wandering livestock—all potentially his doing), one placated the little gnome with a dish of porridge (*julgröt*) every Christmas Eve. Nowadays he has had to shoulder greater responsibility, such as distributing presents to children, and has consequently greatly increased in size, so that he does resemble Santa Claus or Father Christmas.

The climate of Texas mitigated against the fervent celebration of Midsummer which, in Sweden, was as festively celebrated as Christmas, if not more so. But the Dionysian aspects of Midsummer intoxication (literal and figurative), as well as its possible pagan origins, made Midsummer a much less popular holiday in Texas. Although it was celebrated in the Austin settlement, complete with maypole and dancing (a 1900 newspaper account reports that the Swedes partied until 2 a.m.!),[16] it has, for the last 75 years, been equated with the commemoration of the arrival of S.M. Swenson in 1838 and the first group of immigrants a decade later. Texas banbrytareföreningen (Texas Swedish Pioneers Association) has celebrated this historic moment since 1912[17] (see Chapter 20).

Swedish-Texan Architecture

The supposition that Swedes were the exclusive importers of the log cabin to America has generally been discredited. Yet small one-room timbered houses were extremely common on pioneer farms and ranches in Swedish settlements from Minnesota to Texas.[18]

In the unusual climate of Texas there was no need to build stout buildings with massive walls to support steeply pitched roofs strong enough to withstand heavy snowfalls. Instead, the problem was usually the heat, with its attendant dust and discomfort. Swedes quickly adopted local techniques and patterns for their architecture, styles well suited to the environment of Texas.

Many of these styles were, of course, to be seen in Sweden as well, but there they were the franchise of the upper classes, even of the aristocracy. For example, no Swedish farmer (at least in the 1860's) would have dreamt of building the grandiose frame houses with large windows, verandas, and ornamental woodwork in which his Texas counterpart felt most at home.

So far did this ''Americanization'' of architecture go that researcher Carl Rosenquist stated flatly[19] ''there was no attempt made by the Swedes of Texas to set up any of the old-country

Mrs. Carl Gustaf Palm behind log cabin, originally located at Govalle, in which her husband's family lived during the 1850's, Austin, c. 1934. (See p. 248.)

physical arrangements when they organized their communities." The American grid pattern of rectangular 640-acre, square-mile sections did not encourage development of "cluster" communities like the Old World villages which centered on the parish church or a central square. According to Rosenquist, "in no case known to the writer do the . . . buildings built by Swedes in Texas show any trace of Swedish influence whatever." [20]

Yet there may have been just a hint of Old World design in some of the later frame farmhouses, the modest "American" homes that replaced the cruder and intentionally temporary log structures. One such design was the typical "dog-trot" house, quite common throughout eastern and central Texas and parts of the southern United States, from which area it had been imported. Typically such a structure consisted of two "pens" or rooms under a common gabled roof, with an open breezeway between the rooms. Usually a long porch was built along the south side of the building. This type of structure was easily created out of an existing log structure and had the added advantage of providing the maximum ventilation during Texas summers. A number of such houses were built by Swedish farmers in the New Sweden community. [21]

Another variation on this architectural theme was the so-called "double-pen" house, which consisted of two symmetrical ground-floor rooms under a common roof. Similar structures—called *megaronhus* or *parstuga*—are uncommon in Sweden but not altogether unknown. The Andrew Palm House, built in Palm Valley in 1873 and moved to downtown Round Rock in 1976, is a good example of a framed and sided version of a double-pen house built by Swedish Texans. Annie Branham mentions living in such a house near Coupland just before World War I.[22]

Andrew Palm family in front of their residence, Palm Valley, 1900's

In summary, life for the Swedish settlers in Texas was hard but not significantly different from that of other pioneers. Confronted primarily with the necessity of adapting to new conditions of agriculture and climate, the Swedes of Texas also faced the obstacles that all other non-English-speaking immigrants faced: the language barrier and the preservation of their own Old World values in the multicultural arena of the frontier. They were aided in these twin tasks of adaptation and preservation by the institutions they brought with them and the new ones they created when they got here; these will be examined in detail in the last third of this book. But before the chronicle of Swedish settlement in Texas is presented, the vivid firsthand account of the Bergman brothers of Lund will fill out the story of life on the prairies of the Lone Star State.

5

Life on the Prairie

The Letters of Carl and Fred Bergman

Narrative accounts of actual experiences by Swedish immigrants to Texas are extremely few. Swante Palm's incomplete autobiography ceases with his arrival in Fort Bend County. Fredrik Roos af Hjelmsäter's diary similarly stops with his departure for Texas from New Orleans in 1852. Vilhelm Moberg based much of his account of pioneer life in Minnesota in his *Emigrants* tetralogy on the journals kept by Andrew Peterson, who left careful and vivid descriptions of immigrant life in Chisago County over the course of half a century. While Texas produced no Andrew Peterson, it did serve as home to two brothers from Östergötland, Carl Johan and Claes Fredrik Bergman, whose letters home to their sisters in Sweden give almost as colorful an insight into rural life in the Swedish settlements of Texas as Peterson's do for Minnesota.

Carl Johan Bergman was born in 1858 at Hemfriden, a tenant farm dependent on the larger farm Lilla Ånestad a bit south of Linköping, Östergötland. His younger brother, Claes Fredrik ("Fred" in America), was born three years later. Their three elder sisters, Maria Christina (1847-1870), Mathilda Sofia (1850-1923), and Hanna (1855-1915), remained in Sweden after Carl and Fredrik emigrated, but reciprocal letters crossed the Atlantic at regular intervals for nearly 50 years. In Sweden Carl had experienced the bitterness of bankruptcy in the firm which employed him and so decided to emigrate in 1879, taking his younger brother with him.[1]

41

Carl Bergman

They arrived in New York September 8, 1879, on the *City of Montreal*, two of some 500 immigrant passengers about to start a new life in the New World. They made their way first to Bridgeport, Connecticut, where the large Swedish population made it relatively easy to find factory jobs. But they dreamed of owning their own land and fell in with some like-minded Swedes who were discussing the possibility of moving to Texas, where land was said to be abundant and cheap. One of them was Johan Westling, who already had a brother and a son in Texas. Westling journeyed alone to Austin and rented land in New Sweden, east of Austin in Travis County. He kept in touch with his friends in Connecticut and urged them to follow him to Texas. In 1883 the Bergman brothers and their friends August Thornquist and Gustaf O. Seaholm had saved enough money to make their move, and they joined Westling in New Sweden.

They purchased unbroken, thinly forested prairie land just to the north of New Sweden in a tiny Swedish community named Lund after the southern Swedish university city. It was to be their home for the rest of their lives.[2]

The letters of Carl and Fred Bergman to their surviving sisters, Sofie and Hanna (the eldest of the siblings, Maria Chris-

Fred Bergman

tina, had died in 1870), cover the years from 1879 to 1923. The brothers described in formidable detail the arduous life on the Texas prairie and demonstrated the same kind of versatility, ingenuity, and steadfastness that characterizes Moberg's fictional hero, Karl Oskar Nilsson, in a similar situation in Minnesota. But life in Texas was quite different from life in Chisago County.

The terrible heat of Central Texas, more than anything else, caused the immigrants immeasurable discomfort. Their Swedish clothing was designed for much cooler temperatures, and the Bergmans suffered greatly until they were refitted in garments more suitable for the heat. The shifting Texas weather fascinated the brothers:[3]

> I wish that I could describe Texas for you but it
> would be too difficult, for much is still strange
> to me myself. When it begins to rain, it can last
> for long periods of time and the same is true
> for periods of no precipitation, which also last
> for long periods. Swedes who have been here for
> a longer time say there was a period when it
> did not rain for 18 months; there was a terrible
> drought and lack of water. Of course, this was

naturally something unusual, perhaps it has never happened before or may never happen again. The soil here is of such a consistency, that when it rains, we can neither ride nor walk, it becomes so muddy, so then we have to stay inside long hours. Or, if we do go out, we have to ride horses. Winter is variable, sometimes warm, sometimes cold. We have no winter before Christmas.— Now, I have not been to a town in seven months, and perhaps four or five months will go by before I get there again. I don't miss it, we have 18 English miles there, that is about 3 Swedish miles. Fred and I have slept outside on the porch for over a week it is so warm in our room that we can't sleep there. July, August, and even September are usually so hot that one can't go out at midday, but afterwards it gets a bit cooler. I don't think you'd recognize us, we have become brown and lean. . . .

In January of 1885 they moved into their own home.[4]

We have moved from the Swedish family [the Johan Westlings] whom we have talked about before, but we live just ten minutes away from them so that we are in constant communication with them. Our farm is rather large, 65 *tunnland* [about 325,000 square meters, or 67 acres], we have two yoke of oxen and a pair of horses. We have a Swede who works for us [August Thornquist from Bridgeport], he is married and his wife is our housekeeper. We celebrated Christmas in good health, although not so festively since weather was cold and rainy. New Year was the same. The first Sunday after New Year, we were invited to dinner at the home of the man we rent our land from, he is an old colonel [Col. Rayne, who owned a great deal of land in the area around New Sweden and Manor]. There we had a rather good time, he has two sons and a daughter at home, and several other children besides. Now I must close with many warm greetings and wishes for continued good fortune in the New Year.

Your brothers,
Carl and Fred

By April 1885 the brothers had acquired "a pair of donkeys, . . . three cows, two calves, fifteen hens, 17 chicks, and two dogs—a good beginning, all this!" In addition to their cotton and corn production, they were now raising some oats for feed and some typically Swedish food as well: onions, potatoes, and yellow peas. Rain, however, destroyed their cabbage and rutabagas, and the long drought the previous year reduced the cotton crop considerably.[5]

In subsequent letters Carl described the process of cultivating, picking, and cleaning cotton, which was, to the sisters in Sweden, still an exotic, tropical crop. The brothers proceeded to plant apricot, fig, and plum trees but found that apples and pears did not do well under the fierce Texas sun.

By midsummer 1886 they had dug a well, "which produced abundant good, cold water," and procured a third cow, which produced enough extra milk to feed their new pigs. Hail "the size of small hens' eggs" damaged the cotton crop but not severely. In other places, hailstones that weighed as much as "seven *skålpund*" [7 pounds] had totally destroyed all the crops. The wind was so strong that Fred could not open the doors; the hail was so fierce that cattle died in the fields and houses had their roofs destroyed.[6] Despite all this, the Bergman brothers anticipated an excellent harvest, an event which they were rarely to experience in subsequent years.

The daily problems of life on the prairie appear and reappear in the correspondence between Carl and Fred and their sisters. Storms, drought, worms and pests, intense heat and violent winds, swarms of grasshoppers that darkened the sun—all these and more they described and took in stride. But the problem that vexed the bachelor brothers most was where and how could they locate suitable wives? While they searched, they did the "women's work" themselves:[7]

> Baking and washing are the hardest things we
> have to do for they occur so frequently, baking
> every other day and washing once a week.
> Naturally, we don't wash our sheets or things
> that need to be starched, but only our work
> clothes. For Xmas, we slaughtered two fine pigs
> and can you believe that we slaughtered them
> ourselves, without help? We're not afraid to do
> whatever needs doing. It doesn't go as quickly
> here to milk two cows, since here they have the
> stupid idea that the calf must suck down the
> milk first, otherwise the cows will not allow the
> milk to flow. And if the calf should by accident
> die, the cows dry up altogether. Can you guess
> how many laying hens we have now? . . . I
> believe it is about 80 now. We have several
> dozen eggs a day. We cultivate some potatoes,
> but we cannot keep them long because of the
> heat. Sweet potatoes, on the other hand, are
> plentiful. We certainly eat them but we prefer
> the usual kind. Vegetables can be grown but not
> with much success since the summers are so dry.

Late in 1887 the Bergmans bought another piece of land near Johan Westling in the northeast corner of Travis County. They were now senior members of the New Sweden Lutheran congregation, about a six-mile ride from their farm. Gradually their harvests increased; by the fall of 1888 they had to hire five Black laborers to help with the cotton-picking.

Both brothers were gifted musically. They sang in the church and secular choirs and were often sought out to play their violins for dances—song and music were among the few real enjoyments which they had or could afford. They were also still actively seeking wives but so far without success.[8]

The Bergmans received their mail at the post office in New Sweden, which had been established only three years before they settled there; that also became their official address in 1889. Carl Bergman was instrumental in the formation of a local telephone company to serve the Swedish communities in eastern

Swedish Evangelical Lutheran congregation, New Sweden, 1880's

Travis County. The brothers purchased 230 acres of land that year at the rather high price of $12.50 an acre, but under the mesquite and prickly pear it was good land, waiting to be planted in cotton. Carl cooked the food and cleaned the house, but soon a Swedish family came to take over those chores.

The brothers also wisely decided to sell off some of their excess land, retaining 65 acres for cultivating crops and 50 for grazing cattle. "Sixty-five [acres] are all that two men can take care of, but even so they must hire on too many extra workers and you have to work the land just like a garden plot." Eight years after coming to Texas they owned six cows, three yearlings, and five calves, plus pigs, chickens, and laying hens.[9]

> It doesn't pay to sell butter when you can't get more than 8, 10, or twelve cents a pound. We can't sell our milk either because there's no buyer, except in the cities, but we live too far away. There, milk costs 35 to 40 cents per can. One can buy eggs for 6 cents a dozen, so everything is cheap. But this is what it costs during the time when there is an abundance of

these products: in the winter time, on the other hand, prices are driven up: butter 40 cents a pound, eggs 25 to 30 cents a dozen, milk all the way up to 60 cents a can, but I must add that these are the highest prices I have heard paid for these products. . . . We get four pounds of coffee to one dollar, not the best but rather good, sugar, 10 pounds [for one dollar]. Wheat flour comes rather more expensive namely $1.50 per [lis]pund or 20 skålpund [about 20 American pounds]. Potatoes, again, are among the most expensive items, from $3, yes, up to $5 per Swedish bushel. Clothes are also very cheap, but now I'll leave the subject for another time.

By 1892 the Bergmans' crops were more regular and so was their income. The biggest changes had come in the garden that both brothers worked with pride.[10]

We have four plum trees, around 40 peach trees and six mulberry, we will increase them as we can in time with other varieties. Vegetables are nearly the same as with you — potatoes, beans, peas, cabbage, red beets, watermelons, muskmelons, many kinds of squash, as well as some varieties foreign to your climate.

In 1894 it seemed as though at least Fred Bergman's dreams of wedded bliss were about to be realized. He became engaged to Miss Amanda Olson, who was the daughter of Johannes Olson, a pillar of the Swedish-American community in Texas. But the good news was not to last, however, for the engagement was soon broken off by mutual consent. Miss Olson and the Bergmans remained friends for years, however, and often visited one another socially.[11]

The Bergman brothers believed fervently in the idea of the self-made man. And, next to owning land, the best way to become a success in America was to own and operate an independent business. After nearly two decades in America, and despite the rather meager return from their land, they had amassed enough capital by 1897 to underwrite their most daring entrepreneurial venture — taking over management of the post office and the general store in Lund.[12] Within two years their $5,400 investment was bringing in nearly $11,200 a year. They sold groceries, hardware, men's clothing, shoes, hats, and all kinds of dry goods. Soon they were one-third owners of the local telephone company (the other owners being Seaholm and August Thornquist, with whom they had resided earlier in the 1880's).[13] Business kept improving, and by 1902 they even talked of returning to Sweden to see their sisters one last time. But unhappily on February 13, 1903, Carl Johan Bergman died suddenly of typhus and exhaustion.[14]

His brother's death at the age of 44 was a shattering blow to Fred Bergman. They had rented out their land in 1898 to get started in business. They had also invested in the Lund cotton gin and worked to attract more business to the area, which now supported a blacksmith and a second general store. After Carl's death there seemed little purpose in any of it. Fred wrote: "Oh, my sisters, how empty and desolate it is. . . . Oh, how lonesome I am. I want to go home to my fatherland once more."

He wanted to sell the business; Carl's will left him with $10,000, and he wished to liquidate the property as soon as humanly possible, but the tide of events kept delaying his decision, for in February 1904, at the age of 43, Fred Bergman finally got married!

The bride's maiden name was Olga Nygren, and she and her family were all from New Sweden. Olga's father, C.M. Nygren, was one of the "sixty-seveners" who left Forserum, Sweden, under Daniel Hurd's leadership two years after the end of the Civil War. Nygren married Sofia Sandahl of Järsnäs, near Barkeryd, Småland, in Austin in 1870. Eight years later the family moved to New Sweden, where Nygren bought a small farm. He was an active member of the New Sweden Swedish Lutheran Church, where for many years he served as a deacon. He was even able to send his daughter Olga to Bethany College in Lindsborg, Kansas, for a time.[15]

The newlyweds were delighted with one another and with married life; it was something both had looked forward to, and neither was disappointed with marriage or each other. In 1905 the Bergmans' only child, daughter Ruth Hildegard, was born, so Fred Bergman's life was far from over. His interests in "Sandahl and Bergman" were now, in 1905, only nominal, but his business

Bergman farm house, Lund, c. 1905

sense was too strong to allow him to retire to his farm in Lund full time. Within a year he was one of several Swedish immigrants who founded the Merchants and Farmers State Bank in Elgin, the first (and only) incorporated wholly Swedish bank in Texas. For more than 30 years it was to serve the needs of the eastern Travis and Bastrop County Swedes. It weathered a number of local and national recessions, only to be forced into liquidation by the Great Depression. Even so, the Merchants and Farmers Bank managed to hang on until 1936, when it was finally forced to close its doors for good.[16] "Sandahl and Bergman" opened its new headquarters in Elgin in the fall of 1906. The all-brick building had cost $6,000 to build and contained an inventory worth more than $22,000. Almost from the beginning, it was recognized as the best store in Elgin. Bergman remained a full partner until 1913, when he sold his interests to a fellow country-man, Carl Carlson, vice-president of the Elgin National Bank.[17]

He seems to have sold all but the Lund property at about the same time in order to facilitate a move to Austin. There he acted as an auctioneer and served on the Skandia Mutual Fire Insurance Board. He spent his last 30 years in Austin.[18]

Fred and Olga Nygren Bergman and daughter Ruth

He, like S.M. Swenson a half century earlier, never lost his faith in the promise of the New World nor did he ever regret his emigration. He wrote to his sisters accordingly in 1908:[19]

> It is fun to be able to send something to you. If I had stayed home, I probably wouldn't have been able to do anything for you, but Texas is a place for the poor to work their way up by means of work and thrift. Poor Swedes come here practically all the time, and in a few years they are independent. This place is not for a lazy bones but for the diligent.

But he was not wholly uncritical of Texas. The women, he felt, were too small! "Here in Texas, women are in general small and thin, the climate is the reason." His plans for returning to Sweden seemed terminated: "I would freeze to death in an instant if I were at home . . . [and] if a Scandinavian were to come here to Texas in the summer, I don't think he would make it."[20]

In 1910 Bergman bought one of the first cars in the area — an Overland that could seat eight — an event noteworthy enough to make the pages of *Texas-Posten*. Fred found his machine preferable to mules and horses in the almost impassable mud created during Texas winters. On two occasions, he noted proudly to his sisters, the car made it possible for the family to attend julotta services in New Sweden — without the Overland, they would have had to stay at home.[21]

In 1925 Fred Bergman sold his farm in Lund, thus cutting his last tie with the land he and his brother had so laboriously cleared and cultivated for nearly 40 years. His letters to Sweden ceased in 1923 (with a major lacuna between 1913 and about 1922), but he lived on in Austin for 23 years. Finally on July 7, 1946, a fall at home sent him to the hospital with a broken hip. There he suffered a heart attack and died on July 11 at more than 85 years of age.[22]

The record of the Bergman brothers is unique in that the original sources — their "America letters" — have survived, but their story was typical, even archetypical, of the aspirations of the Swedish immigrants who settled in Central Texas.

Sandahl and Bergman Store with crowd listening to Buster Brown salesman, Elgin, c. 1910

The Trailblazer

Swen Magnus Swenson

T housands of Swedes who turned their backs on their homeland to strike out for the Promised Land on the other side
of the Atlantic did so in response to the urgings of a handful
of extremely persuasive individuals. Per Cassel led his small band
from Västergötland to the prairies around New Sweden, Iowa.
Gustaf Unonius's less successful Utopia, "New Uppsala" at Pine
Lake, Wisconsin, nevertheless inspired several subsequent groups.
And Erik Jansson's religious fervor convinced more than 1,200
of his followers from Uppland and Hälsingland to join him in
the arduous trek across the Midwest to the fertile fields of Henry
County, Illinois, where he established his "New Jerusalem," the
colony of Bishop Hill.

But all these ventures—the earliest in 1844, the latest in
1846—had been anticipated by a young Swedish merchant from
northern Småland named Swen Magnus Swenson, whose plan
it became to build a Swedish colony in the Republic (ultimately
State) of Texas. He was among the first of a new kind of entrepreneur—the "emigrant agent"—whose charm and persuasion
convinced hundreds of his countrymen to risk the hardships of
emigration for a better life in the New World.

Many details of Swenson's life have been lost or confused,
and some have entered the realm of legend. One story, for example, alleges that Swenson spent three years as an English merchant
seaman before coming to America, even though his emigration

Swen Mangus Swenson

from Sweden and his arrival in New York are known to have occurred in the same year (1836). Many such tales can be traced to August Anderson's fictional biography *Hyphenated: The Life of S.M. Swenson,* which blithely perpetuates the legendary aspects of Swenson's life. But Swenson's life did generate colorful stories, and his extraordinary accomplishments are the kind that lend themselves almost naturally to embellishment.

Swen Magnus Swenson[1] was born February 24, 1816, the second son of Sven Israelsson and Margareta Andersdotter in the parish of Barkeryd, Sweden, which lies midway between the cities of Nässjö and Jönköping in northern Småland.[2] Swen Israelsson was a member of the jury of the local assizes and also a *rusthållare,* or local cavalryman. In return for providing part of the parish's military contingent, the family was given a small farm named Lättarp about five miles west of the village church on the banks of Lättarpssjön (Lake Lättarp). But life was hard, especially for a farmer trying to till the rocky soil of Småland, some of the stoniest ground in all of Sweden. A small annual allowance barely paid for Israelsson's uniforms and the upkeep of his military equipment and horse. By 1829 there were five children in the family, and feeding them all adequately was something the parents were finding increasingly hard to do.

So, at the age of about 13, Swen Magnus was sent as a foster child to his paternal relatives at Älmeshult, a small ironworks in nearby Solberga parish. In 1831 he found employment as a clerk in the shop of J.M. Bergman in Eksjö, some 40 miles from the home farm. A year later he left for the port of Karlskrona, where he worked for four years. There he was employed by N.H. Hedin, an iron merchant. Swenson was industrious and clever and especially adept at keeping accounts, so that by 1836 he could describe himself as a *bokhållare* (bookkeeper).

According to one account, a "box on the ear" caused Swenson to hurl his cap to the ground and swear that he was headed for America where there were "no more masters!" But there is no evidence that Swenson was ever bitterly disenchanted with his homeland. On the contrary, he was almost classically afflicted with the immigrant's "divided heart." As late as 1840, for example, he wrote home to a friend that he still considered America to be his *temporary* home.[3] He returned to Sweden 16 times and always expressed the deepest love for his homeland. But an odd and seemingly unrelated footnote to Swedish-American history may provide some evidence at least for Swenson's initial departure and destination.

While in Karlskrona, he had become acquainted with the commandant of the naval base, Admiral C.R. Nordenskiöld, who had earlier served as captain of the Swedish frigate *af Chapman.* This ship and the Swedish man-o-war *Tapperheten* had been pawns in a complicated game of international intrigue which eventually encompassed both Swenson and his uncle Swante Palm.

In September of 1826 Nordenskiöld was ordered to sail to Cartagena, capital of the new republic of Colombia. There, his ship and *Tapperheten* were to be sold to Colombia in a complex deal engineered by Sweden's King Carl XIV Johan and worked out by Swedish-Norwegian consul-general in New York Severin Lorich. The idea was that, in exchange for Colombia's purchase of the ships, Sweden would officially recognize Simón Bolívar's revolutionary government and would, in return, receive favorable trade arrangements for Swedish iron through the Swedish West Indian colony at Saint-Barthélemy. Unfortunately for King Carl

Johan and his henchman Lorich (who had worked out the naval sale and the secret trade agreement over several years in Colombia), the Russian czar, Alexander I, learned of Sweden's intention to recognize a revolutionary government. This was a violation of the Holy Alliance, and Sweden was effectively ordered to cease immediately as were the governments of the Netherlands and France, on whose backing the Swedish king depended. So, having sailed for three months, Captain Nordenskiöld reached Colombia only to find his orders countermanded: the Colombian government had no intention of buying the Swedish ships without getting badly needed international recognition from Sweden. In frustration Captain Nordenskiöld and a depleted crew (some had gone ashore in Cartagena and had not returned) turned north to New York. There his little fleet was put on the auction block and sold for a fraction of its actual worth. More seriously, the funds raised from the ignominious sale were insufficient to pay the return passage of the remaining 700 crew members. Put ashore in New York, they became involuntary immigrants since they had no way of paying their own passage home to Sweden.[4]

Now, ten years after the fiasco, Admiral Nordenskiöld expressed his concern about the fate of his former crew to young S.M. Swenson, who was about to depart for New York. Swenson carried a letter of introduction from Admiral Nordenskiöld to the Swedish-Norwegian consul in New York, the same Severin Lorich who had put together the disastrous Colombian deal for King Carl Johan a decade earlier. Lorich was to become a close friend and business associate of Swenson's in later years,[5] but as late as 1845, still plagued by the repercussions of events now 20 years in the past, Lorich enlisted the help of Swenson's uncle, Swante Palm, in the protracted search for the stranded Swedish sailors.[6] While this is hardly a substantive explanation for Swenson's emigration—his decision seems to have been reached before Nordenskiöld contacted him—it at least provided him with an excuse to sail to New York and also furnished him with an influential contact in the New World.

So, his mother and sister waving farewell, S.M. Swenson left Sweden on board the brig *Rhine* on February 13, 1836, just a week before his 20th birthday.[7] The ship docked in New York on June 20 after more than four months at sea. Swenson's ship did not sink or explode immediately after his arrival in New York, as one story had it, although there *was* a fire on board the *Rhine* that destroyed the cargo, some of which was Eskilstuna iron consigned to Swenson for sale by his Swedish employer, Mr. Hedin. But all these elements have worked themselves into the romantic fabric that was to be Swenson's life.

Using his introduction to Consul Lorich, Swenson was soon working as a clerk for $15 a month. After studying English intensively for two months, he found a better job with the Baltimore and Ohio Railroad in Maryland. In 1838, after two years in America, Swenson was sent by his railroad to Texas to investigate possibilities for expansion into the vast area claimed by the newly independent republic.

It was a fateful assignment, but not so dramatic as some stories have it. The ship that brought Swenson to Galveston did not sink in Galveston Bay, nor did Swenson swim ashore, like Robinson Crusoe, the sole survivor, and get his start as an itinerant peddler by salvaging the cargo from the wreck. But he seems never to have given Baltimore or the B&O Railroad a second thought. Soon he had formed a partnership with well-to-do merchant John Adriance in Columbia, Brazoria County. The alliance was an excellent one, with Swenson on the road as a traveling merchant and Adriance minding the store in Columbia. Swenson prospered and, within four years, concluded a second business arrangement, this time with George W. Long, a wealthy physician.

Dr. Long was one of the first doctors to serve in Fort Bend County. He had come to Texas from Tennessee because of his wife's and his own fragile health in October 1837: both Longs were consumptive.

Like many wealthy Southerners, Long had come to Texas to increase his fortune by becoming a gentleman farmer. He planted his fields in the crop that he knew best and that was beginning to pour wealth into the impoverished Texas republic—cotton. Long's plantation, Finckley, was outside Richmond in Ft. Bend County. He owned some 400 acres of bottomland across from the Big Bend of the Brazos River. Long ran the entire operation with the labor of slaves. Swenson came to know Long when he stopped periodically at Finckley during his travels for Adriance around Texas. Long was so impressed with Swenson's diligence and ability that he wanted to make him overseer of his cotton plantation as well as his business partner, but Swenson was too busy on the road to settle down just then.

In December 1842 Swenson was transporting merchandise from Houston to Richmond by ship when one of the vessels ran aground and broke up, resulting in heavy losses. Swenson tried personally to salvage what little was left of his goods and so may have inspired both the legend of his losses in New York and the shipwreck in Galveston upon his arrival in Texas. He turned over his peripatetic traveler's rig to John Adriance, accepted Dr. Long's offer, and settled down to run Finckley.

The tuberculosis which had driven Dr. Long to seek refuge in Texas finally claimed him near Christmas 1842. His young widow, Jeanette, spent four years after her husband's death with family in Tennessee, while Swenson moved into Finckley to manage the estate in accordance with Dr. Long's last wishes. But, through a frequent exchange of letters, Swenson and Jeanette declared their mutual attraction. Jeanette remained in Tennessee, where, in the fall of 1843, she and Swenson were wed. Although their marriage was to prove short-lived, it was a genuinely happy one, with busy years filled with bustling activity and growth.

The Finckley plantation became the staging area from which Swedish immigrants, brought by Swenson, entered other parts of Texas. It was here that Swante Palm, Swenson's uncle, came in 1844, to be followed by Swenson's sister, Anna Kristina, in 1847. She became the second Swede in Texas to marry an American (her brother, of course, had been the first). In the summer of 1850, less than a year after coming to America, Anna Kristina married William Dyer, Swenson's overseer. The Dyers were the first to leave the Finckley estate, settling on a tract of land owned by Swenson on Brushy Creek north of Austin.

At Finckley, Swenson dealt with America's ugliest institution—slavery—daily and at close range. As owner of Finckley, he owned some 40 slaves and a plantation of 400-500 acres, almost all of which was devoted to cotton production. His attitudes toward the institution seem to have been, at best, ambivalent. Though he did not, like Swante Palm, ever defend slavery (see Chapter 10), S.M. Swenson depended on slave labor for the prosperity of his plantation. But he was apparently concerned about the physical well-being of his slaves, opposed their maltreatment, and strove to keep slave families together whenever possible.

In addition to operating his cotton plantation, Swenson had been busy buying up land anywhere it was cheap, but especially along advantageous routes to expansion. A friendship with Sam Houston, dating back to S.M.'s first year in Texas, allowed Swenson to purchase land along what would eventually become the right-of-way for the Buffalo Bayou, Brazos, and Colorado Railroad. In 1839 he learned that the permanent Texas state capital would be relocated to Austin from Columbia, so he bought enormous parcels in advance of the relocation and subsequent sharp rise in land values.[8] By 1860 he had accumulated over 128,000 acres in Travis County.[9]

First he established his mercantile business, which he operated with his uncle Swante Palm as junior partner; by October 1850 he was already running advertisements in the *Texas State Gazette.* From the beginning Swenson was known as a shrewd businessman, one who was willing to take risks in inventory to stock new items which he felt the public might buy. (Swenson is usually credited with being the man who introduced Mr. Colt's revolver to Texas in his Austin emporium: he advertised the fact in the May 10, 1851, issue of the *Gazette.*) Swenson noted that he stocked, among other things,

> boots and shoes, Hats, Hardware, Holloware, Earthenware, Woodware, Blacksmith's tools, Iron, Steel and Nails; a General Assortment of Groceries, Flour, Tobacco, Rice, etc; whiskey, brandies, Holland gin, Rum, Sherry, Madeira, Port and Claret wine by the box or the barrel, oils, Paints, Window-Glass and Putty, Bagging and Bale Rope, Powder Shot and Lead; cooking stoves and office stoves, ploughs, hoes, etc.[10]

Soon he began construction of the Avenue Hotel downtown, which would soon be the largest hotel in the capital city. Austin had a total population of just 629 in 1850, but Swenson had faith in the city's growth potential. As soon as "Swenson and Co." was turning a reasonable profit, he began acquiring even more downtown properties, concentrating on Congress Avenue. By the outbreak of the Civil War he owned the equivalent of 12 square blocks of prime mercantile real estate in the heart of the growing capital.

Jeanette Long Swenson never recovered her health, and in November 1850 she died in her family home in Tennessee. Swenson had, on numerous occasions, met her dearest friend, Susan Hudson McCready, an orphan who had grown up on the plantation which adjoined that of Jeanette's family in Tennessee. His burgeoning business ventures had kept him in Austin during his wife's final illness. To his great chagrin, he was not even able to make it to Tennessee in time for her funeral. But by correspondence S.M. Swenson was able to make his interest clear to Miss McCready, and she agreed to marry him as soon as he was able to put aside his frantic preparations to open his Austin business. Anna Swenson Dyer and her husband came to Austin to help her brother set up house. Finally in 1851 he was able to go to Tennessee, where he and Susan McCready were married.[11]

Susan McCready Swenson

As for the purpose of enticing Swedes to Texas, more significant than his business operations was Swenson's October 3, 1850, purchase of a 182-acre tract of land one and a half miles east of Austin from Thomas T. Fauntleroy, a former army colonel. Acquisition of the adjoining parcels quickly increased the size of the estate to nearly 400 acres on a plateau overlooking the Colorado River; here Swenson would build his Austin home, which would also be the first American home for many Swedish immigrants. He named the place "Govalle."

There has been considerable misunderstanding about the nature of Govalle and the origin of its unusual name. The usual explanation—not very linguistically convincing, but commonly repeated—is that "Govalle" came from the Swedish Småland dialect verb phrase *gå valla*, "graze, or tend cattle, sheep, etc." Another derivation has it stemming from the noun phrase *god vall*, "good pastures." [12] In either case, it would seem that Swenson intended Govalle to be as much (or even more) a sheep and cattle ranch as it was a cotton plantation. The small number of hands that worked there in the 1850's and 1860's—never more than a dozen or so—was in marked contrast to the 40 slaves he had needed to work the Finckley plantation. The geography of the area must also have suggested sheep and cattle grazing as more natural and practical than cotton production. By 1862, for example, Swenson was grazing more than 1,500 sheep and an unknown number of cattle at Govalle. [13]

Govalle was to be Swenson's home for over a decade. There his five children (Sarah, 1852-1879; Eric, 1855-1945; Ebba, 1858-1879; Swen Albin, 1860-1927; and Mary Eleanora, 1862-1958) were born. [14] Even after Swenson's secretive departure for Mexico in 1863, Mrs. Swenson and the children continued to live at Govalle until the end of the Civil War, when they joined Swenson in New Orleans.

One researcher states [15] that Swenson sold his slaves just prior to the Civil War and implies that some of them had been working in Austin. While Swenson had sold his own slaves before moving to Austin, the new Govalle enterprise apparently still required some slave assistance. A contract in Swenson's handwriting records his need of two male slaves, named Tom and Dan, whom he hired for a period of four months in 1854 from Mr. E.M. Renie of Austin. [16] He renewed the contract twice, keeping

Swen Albin Swenson

the slaves until August 1855. By then there were more than 100 Swedes in the Austin area, some of whom were now settling down on land of their own. Thus there may have been a temporary labor shortage at Govalle, which Swenson had to make good with slaves. But his ideal was to operate Govalle with Swedish labor, constantly cycling immigrants onto his lands to work off their passage and then moving them onto land of their own, purchased at favorable but still profitable rates from Swenson himself.

It is impossible to state with any accuracy how many Swedes arrived in Texas as contract laborers or even how many arrived on prepaid tickets sent from Austin by Swenson to his brother Johan Swenson in Barkeryd, but it is known that three-fourths of the 100 immigrants who arrived in 1867 worked a year for Swenson or his agents to repay their passage to Texas. The out-of-pocket expenses for prepaid tickets could tie up a considerable amount of capital for some time: for instance, another large group of 70 to 80 immigrants cost Swenson more than 10,000 *riksdaler* (over $2,500) in 1870.[17] The economic crises associated with the depression of 1873 ''cut short the flourishing career of Swenson's [immigration] bureau.''[18] Perhaps even more important was the step-by-step curtailment of contract labor that culminated in its total abolition in the Foran Act of 1885. But, by that point, the emigration was self-sustaining: 5,000 more Swedes arrived in Texas over the next 20 years without Swenson's help.

The nagging problems—moral and economic—raised by slavery had lain behind Swenson's decision to sell his Richmond property (with its attendant slaves) and to start over in Austin, employing mostly hired or indentured labor from Sweden. But the growing sense of fear and division that spread through the state in the 1850's did not leave S.M. Swenson, as a former slave owner, untouched.

Pro-Southern sentiments were strong in Texas and growing stronger. Men like Swenson and Governor Sam Houston tried desperately to stem the secessionist tide, but in vain. Soon violence was close to the surface, and the divisiveness became open. The Epiphany Episcopalian Church in Austin, for example, of which both Swenson and Palm had been members, split in two over the secession question; Swenson joined the ''rich, influential Northerners'' who established Christ's Church (eventually reunited with Epiphany as St. David's) in 1856.[19]

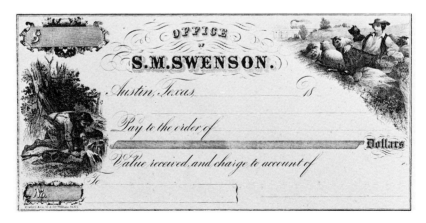

A "Vigilance Committee" was formed in Austin to keep an eye on citizens with pro-Union sympathies. Swenson realized that his outspoken attitudes were now endangering his life and his family.

On April 1, 1861, just a few days before Fort Sumter was attacked, Carl Gustaf and August Palm borrowed $30,000 from Swenson to start "Palm Brothers and Company."[20] Their intention was to transact "business of a mercantile character" for six years. By that time the impending war should be over. Swenson rented his own storehouses and warehouses in the Swenson Building on Congress Avenue to his cousins for $1,200 a year, payable quarterly. Some $26,000 in insured goods—Swenson's entire inventory in 1861—were also to be turned back to him after six years. This silent partnership not only made the Palm brothers the richest Swedes in Texas (for six years) but also transferred Swenson's vast financial responsibilities to his relatives, who now had to act in his stead and on his behalf, since uncle Swante Palm also held Swenson's power of attorney.

One of the most colorful stories told of S.M. Swenson's last days in Texas concerns the hiding of his hoarde of gold:

> [Swenson] pried loose the bricks in the fireplace and picked them out one by one. Then he started to dig a big hole underneath. It was rather soft and not as hard as he imagined it to be. He dug until he thought it was deep enough, then he deposited one of the heavy tin boxes in the hole. He looked into the box to see that everything was all right. That [sic] the slip on which was written, ["] $10,000 by actual count," was laid on top. Then he covered the box with a piece of ducking and put the dirt back. He tramped and tried to get the dirt back again, but he had a considerable heap of it left.[21]

The story goes on to relate how Swenson then buried a further $10,000 in gold under the other fireplace and had the entire area mortared over the next day, with no one the wiser. After the Civil War he sent word to Palm of the cache. Palm then went to Govalle and dug up the fortune and returned it to his grateful nephew. (Another version of this story has Swante

64

Palm hiding S.M. Swenson's gold under his own hearth at the "consulate" on E. Ninth Street—that version insists that $40,000 in gold rested under the fireplace for four years.)[22]

Oddly enough, this colorful story is probably true because an eyewitness recorded her own version. In the account that she wrote to correct the errors in August Anderson's biography of her uncle, Jeanette Dyer Davis, daughter of Anna Kristina Swenson and William Dyer, states that the sum buried was unquestionably $40,000 in gold but that it was buried at Govalle, not in Austin: "I was there, and I remember it well."[23]

Realizing that his continued presence in Austin also endangered his wife and children, Swenson planned his escape. Using his rheumatism as a pretext for visiting the hot springs of Monterrey, Mexico, he applied for and received permission from the governor to leave Texas for Mexico. In the company that was to travel with him were Judge Amos Morrill and a "fervent unionist," Sam Harris, as well as Morgan Hamilton, the brother of Jack Hamilton (later governor of Texas). Swenson crossed into Matamoros just ahead of army patrols sent out particularly to seize him.[24]

Despite the presence of thousands of Texans in Mexico, Swenson was uncomfortable and uneasy being away from his family and business. He eventually arrived in Monterrey, where the governor and president received him courteously, but the war and the struggle over the succession to the crown of Mexico meant further difficulties. Continuing to buy cotton, Swenson stored it in warehouses until a break in the fighting (and the aid of his old friend Consul Lorich in New York) permitted him to ship some 4,700 bales at a profit of more than $25,000. One shipload of this cotton was even sent to Sweden and sold in Göteborg. In the summer of 1864 Swenson managed to make another trip to Sweden to see his mother, stopping in Washington on the return voyage to visit with President Abraham Lincoln, who commented on the vital and strategic importance played by Texas in the closing phases of the war. Swenson returned to New Orleans, where he was quarantined because yellow fever was raging there as well as in Galveston. New Orleans was like a city besieged—children roamed the city in packs begging for food.

After the war's end Swenson decided not to return permanently to Texas, where he still had enemies. The house he had been building in Austin since 1860, on a scale and in a style to rival the Pease mansion, remained unfinished and soon became a picturesque ruin. (Local tradition says that the main building of Huston-Tillotson College was built on the site of "Swenson's Ruin.") Govalle itself was sold in 1871 for more than $50,000, and soon almost every trace of Swenson's presence on the land had apparently disappeared.[25]

Despite his losses during the war, S.M. Swenson was still one of the wealthiest men in Texas, with cash assets valued at over $275,000 and vast landholdings in Austin and North Texas worth even more.[26]

But Swenson decided to settle in New Orleans, where he had already established a large mercantile business with William Perkins. A sugar plantation in Texas (purchased in 1860) near the Louisiana border was proving to be very profitable. By 1880 Swenson had become sole owner of four sugar plantations, and by 1891 each was producing what was generally regarded to be "the finest sugar in Louisiana."[27] The "Swenson touch," evident from his earliest days in Austin, when "the day Swenson did not make $1,000 profit was reckoned a failure," became, if anything, even surer after his departure from the Lone Star State.

Ultimately Swenson decided to manage his combined southern operations from outside the region; he moved his base of operations to New York in 1866. There he and Perkins reopened the Swenson, Perkins Co. on Wall Street. That soon became the banking firm of S.M. Swenson & Sons, which later merged with National City Bank to become the First National City Bank of New York, the second largest bank in America.[28]

With Swenson's move to New York, his pioneering days as a Swedish colonist were over. His next enterprise was the creation of the S.M.S. cattle ranches, one of the greatest cattle empires in the history of the state.

7

The First Immigrant

Swante Palm

With the notable exception of his nephew, S.M. Swenson, no one did more to encourage immigration to Texas or to nurture the aspirations of the immigrants than Swante Palm. He pioneered the pathway to Texas and played a major role in the development of Swedish-American cultural life in the Lone Star State. Much of what he did has been inaccurately reported, often even in the standard sources. Palm's life, however, was a fascinating one, even without embellishment.

Born on January 13, 1815, at Bästhult, a farm just south of Barkeryd Lake, Swante Palm showed early signs of intellectual promise.[1] He was tutored by the sexton of the Barkeryd parish church in Swedish, Latin, English, French, German, and mathematics. Although this was the only formal education he received, it stood him in good stead and permitted him to leave the family farm and strike out on his own. While his nephew Swen (whose mother, Margareta, was Palm's sister and elder by some 20 years) was working as a bookkeeper in Eksjö, Palm was riding the circuit of local courts in three districts, first as apprentice scribe, then scribe, to the bailiff. These positions demanded a quick mind and a quick pen (as well as decent handwriting), for much of the work consisted of recording the proceedings of the various judicial courts. Finally, in 1841, Palm became rural clerk (*landskanslist*) for the cities of Kalmar and Jönköping, which were much larger than the villages of Småland in which he had worked up to that time.

Swante Palm

Kalmar—in the 19th century it was spelled "Calmar"—soon became his permanent home, when he was appointed to the Göta Court of Appeals, one of the high courts of Sweden, similar to an American federal court.[2]

Sometime during the next three years he created the surname by which he was henceforth known. He was christened Swen Andersson, following the traditional patronymic system common in Sweden a hundred years ago and still in use today in Iceland (see Chapter 6, note 1). Swen Andersson did as so many other immigrants were to do after him: he invented a new name. Actually, there was a native precedent for taking a name like "Palm." The military authorities were also dismayed by the repetitions created by the patronymic system and often issued new *soldatnamn* or "soldiers' names" (usually one brisk syllable in length, like "Brand" or "Frid") to new recruits.

The Christian name "Swante," as we have seen with his namesake Swen "Swante" Magnus Swenson, is a diminutive, like "Jimmy" or "Tommy" in English; in the extended Swenson-

Andersson family, it clearly helped to distinguish nephew from uncle. And the Palm name became normative for all of Swante's brothers who followed him in the chain migration to Texas; they stepped on board the emigrant ship surnamed Andersson and arrived in America named Palm.

Swante Palm edited the weekly newspaper *Calmar-Posten,* in Kalmar between 1841 and his emigration in 1844. It was largely an honorary position, but one which supplied a small and badly needed income. During this same period he also fell unhappily in love. By the beginning of 1844 neither his debts nor his romantic prospects seemed to show signs of improvement, so his thoughts turned to his prospering nephew's entreaties to join him in the Republic of Texas.[3]

According to a story which Palm himself may have helped circulate, the waning days of King Carl XIV Johan were fraught with difficulty for publishers as the increasingly paranoid monarch saw cabals and conspirators everywhere, their every move supposedly reported to and supported by the public in the pages of the popular press. Carl Johan invoked 100-year-old sedition and censorship laws to suppress the newspapers for the first and only time in Swedish history, a dark era for Swedish journalistic freedom. Palm, as editor of *Calmar-Posten,* may have tangled with the law, but a perusal of the issues he edited shows only three or four mild editorial comments (signed "Najad"—"Naiad," Palm's nom de plume) in the three years of his editorship. Most editorial energy was expended in a seemingly endless diatribe against the rival Kalmar newspaper, *Barometern,* over subscription tactics and the personal political convictions of the respective editors. *Calmar-Posten* was, in fact, quite conservative, while *Barometern* espoused the more radical views of its editor, Dr. Engström.[4]

For these reasons, in addition to the warm and genuine respect his private writings always displayed toward the Bernadotte dynasty, it seems hard to credit trouble with the censor as a major factor in Palm's decision to emigrate. He himself mentioned only his debts and his unrequited love affair, but perhaps Dr. Engström's attacks on him (he was called a "little boy" and a "young bantam" in the pages of *Barometern*) might have helped his decision.

S.M. Swenson contacted both Palm and Palm's elder brother, Gustaf, almost immediately after his own arrival in

Texas, asking them to join him in his new business ventures. Their response must have been positive, for in March of 1839 Swenson wrote to no less a partnership than McKinney and Williams,[5] two of his oldest friends in Galveston, to introduce "my uncles Gustavus and Swen Palm" and to request that the wealthy Texans advance the Palms money "sufficient for expenses to this place [Richmond]."[6] But it was to be five years before "uncle Swen" arrived and a full decade until "uncle Gustavus" joined him. By then Swen Magnus Swenson was well on his way to becoming a millionaire.

Swante Palm sailed from Kalmar on board the copper-hulled brig *Superb* on May 1, 1844, bound for New York. His account of that voyage is one of the earliest made by an actual Swedish emigrant and provides a few intimate glimpses into life aboard an emigrant vessel in the earliest days of the Scandinavian transatlantic migration.[7]

There were 13 passengers, emigrants all, three of whom were returning to North America after a visit home. One of these was J.P. Hägerlund, a former merchant seaman aboard the Swedish frigate *af Chapman* and now a merchant in S.M. Swenson's employ. He had lived in Richmond, Texas, for several years after being stranded in America in 1826 when the *af Chapman* was sold. Another veteran was James Brodie, whom Palm incorrectly identifies as a Swede: he was actually born in Scotland. Like several of the crewmen, Brodie had quite a drinking problem during the voyage, and drinking seems to be about the only vice sternly condemned by the otherwise tolerant Palm.

Finally, there was Palm's friend and traveling companion, Eugen Conrad Gullbrandsson, a rather shadowy figure about whom little is known. It is uncertain exactly where in Sweden he was born, but in 1844 he was just over 19 years old. He must have been a good friend of Palm's, because a mutual acquaintance read a farewell poem composed especially for their emigration from Kalmar, addressed to both Gullbrandsson and Palm. It is quite likely that Palm had persuaded young Gullbrandsson to join him on the long road to Texas.[8]

On May 3 the *Superb* passed the Norwegian coast with a good southeasterly breeze. The captain, a Swede named Nissen, was a devout Methodist and held divine worship on the afterdeck. By May 6 they were passing the Shetlands and the Orkneys and heading out into the Atlantic. An imaginary hunting society leveled "fines" for shooting imaginary game—fines levied in ''liquid goods,'' sherry or port. The players soon ran out of capital, however, and the drinking society foundered.

> During the following five weeks, my diary is concerned only with storm, sea-sickness, and calm, whales, porpoises and terns. . . . Any specific "dangers at sea" I cannot recall and only a couple of hard storms, during one of which the boatswain got a rope wrapped around his neck and remained hanging awhile in a situation which suggested that he would be either hanged or drowned. Another night we lost part of the foremast. . . . At 7 in the morning on the 18th we had land in sight on both sides of the entrance to New York harbor. The coastlines wore their prettiest greenery. Highlighted by dark-green, white and pleasant, the groves of trees and everything seemed to beckon us welcome.[9]

After coming ashore at Castle Garden, Palm wandered out into the streets of New York, where the bustle and spectacle fascinated him — from glassblowers in the streets to massive political rallies. A few days later he traveled by steamer up the Hudson to Albany and Buffalo, where his meager funds dried up. But soon, "like some kind of Swedish-American Peddler," he got a traveling sales job, covering the countryside for Swedish businessmen in Buffalo. It was now high summer, and he was wary of heading directly into the brutal Central Texas heat, so he spent the next five and a half months covering 700 miles on foot and another 425 miles on the decks of steam and canal boats in New York, Pennsylvania, Ohio, and Kentucky. Palm's friend Conrad Gullbrandsson, meanwhile, remained in New York working for a tanner; he, too, wished to await cooler weather before heading west. Finally on December 9 the friends decided that conditions in Texas were satisfactory, so they met in Louisville and boarded a steamer bound for New Orleans. There they found letters from

S.M. Swenson welcoming them to Texas. On December 20 they boarded another steamship in New Orleans and landed in Galveston on the 23rd. They reached Houston on Christmas Day, and by twilight the next day they had ridden to Swenson's plantation, Finckley.[10]

"Uncle Palm" helped Swenson with his accounts and books and maintained a correspondence with Sweden, keeping their relatives informed of Swenson's steady successes in America. Plans were already under way in 1845 for Swenson's first return visit to his mother country, but, because of his burgeoning business activities, the trip had to be postponed for two years.

Less than two years after his arrival Palm had formed a mercantile partnership of his own with C.P. Flack of Seguin. Swenson helped finance "Flack and Palm Co." of Columbia in September 1846. They were to deal in "vending goods, wares and merchandise," and Palm was to be the junior partner. But in May 1846, less than four months before going into business with Flack, Palm had become postmaster in La Grange. Because of the constant traveling and the demands of his new job, he decided to sell the business (and inventory) to his partner. Flack's share was $1,919 and Palm's a meager $163.04. Despite his skill in managing Swenson's affairs, this entrepreneurial fiasco might have given rise to the stories of Palm's financial fuzzy-headedness and the image he was later to project of an impractical, absent-minded bookworm.[11]

Before leaving Sweden in 1836, S.M. Swenson had made the acquaintance of Admiral, later Baron, Nordenskiöld, the former commander of the Swedish frigate *af Chapman*. Nordenskiöld was, in turn, a good friend of Baron Gyllengranat, the former commander of the other Swedish warship, *Tapperheten*, which was to be sold with *af Chapman* to the new republic of Colombia by the Swedish government in 1826. Because Sweden was unable to recognize diplomatically the revolutionary government of Colombia, however, the sale was stopped, and the vessels sailed to New York, eventually to be sold at auction. Many of the nearly 700 Swedish crew members were stranded in the New World without the funds for repatriation. Many, like Palm's traveling companion in 1844, the plucky J.P. Hägerlund (a sailor from *af Chapman*), went ashore in New York and made their way westward. (By a strange turn of fate, Hägerlund wound up in Texas in 1837 and within two years was working for none other than S.M. Swenson.)

A few of the stranded sailors stayed in New York itself. The most famous of them was Olof Hedström (from *af Chapman*), who married an American girl, converted to Methodism, and opened a Methodist seamen's hostel in a demasted ship right in the harbor. Hedström's kindness to arriving immigrants was soon well known; he and his brother, Jonas, were largely responsible for routing immigrants (among them Erik Jansson and his followers) to Illinois and the Midwest. More important for Swedes bound for Texas was the friendship struck up between S.M. Swenson and Olof Hedström in the 1870's. Many of them were met at the pier by Hedström and taken to Swenson's New York immigrant hotel before they set out for Texas on the train.

Other Swedish sailors, such as Gustaf Ceder, a seaman aboard *Tapperheten* who was the son of Palm's former tutor, did not fare as well. Some were sent ahead to Colombia, probably to await the arrival of their vessels after the intended transfer to the Colombian fleet. Many of these seamen were never heard from again. Ten years after the so-called "*af Chapman* affair," both former commanders were still quite concerned about the fate of their shipmates and urged Swenson, while he was in America, to find out all he could about their whereabouts. He relayed the little he was able to discover to Nordenskiöld in 1840 after he reached Texas. Nearly a decade later, since Swante Palm was acquainted with one of the hapless Swedes — Gustaf Ceder — Swenson pressed his uncle to help find them.[12]

This was the background for one of the strangest incidents in the early days of the Swedish colony in Texas, Swante Palm's departure for the Isthmus of Panama in the spring of 1849 as a "secretary in the diplomatic service." Palm's stay in Panama has long been somewhat puzzling, if not outright mysterious, but the basic facts are now available.

In the 1840's the Isthmus of Panama belonged to Colombia, a new republic carved out of the last remnants of the old viceroyalty of Nueva Granada. The redoubtable Captain William "Peg Leg" Ward, colorful politician and hero of the Texas Revolution, was heading for the Isthmus of Panama on a diplomatic matter, according to one source, as a military adviser to Colombia. Palm's mission had nothing in common with Ward's, save the destination, but the Texan's presence certainly made the long trip a bit less dangerous for Palm.

Swante Palm was an unofficial representative of the Swedish diplomatic corps, urged to undertake the journey by Consul Severin Lorich in New York on behalf of the Swedish captains, Nordenskiöld and Gyllengranat. Lorich was an old friend of Swenson's, too, so the mission must have been undertaken more out of a sense of personal honor than official diplomatic necessity. Palm's contact in Panama was Consul Charles Zachrisson. The mystery surrounding Palm's journey arises from its sensitivity: why did Lorich not write his counterpart, Zachrisson, for information about the missing sailors instead of asking Palm to make the long and hazardous journey in person?

But perhaps it was Palm's irrepressible curiosity that sent him forth. He must have relished the chance to see such exotic places—and read about them: Harry Ransom remarked that Palm wanted to take a wagonload of books with him but was eventually dissuaded by Captain Ward.[13] At any rate, he reached the isthmus in the spring of 1849 and made contact with "Don Carlos" Zachrisson. He soon learned that his old friend Ceder had died of yellow fever in 1827, shortly after arriving in Cartagena. He had written a number of letters to his father (Palm's former tutor), but they had been intercepted by the authorities and suppressed, so no one in Sweden had heard of his fate. (Another aspect of the mystery is who in Cartagena, besides Zachrisson, could have read the contents of Ceder's Swedish letters!)[14]

After learning of his friend's sad fate, Palm stayed a year in Panama as secretary to Consul Zachrisson before returning to Texas. By 1850 he was back in the Lone Star State, where, save for two trips back to Sweden, he was to remain for the next 50 years. Panama apparently cured his wanderlust.

On his return from Panama in 1850, Palm settled first in La Grange, then for a time at Govalle. S.M. Swenson's Austin business interests were expanding rapidly and needed the attention of both men. In the fall of 1853 Agnes Alm and her sister, Laura, came to Texas from Kalmar. It is possible that Agnes was the "unrequited love" of Palm's early manhood. If she was not, they soon fell in love, in any case, and early the next year Agnes Alm and Swante Palm were married in La Grange in Palm's former home, fondly known as Nya (New) Bästhult, after the family farm in Sweden. But as soon as their house on 9th Avenue in Austin was ready, the newlyweds moved in.

The Palms' move to Austin was to be the last one in both their lives. Swante Palm settled down to a more sedentary life, working for Swenson until the latter's departure for the East Coast after the Civil War and at the same time pursuing his various interests, many of which centered on the fledgling Swedish colony in Texas, less than a hundred strong in 1853. The Palms and the Swensons joined the Episcopal Church, which satisfied Swenson and his wife, who remained lifelong Episcopalians. Palm, however, was interested in obtaining the services of a Swedish Lutheran minister as soon as possible and in founding a Swedish Lutheran congregation in the capital city. His labors eventually bore fruit, but it was to take nearly two decades.

The Palms' only child, Swante Sture, died in infancy. His death was a blow from which neither parent ever truly recovered. Perhaps to assuage his grief, Swante threw himself into a welter of activity. In 1868 he began to lay the groundwork for the congregation that would later become the Gethsemane Lutheran Church by convincing an itinerant pastor of the Swedish state church to hold the first Swedish-language worship service in the Lone Star State.

Palm resumed his interest in the postal service and for four years acted as postmaster of Austin. He also served as justice of the peace and was elected to several terms on the Austin School Board. To commemorate his service to the schools of the city, Palm Elementary School, now Palm Center, was named in his honor in 1902. (More recently, in 1987, a new elementary school was named for Swante Palm.) His political career also included two terms as alderman, or member of the City Council.

Much of Palm's time was his own after Swenson's removal to New York, although he continued to represent Swenson's interests in Austin and to derive a modest income from the various businesses in which both men had been involved. But after he was named honorary vice-consul for Sweden and Norway in 1866, more and more of his energies went into representing Scandinavian interests in Texas, primarily by arranging prepaid passage for the growing number of Swedes wishing to immigrate to Texas. Throughout the decades of the 1860's and 1870's he also acted as an emigrant agent for Swenson and Swenson's brother Johan Swenson back in Småland. During this period the number of Swedes in Texas — 80 percent of whom were still related either by blood or marriage to Swenson or, at least, had lived in or near Barkeryd parish — rose from 153 to nearly 1,300.

Palm returned to Sweden two times, in 1873 and 1884. He visited Barkeryd in 1873 and spent most of his time during that visit home working on supplementing his library. He and his wife were warmly received in Kalmar, their former home, and friends of 30 years wrote a long poem of farewell on the Palms' departure, just as they had when Swante Palm had emigrated in 1844.[15]

Agnes Alm Palm died in July 1881 and was buried in Austin. Her death, after nearly 30 years of marriage, deeply affected Palm, and he undertook a second trip to Sweden in 1884, in part to rid himself of bad memories. On this visit home he was received by King Oscar II (technically Palm's "boss," since Palm, as vice-consul, was a member of the Swedish Royal Diplomatic Corps), who presented him with the Order of Vasa. People in Texas incorrectly inferred that Palm had been knighted, and he was often called "Sir Swante" (against his wishes) in his last days. (The Vasa Order is a life honor and does not confer a title on the recipient.)

In addition to being Swedish and Norwegian vice-consul, which post he held for more than 30 years, Palm was a member of many national and international organizations. Almost from his first day in Texas he had been fascinated by the weather in the Lone Star State and kept meticulous meteorological notes. He was later named Austin's first official meteorologist and worked on one of the earliest geological surveys of the state in the 1850's. He belonged to such diverse organizations as the Masons (at one time during the Civil War he was said to have been the secretary of all five Austin lodges simultaneously), Fornskriftssällskapet (The Society for Medieval Literature) in Stockholm, as well as Geologiska föreningen (The Geological Society), Svenska Geologiska och Anthropologiska Sällskapet (Swedish Geological and Anthropological Society), and Oskar och Josefine Sällskapet (King Oskar and Queen Josefine Society) in Stockholm, among others.[16]

But what made Swante Palm famous throughout Swedish America (and even outside it), and what really occupied most of his time in Austin during his last 40 years, was his incomparable library. He was an inveterate reader and collector, many of his volumes having crossed the Atlantic with him in 1844. He annotated his books, underlining, punctuating, and commenting. He read and reread them until they sometimes fell apart from overuse. He bound them in practical, if not aesthetic, little volumes of varying format and length. He was a constant notetaker and observer, jotting down his findings on the flyleaves of his books and the endpapers of his pocket almanacs. For nearly 60 years he carried out a far-flung correspondence with book dealers and book lovers, trading, buying, selling, or simply chatting about books.

The full range of Palm's library is too great to be discussed here. We can simply note that his taste was wide-ranging but only somewhat eclectic. He loved the classics of English and Scandinavian literature: Shakespeare and Strindberg, Thackeray and Tegnér, Goldsmith and Andersen, Dickens and Ibsen, were all represented in well-worn editions, each as complete as possible by 1899, the year of Palm's death. He loved large editions of plates and engravings of city views: he had many of Sweden and Texas and also of Paris, Berlin, London, and other cities that he had never seen. History, especially English, Swedish, and American history, fascinated him: from ghost stories to the Federalist papers, Macaulay to Mark Twain, Palm loved it all. His collection

Swante Palm with his book collection

of theology (Swedish and English) is perhaps not so surprising, considering his deep lifelong piety and scholarly interest in religion, but one is also struck by his open-mindedness, as witnessed, for example, by a number of works by the youthful, atheistic August Strindberg. His tolerance, his unbridled curiosity, and his strongly empirical, or scientific, bent are attested to by the heavily annotated volumes of Darwin's *Voyage of the Beagle* and *Origin of Species.* Clearly the acquisition of some 12,000 to 12,500 volumes was a remarkable achievement for any early American book collector, but in the case of a frontier immigrant, it is amazing. Swante Palm's library was a monument to the collector, who intended it to be a legacy to Texas Swedes.

Before they had a chance to appreciate it, however, they had to fight to keep Palm and his treasure in Texas. The library's existence was no secret: on the contrary, a number of institutions were lining up in the 1890's to try to get it for themselves.

The fight for Palm's library was a long and often bitter one, with the fledgling University of Texas and Gethsemane Lutheran Church of Austin the eventual winners. Bethany College, a tiny and, at that moment, financially strapped Swedish-American institution in Lindsborg, Kansas, was the chief rival for the collection. Carl Swensson, the president of Bethany, had been begging Palm for years to at least *consider* Bethany before committing himself, since Palm on several occasions had visited the school and encouraged its development.[17]

As early as 1891 the college had honored Palm by bestowing an honorary doctor's degree (*filosofie heders-doktor*) upon him. On subsequent visits he donated some small sums to the struggling school, which were gratefully received and acknowledged. Then, on May 15, 1896, President Carl Swensson offered to build the Swante Palm Library at Bethany, a roomy, fireproof building with an apartment for Palm in the same structure, as well as to provide food, heat, light, and care for the aging scholar. Palm would be named librarian of the collection, and he and his goods would be moved without charge to Lindsborg, if only Palm would bequeath the library to Bethany.

Despite the pleas of Carl Swensson, Palm seems never to have seriously considered moving to Lindsborg. In a note appended to Swensson's last appeal, he comments: "Back in Austin,

Library, Swante Palm residence, Austin, 1894

Swante Palm in his garden, Austin, 1894

I am now living in very tight quarters with the books and need to build my present library in Austin. We talked about this (in Lindsborg)."[18] In fact, so tight had quarters become in Palm's Austin home some time earlier that he had already built an addition onto the residence, and by the 1890's the *addition* was too crowded. He needed to move his books somewhere, but he wanted to be close to them as well. Finally he agreed to donate the bulk of his library to the University of Texas; some 2,000 to 2,500 works on theology (many in Swedish) would go to Gethsemane Lutheran Church to which he belonged and which he had helped found.

Beginning in February 1897, with the appropriate fanfare, Palm and his library moved into the original Main Building on the campus of the University of Texas at Austin, then only 15 years old. The 10,000 volumes in the Palm collection more than doubled the original library holdings.[19]

On June 22, 1899, Swante Palm died at the age of 85. He was given one of the largest funerals in the history of the Swedish-American community in Texas. In essence, the mourners were paying tribute both to the old consul and to his legendary nephew, S.M. Swenson, who had died in 1896 and been buried in New York. Palm was named "benefactor of the year"

*Bust of Swante Palm
by Elisabet Ney*

in the 1899 University of Texas yearbook, *The Cactus.* Admiring students had even led a torchlight parade to "the consulate" at 9th and Guadalupe to celebrate the "man of the hour." A collection was taken up among the students to pay for a bust of the benefactor, which was executed by Elisabet Ney, one of the most renowned sculptors of the day. (Kaiser Wilhelm I and Bavaria's King Ludwig II had sat for her, among other notables.) Her hauntingly romantic bust is now in the library of the Eugene C. Barker Texas History Center on the Austin campus of The University of Texas.[20]

Palm's extraordinary largess was widely discussed in the *dödsrunor* (obituaries) which appeared in the Swedish-American press from coast to coast. Austin's own *Texas-Posten,* then only three years old, took the opportunity to extol Palm's role as molder and shaper of the spiritual and cultural life of the Swedish-Texan immigrants.[21] "Above all," declared *Texas-Posten,* "Consul Palm was, in his heart and soul, a Swede. Swedish literature, the Swedish language, and the Swedish people were always closest and dearest to him."

Other papers, such as *Svenska-Amerikanaren* in Chicago, reminisced about the absentminded book collector who fit so many stereotypes and stirred so many imaginations.[22] His wisdom and acumen were what editors wished to remember Palm for, and these qualities were epitomized — even immortalized — in the Swante Palm Library.

8

The Nomads

Other Early Swedish Settlers in Texas

S wen Magnus Swenson is often called "the first Swede in Texas," but that was a designation he himself never used. In his early years Swenson met a number of Swedes who were more or less wholly acculturated to Texas, but who nevertheless remembered their homeland and mother tongue. Others preceded him and then vanished with hardly a trace.

One of the latter was the shadowy John R. Reagor, or Reager, allegedly a Swedish sea captain who settled near present-day Ennis in Ellis County about 1806.[1] The Carpenter Land Grant of 1850 perpetuated the sailor's name in "Reagor Springs." Almost as mysterious was one Jan Jacob Lundquist, who disguised his Swedish origins behind the faceless name of "Joe Smith." He may have reached Texas as early as 1822. In later years he told people he was from Halmstad in southwestern Sweden, where he claimed to have been born in 1794.[2] No less a figure than Sam Houston, leaving Nashville to live out west among the Indians, traveled with a Swede named H. Haroldson as far as Texas.[3]

Another early Swede in Texas was John Peter Hägerlund, or Hagerlund, who arrived in Texas in 1837, at least a year before Swenson. He was born in the coastal town of Karlskrona in southern Sweden in 1805 and had been a cadet aboard the Royal Swedish Navy vessel *af Chapman* until 1826 when it was sold in New York, leaving Hägerlund and a number of fellow countrymen stranded in America. But Hägerlund must have been a resilient sort, for he came to Texas and soon ran a mercantile business in Richmond, not far from Swenson's plantation in Fort Bend County. He returned to Sweden several times and accompanied Swante Palm to New York aboard the *Superb* in 1844.[4]

The continuing skirmishes with Mexico that followed Texas independence finally erupted into full-scale war in 1846. As is always the case, combat drew eager young soldiers to both sides of the conflict. A number of these mercenary types were from Sweden, some of them aristocrats or other unblooded soldiers of fortune looking for action in the war with Mexico.

Historians have identified a few Swedish names: William Peterson and a man named Hallmark, for example, were residents of Texas in 1846 and fought with American forces in Mexico. Other Swedes were already serving as officers and enlisted men in federal forces and saw action against Mexico. These included Captains Oscar Malmborg, Fabian Brynjolf, and Ernst Holmstedt, whose experience in the Mexican War later enabled them to earn commissions in the Union army during the Civil War. The best-known name among this tiny group was John Ericsson, later designer of the *Monitor* during the Civil War, who served as a consultant to the War Department during the Mexican War and presented the government with a plan for an iron steamer which could navigate the Rio Grande as well as the Gulf of Mexico.[5]

Swante Palm painted vivid portraits of several such Swedes some time after their deaths for the readers of *Hemlandet,* the leading Swedish-language newspaper in America for many years. In these articles, Palm recalled that "3 or 4" Swedes had participated in the battle of San Jacinto and may have fallen there. Sam Houston remembered too that "there were brave Swedes there" but did not recall any names. Count Arvid Posse (1782-1831), for example, fought for Texas in the battle of San Jacinto. He came from a fine family in Sweden and was known for his "exquisite manners." Nevertheless, money problems and a general depression finally drove Count Posse to a grim and ironic end. He shot himself in the head on the banks of the San Antonio River, but his body fell backwards onto the riverbank, not into the water where, he had hoped, it would be washed away to sea. Alas, only the vultures (and the vivid imagination of Mrs.

Mary Austin Holley, from whom Palm got the story) seem to recall the last resting place of one whom Mrs. Holley rather fancifully called "a brother-in-arms to Napoleon I."[6]

Less macabre was the story of Adolf von Wolfcrona, a German-Swedish aristocrat who had been in Texas since the revolution when Palm first met him in 1847. At that time von Wolfcrona thought himself to be the only Swede in Texas. His father owned a *fideikomiss*, or entailed estate, in Skåne in southern Sweden, but most of his youth had been spent in Germany at the home of his mother's parents near Hamburg. For a while, he was a kind of foreman for his elder brother, who had inherited the estate, but soon Adolf decided to try his luck in America. He made his way to Texas in time to join General Taylor's army for the siege of Monterrey. He became ill and settled for a while in Industry, Texas, where he developed a good business breeding chickens. He soon returned to military life, however, and to the war in Mexico. He became an officer in a company commanded by a Captain Evans but was taken ill again at the battle of Mexico City near Jalapa, where he died on January 16, 1848.[7]

Palm mentions another early Swedish aristocrat in Texas, one whom he knew intimately. This was the young Johan Fredrik Roos af Hjelmsäter, some of whose papers, including his travel diary of 1850-1852, have survived to give us a detailed portrait of a Swedish officer/gentleman/immigrant in the early days of the Lone Star State.[8]

Johan Fredrik Roos af Hjelmsäter was the illegitimate son of Elaias Roos af Hjelmsäter and Mathilda Frederica, née Dahlgren. The young man grew up in a military home—his father was an officer in the Götha Royal Artillery. Johan chose the military life over a life "intended for business" and entered the Swedish army as a second officer. He volunteered for duty in Denmark and saw action in the battle of Fredericia.

But Roos was soon out of work after the Prussian withdrawal in 1848, so he made his way to Germany, hoping to find some military employment there. In Hamburg he met a Swedish businessman from Kalmar, one Herr Båth, who was on his way to dig for gold in California. Since Roos had just sold his gold watch to pay his hotel bill, Båth's adventure may not have seemed so rash.

Two days later Roos bought a ticket for New York aboard a ship which was to sail within 48 hours. On October 19, 1850, Roos left Hamburg with a "cargo" of 70 emigrants, all the rest of them German. The ship, the bark *Mellis Sloman,* met generally beautiful weather except in the North Sea. Beautiful, too, were the daughters of a minister from Hannover, "who made my journey most enjoyable."

On December 10, 1850, the *Mellis Sloman* docked in New York after a voyage of some seven weeks. The next day Roos moved into a Scandinavian hotel in "Grönwish Strit" (Greenwich Street) and immediately began to look for a job. He worked as a bartender for a few days but was never paid, so he moved on to Cumberland with two Germans who liked the penniless Swedish soldier of fortune. He and his German friends worked for food and a night's lodging, moving from one farm to another. One night Roos was asked to go to church before the evening meal. Although tired and hungry, he agreed. The church was crowded, he noted, and when he walked in, "I believed at first that I was in a madhouse, but later I understood that we had come among Methodists, who pray to God with much bending of the knees, and they beat their hands and heads so hard against chairs and pews that blood flew everywhere."

From March until the middle of May Roos served as a kind of secretary to one "Doctor" C.W. Roback, a Swedish snake-oil salesman, mesmerist, quack, and crackpot. Roback was arrested and fined $7,000 for deceitful practice, but Roos followed the charlatan to New York despite Roback's astrological pretensions because he desperately needed the $18-a-month wages. In September 1851 Roos sailed to Richmond, Virginia, in an old schooner. He stayed in Richmond—a town much to his taste—for more than a month, largely in the company of generous Swedes. Then, in October, he began his wanderings again, ending up stranded in Key West. There he gave guitar lessons, watched the huge flocks of birds, and observed the people, among whom were Spaniards, Turks, and Malaysians, as well as many slaves. After staying a month in Key West he sailed up the coast to Apalachicola, working his passage. He saw his first cotton being loaded aboard, cotton from Alabama, Georgia, and perhaps even Texas. From Apalachicola, he made his way to Columbus, Georgia. There he was made "second steward" aboard

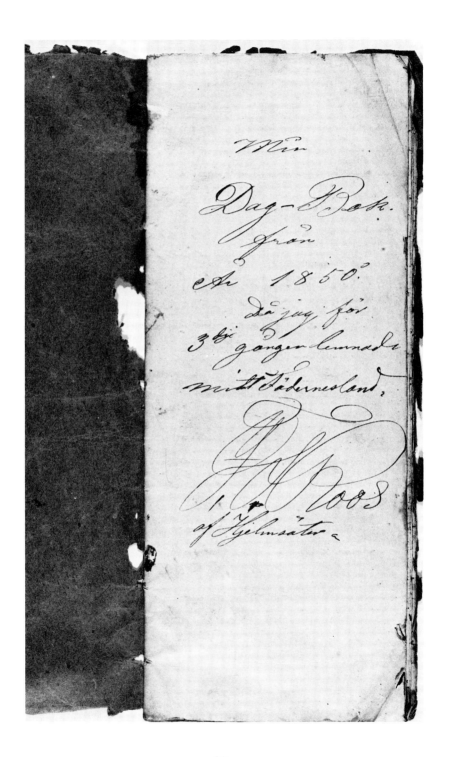

Min

Dag-Bok.

från

År 1850.

då jag för
3dje gången lemnade
mitt Fädernesland;

[signature]

af Hjelmsäter.

the steamboat *Swan,* on which he worked for two months until he earned enough money to get to New Orleans. He arrived there aboard the steamer *America* on March 29.

Although Roos af Hjelmsäter's diary stops at March 29, 1852, it is clear that he headed almost immediately for Texas from New Orleans. Swante Palm remembered meeting him in "late spring or early summer" that year in La Grange. Palm, in fact, thought that exaggerated reports of a gold strike near Austin, which appeared in many newspapers across the country, were the initial factors in Roos's trip to Texas. Soon the young Swede had found a job in Austin working for a German food merchant named "Dutch (i.e., Deutsch) John."

Johan Fredrik Roos af Hjelmsäter now changed his name to "J.F. Hamilton." He became a volunteer in one of the four horse companies established by the state to guard against attacks by Comanches in West Texas. He served six to eight months as a Texas Ranger in 1854 and traveled as far south as Monterrey, Mexico. He became known for his constant good humor and his honesty, and Palm was also impressed with his natural abilities as a military man.

Finally it seemed as though this wanderer was able to find a home and put down roots. In October of 1856 Hamilton began work as a chief clerk for Swenson and Palm at a salary of $45 a month. He moved in with Daniel Hurd, one of the original 25 Swedish immigrants who had come from Barkeryd parish in 1848. Hurd was, in the mid-1850's, S.M. Swenson's foreman at Govalle in Austin. Perhaps with Hurd's influence, Hamilton was able to buy a 160-acre homestead from Swenson on January 14, 1857. A week later, he was dead.[9]

Palm explains that a "lilac-like" bush (possibly mountain laurel) grew in Texas and reminded the Swedes most poignantly of their distant homeland. In January of 1857 he and several other immigrants, including Hamilton, were transplanting some of these bushes. The weather, Palm noted, was cold, wet, and raw—especially so, says Palm, "because [our] blood was now thin as water." Hamilton became ill, seemed to recover after a few days, then caught pneumonia and died on January 21, 1857. He was only 36 years old.

The funeral of Johan Fredrik Roos af Hjelmsäter, now John F. Hamilton, was held in S.M. Swenson's Avenue Hotel

FUNERAL NOTICE.

The friends and acquaintances of

JOHN F. HAMILTON,

are requested to attend his funeral at Mr Swenson's building, Room 26, North wing, to-morrow, at 10 o'clock A. M.

Austin, Friday, 23d January, 1857.

at 10 o'clock on January 23, 1857, at Swenson's expense. In an account book found with his papers, Hamilton left his estate, valued at $261.73, to S.M. Swenson. A list of the estate, in Palm's handwriting, reveals that he left behind some used clothing, an old gold watch, an old saber, a dress sword, and a signet ring with the Roos af Hjelmsäter crest "to be sent to his parents."[10]

The sad ending to such a promising new life was felt especially keenly by Swante Palm and S.M. Swenson. They buried the young Swedish aristocrat under a Texas live oak, but it was nearly ten years before Palm was contacted by Hamilton's parents, who had read an earlier letter by Palm in *Hemlandet*. So the young man's few possessions and his account book ultimately found their way back to Göteborg in 1867. At Hamilton's funeral, Palm read the following poem, which well summed up the hopes and promises of Hamilton's nomadic life:

> He left his home with a pounding heart,
>   For the world was all before him,
> And felt it scarce a pain to part
>   Such sunbright beams came o'er him.
> He turned him to visions of future years
>   —The rainbow's hues were 'round them—
> And a father's bodings, a mother's tears
>   Might not weigh with the hopes that
> crowned him.[11]

9

The Pioneers

The Immigrants of the 1840's and 1850's

Swen Magnus Swenson's first visit home in 1847 inspired only one emigrant, his younger sister, Anna Kristina. But he had planted an idea, and the imaginations of the farmers of Barkeryd proved fertile ground. By spring of the next year "Texas fever" had spread for the first time through Barkeryd and the neighboring parishes.

The company that made the first voyage consisted of members of three large family groups from the same area. They not only grew up with one another and emigrated together, but, more importantly, they remained together in Texas, settling near one another in a pattern similar to that at home. They also married within the larger extended family group and saw to it that other members of their family circle emigrated as well.

The *de facto* leader of the group was Anders Andersson, a 52-year-old farmer and elder brother of Swante Palm, who had by then been in Texas for nearly four years. With Andersson was his brother Gustaf and both of their families. Gustaf and Anders quickly adopted Swante's practice and called themselves "Palm" after they came to Texas.

Anders's wife, Annika or Anna, was 12 years his junior. They had six sons ranging in age from 16-year-old Johannes to 3-year-old Henning. The other children were August, Carl

Anna Palm

Gustaf, Anders Johan, and Swen Wilhelm, all of whom were to become leaders in the Swedish community in Central Texas.

Gustaf Palm was a year younger than his brother Anders, and his wife, Emilia, at 26 was considerably younger than Anna Palm. The eldest of Emilia's four children was only seven. The youngest, Johan Gustaf, was barely a year old when the family set out across the Atlantic. Gustaf Palm was unusual among the emigrants in that he had received training as an oboist and organist; by profession, he was a skilled watchmaker, not a farmer. But he was headed for Texas to acquire land and raise his family, just as the rest of the company dreamed of doing.

Two other brothers were taking their families to the Lone Star State. Carl Johanesson was 32 in 1848 and a native of Forserum parish just west of Barkeryd. He followed the example of the Palm families and dropped the patronymic "Johanesson," changing his name to "Hård." Other family members did the same thing, but the spelling was soon changed to "Hörd," then

"Hurd" or "Heard" to conform with American orthography. Carl was Anna Palm's younger brother, so the Hård emigration was directly linked to the Palms and thus indirectly to Swenson. Carl and his wife, Maria, invariably known as "Maja Lisa" in Texas, had two sons with them on the voyage to America: Johannes, nine, and Swen August, two years old.

With Carl Hård came his younger brother, Daniel, then 23. He met a girl from home on the ship, and, by the time they reached America, they were engaged. Daniel Hård and Hedvig Lönnquist (who had emigrated with her sister, Anna Stina) were the first Swedish immigrant couple to be married in Texas.

The most eminent member of the emigrant party was no less a personage than S.M. Swenson's mother, the redoubtable Margareta Andersdotter, who was yet another of the myriad Palm siblings; she was the elder sister of Anders, Gustaf, and Swante. At the time of her emigration she was a hale 53 years of age. The reasons for her emigration are unclear. Her husband, Sven Israelson, was still alive (he did not die until 1871 at the age of 80). The romanticized account given by August Anderson hints that she wished to be reconciled with her daughter, Anna Kristina, who was said to have emigrated without seeking or receiving the family blessing. (Jeanette Dyer Davis refutes this completely; she says that her mother had emigrated with the family's blessings for reasons of health.) Whatever reasons she may have had for leaving Sweden, Margareta did not stay away long. She found the climate of Texas too hot, and she did not approve of the fact that Swenson's cotton plantation was worked by slaves. In 1850 she returned to Sweden, where she remained for the rest of her life.

Twenty-three years after her return from Texas and two years after the death of her husband, Margareta Andersdotter was visited by her rich son from New York. Swenson installed her in a magnificent estate called Ingsberg in the heart of the city of Nässjö. Ingsberg was one of the finest houses in the entire region and was situated on a lake (called Ingsbergssjön, or Lake Ingsberg) with huge park-like grounds bigger than any farm in Barkeryd. There Margareta i Ingsberg, as she came to be known, lived in Swedish splendor paid for with American gold for 20 years. Swenson made Ingsberg his Swedish "home away from home" and a gathering place for future immigrants to Texas.

Margareta Andersdotter

More than 450 young people emigrated from Ingsberg and the surrounding Nässjö region. The grand old lady lived until 1894, one year short of a century. Over her grave Swenson and his brother, Johan, raised a large marble marker on which their parents' skills are extolled in a few lines of homespun doggerel:

> hans krafter ägnades åt
> skulder och skatter
> hennes i att vävfa matter.
>
> (His energies were expended on
> taxes and debts,
> hers in weaving rugs.)

Another passenger sailing on the *Augusta* in the spring of 1848 was Gustaf August Johanesson from Forserum parish. He was only 16 years old, single, and listed on the *Augusta's* manifest as *dräng,* farm laborer. In fact, he was one of the 12 sons and daughters born to Johannes Samuelson of Forserum, who was a member of the national parliament representing his constituency in the Fourth Estate (landed peasants). Despite his father's prominence, young Johanneson had heeded the siren call to Texas. Eventually seven of his brothers would follow him there. And, unlike the rest of the "forty-eighters," he does not seem to have been very keen on farming or rural life in general.

On his arrival in Houston, he chose to stay there rather than follow the group to Finckley and points west. He went into business, hoping perhaps to duplicate the luck of S.M. Swenson. He changed his name to Forsgård, a practice his siblings were to follow as they emigrated one by one. He became an outstanding businessman, but he never forgot that it was Swenson who had made it possible for him to come to Texas in the first place. For years he served as Swenson's agent-in-place on the coast, the semi-official liaison between the Central Texas Swedes and those arriving by ship from Sweden via New York. He greeted each group, however tiny, and arranged for housing in Houston until they could begin the next, and last, portion of their journey to homes in Central Texas.

There were nine other *drängar* on the *Augusta*, ranging in ages from 18 to 36, and two *pigor* (unmarried servant girls), besides the Lönnquist sisters. Altogether there were 30 men, women, and children bound for Texas.

The emigrants sailed from Göteborg in July 1848. A story often related by Gustaf Palm described the *Augusta* as so battered by storms and heavy seas that her cargo of Swedish iron shifted, putting the ship in immediate danger of capsizing. At that point, Margareta Andersson led the emigrants in prayer on the heaving deck, supported by her brothers Anders and Gustaf Palm, until the weather broke and the cargo could be secured. The story goes on to say that the *Augusta* was demasted in Boston and converted into a floating seaman's chapel, but here the aged Palm must be confusing the *Augusta* with the so-called "Bethel Ship," the Swedish Methodist chapel moored in New York harbor; the *Augusta* was still plying the Atlantic as late as 1852.

The *Augusta* reached Boston after 90 days at sea. Then began the equally long voyage to Texas—at Boston the emigrants transferred to a coastal steamer, the *Stephen F. Austin*, which took them as far as Galveston; from there they steamed up Buffalo Bayou to Houston on the *Reliance*. They arrived November 22, 1848, were met by Swenson and Palm, and wintered at Nya Lättarp in Fort Bend County.

Just a few months after their arrival in Fort Bend County, Anders Palm—the group's leader from Sweden to America—died of a fever, leaving his widow, Anna, with six children. But Anna Palm, like most pioneer women, was made of stern stuff. They had come to America to settle, and there would be no turning back. In 1849 she rented land on a small farm near New Ulm in Washington County and began to support her family—the first of the "forty-eighters" to set out on her own.

The homesteads of the "forty-eighters" acted as magnets, drawing later immigrants to the areas they had settled. These farms, in turn, provided a place for the contract laborers who came in the 1850's and later to work off their passage. Forsgård in Houston transshipped arriving immigrants to Austin, where some of them (such as Gustaf Palm) lived and worked at Swenson's ranch before moving into Austin or renting land along Brushy Creek.

Following the example of Anna Palm, most of the "forty-eighters" soon left Fort Bend County for Travis County and began working off their passage at Govalle. Swenson's sister, Anna Kristina, and her husband, William Dyer, settled in 1852 on some land which Swenson had purchased for them on the south bank of Brushy Creek in Williamson County. The land was already a well-known local landmark called Kenney's Fort (it had been the site of the end of the "Archive War" of 1842), but it soon began to attract newly arrived Swedish immigrants as well, for land in Travis County was rapidly rising in price while it was relatively cheap in Williamson County. The area was still largely uninhabited, except by Indians who would occasionally attack and rob new settlers in the area around Kenney's Fort.

The 1850's were decent harvest years in Sweden with relatively stable economic conditions which tended to hold emigration down. In America, fears over a divided nation's plunge into civil war were growing, which also discouraged immigration. Still, some came. And what was more important, they stayed, married (most were under 30), and settled down.

During the 1850's other Swedish immigrants moved into Travis and Williamson counties. A few of them became as influential as the "forty-eighters." Foremost among these were Arvid Nilsson and his family, who emigrated to Texas from Öggestorp Parish, Småland, which lay some six miles west of Barkeryd.

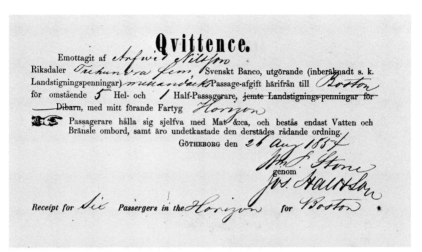

Arvid Nilsson's receipt for passage from Göteborg to Boston, 1854

Arvid Nilsson was among the first emigrants to be infected with "Texas fever" who was not related to the extended Swenson-Palm-Hörd clan, although his wife was a native of Barkeryd parish. In the fall of 1854 Nilsson, a respectable 52 years of age, boarded the sailing vessel *Horizon* in Göteborg bound for Boston. Accompanying him were his wife, Anna Lena, herself over 40, their two sons, Anders Johan, 19 years old, and August, 14, and daughter Carolina, 3. The voyage must have been an unusually somber one, for the Nilsson's eldest daughter, Lena Stina, had died in Göteborg while the family awaited passage to America. With them traveled Swen Larson of Lekeryd parish (where Arvid Nilsson was born), his wife, Johanna, and their daughter, Edla, aged nine.

Eventually the Nilsson party reached Boston, transferred to a coastal steamer, and finally arrived in Galveston, where Gustaf Forsgård met them. They moved onto some rented land near Port Lavaca for a short time, but, by the end of the year, they had relocated to a homestead south of Georgetown on Brushy Creek. The Larsons settled nearby in the area which later came to be known as Palm Valley.

The Dyer settlement at Kenney's Fort on the south bank of Brushy Creek, followed by Anna Palm's arrival a year later and the advent of the Nilsson party in 1854, defined the boundaries of the Swedish colony in Williamson County. The original settlement was referred to as "Brushy" (the earliest name for Georgetown until the present name was adopted in 1848), and the name endured as a general term for all the Swedish settlements even remotely near Brushy Creek. Actually, "Brushy" was an area bounded by Georgetown on the west, Jonah on the north, Hutto on the east, and Palm Valley on the south. The area just to the north and south of Brushy Creek later came to be called Palm Valley, when the Lutheran church took that name in 1896, but since the congregation was still referred to as "Brushy-församlingen," the settlements along the creek continued to be referred to collectively as "Brushy Creek" by many. That name, in turn, was changed as early as 1854 to Round Rock, but Swedes used the old terminology well into this century.[1]

The Nilssons, reliable but unverifiable sources say, had a sturdy wagon which they had brought with them from Sweden at great cost in money and labor. But all their efforts paid off almost immediately—they used the last of their funds to purchase a yoke of oxen and began hauling goods from Central Texas to the coast and back. Arvid and his sons were paid in gold, much of which went back into the drayage business to purchase additional wagons and oxen. The rest was carefully hidden and used to buy the one commodity Swedes never seemed to get enough of—land. Anders Johan Nilsson, later known by the anglicized Andrew John Nelson, became the head of the second Swedish "empire" in Texas and second in wealth only to S.M. Swenson himself. The vast Nelson landholdings in Williamson County centered on the little town of Round Rock, which became, as a consequence, the focal point of intense Swedish agricultural and mercantile activity from just before the turn of the century to the Great Depression. Like Swenson, the Nelsons were eager to help Swedes come to Texas, and, again like Swenson, they had land to rent or sell to their countrymen. Another parallel between the two richest Swedes in Texas was that both were affectionately known as "Rike" ("Rich Man") by their fellows.

In all, more than 100 Swedes arrived in Central Texas from Småland during the 1850's. Most of them still came from Jönköpings län and were thus swayed by the direct appeals of S.M. Swenson. But after a time the emigration seems to have become self-sustaining: a small but steady stream of arrivals— channeled from Barkeryd through New York, Houston, and

Redvig and John Rosengren (right), who immigrated to Austin from Småland in the early 1850's

Austin—kept feeding the colonies in Travis and Williamson counties. They worked off their passages, passed on to land rented from Swenson, the Palms, or the Nelsons, purchased land of their own, married within the Swedish group, and began raising families. This pattern remained unchanged throughout the pioneering period, for nearly three generations. Only age and urbanization hastened the process of "Americanization" and cultural adaptation.

The Swedish-born inhabitants of Texas had, by 1860, more than tripled their numbers, from 48 (30 of whom had arrived together only two years earlier) to 153. The difficulties of the Civil War years virtually closed the state to immigration. In fact, not until 1867 were conditions favorable for immigration, which then resumed on a relatively large scale.

10

Swedish Texans, Slavery, and Civil War

The attitude of S.M. Swenson toward the slave system was ambiguous, but it was an honest reflection of the confusion he shared with many of his fellow Swedish Texans. Before the Civil War hardly any Swedish immigrant openly defended slavery. Swante Palm's letter to *Hemlandet* in the summer of 1855 is thus a unique exception and one vigorously denounced by other Swedish settlers in Texas.

T.N. Hasselquist's influential newspaper *Hemlandet* began publication in Galesburg, Illinois, in 1855. Its editor was a fervent Republican, fervent abolitionist, and fervent supporter of Abraham Lincoln: he urged his fellow Swedes to believe as he did, and most of them concurred. Strong personal identification with Lincoln (he too had lived in a humble log cabin, for example) made Hasselquist's job easier. In the election of 1860 most Swedes in the Midwest voted for Lincoln.

Swante Palm had written to Hasselquist in 1855, and his letter was published in the July 7 edition of *Hemlandet*. In addition to some highly interesting views on contemporary topics (the "Know-Nothing" party, Freemasonry, American religious denominations), Palm finally got around to the question of slavery, "in which we [i.e., all Swedish Texans] are of a completely different opinion from yours." Palm went on to say that:

We live in a slave state and therefore have personal experience in seeing how slaves are fed, treated, housed, and cared for. . . . We find that the slaves receive better food, better treatment, and better care than the working classes in Sweden. . . . Many of us own slaves and all of us want to own such as soon as we are in a position to buy some. It is an advantage in a slave state to be white. . . . Several countrymen write to us from the North that they are worse treated and sometimes suffer more than our slaves do here. In general, our slaves do not suffer any kind of lack or abuse and times of want do not exist for them. Workers here are not punished physically and are not let go, they earn good wages and their prospects for the future are good.[1]

The letter sparked indignant comments not only from Reverend Hasselquist ("Should we not then all race to Texas and sell ourselves there as slaves?") but even from the tiny Swedish-Texan community. In the next issue an unidentified Austin Swede stated most emphatically that Swante Palm did *not* speak for *all* Swedes in the Lone Star State.[2]

Not only were Swedes faced with the moral issue of one human being's ownership of another, but they were also instinctively distrustful of the social hierarchy of the plantation system itself, which reminded them of the feudal estates back home. Another aspect of slavery that many Swedes disliked was the hypocritical nature of American liberty it presupposed: here, where all men were presumed to be equal, the "colored" portion of society was everywhere in chains.[3]

Prior to their emigration, however, Swedes had little knowledge of Black Americans, and most of them had little contact with Blacks even after they arrived. As a group, Swedes were temperamentally inclined to oppose slavery in any form, largely because of their dislike of the rigid Swedish class structure, but they had difficulty accepting Blacks as full and equal fellow human beings. In fact, those few Swedes who regularly came in contact with Blacks—many of these were in Texas—began to modify their earlier attitudes as a result of the beginning of the enforcement of the Emancipation Proclamation in 1865. Southern Swedes, including those in Texas, quickly decided that "the question of racial equality was not debatable."[4] No disagreement on the inherent inferiority of Blacks was tolerated, and Swedes were quick to fall in line with their White American neighbors. After one Swedish settler had been murdered in eastern Travis County and another raped, allegedly by Blacks, a few Swedes actually tried to lynch the presumed perpetrators and were stopped at the last second by a Swedish-American sheriff.[5] By the turn of the century Swedish attitudes toward Blacks were virtually identical with those of other Whites.

There is some evidence that a few freed Blacks, formerly owned by the handful of Swedish slaveholders in Texas, stayed on with their former masters and their families after Emancipation. One source mentions a Black family which had married into a Swedish family, learned Swedish, and become members of the Swedish Lutheran church.[6] A widespread item of Texas folklore concerns a young Swedish-speaking Black sent to meet immigrant trains in Austin and banter with the *smålänningar* in their own dialect about the deleterious effects of the hot Texas sun. "Are you Swedish?" asked the confused immigrants. "Yes, indeed," answered the young man, "and after a few Texas summers, you'll be just as black as I am!" [7] This ubiquitous tale — a version from the Swedish settlement in Lindsborg, Kansas, recently turned up — has been retold numerous times but may actually have had some foundation in fact — a young Swedish-speaking Black named Will Palm, raised by William Palm of Round Rock, may have been the source of the story.[8] And there is another tale of a Black raised among Swedes who not only spoke Swedish with a Småland accent but also subscribed to and faithfully read *Texas-Posten* every week.[9]

These instances of cultural interaction between Swedes and Blacks tend to enhance a perceived amity between the races which probably never existed. Researcher Carl Widén stated on numerous occasions that "the relationship between the Swedish landowners and the Negroes, who furnished the knowhow in the raising of a crop, was always very, very satisfactory." One of the reasons usually given for the Blacks' preference for Swedish employers was the abundant food given them at Swedish farms. "They loved very much to go to the Swedes because they always had plenty of chickens and milk for their babies," said Widén.

But writer Folke Hedblom is certainly as naive as Widén when he states that "in Texas, there occurred no segregation of the kind that characterized the other southern states."[10] Few rural Blacks owned their own land. Like itinerant Mexicans, they were available, cheap, and *indispensable* labor; no Central Texas cotton farmer could realistically consider raising his crop without them. But despite their willingness to work for extremely low wages, some Swedish farmers were displeased with them.

As Magnus Mörner understates it, relations between Swedes and their hired Black and Mexican migrant workers were "at times, less than harmonious."[11] As early as 1902, when cotton prices were extremely low, Bror Hintze, a scientifically trained Swedish agronomist, wanted to found the *Svenska Lantbruksföreningen af Texas* (Swedish Farmers Association of Texas) to protect farmers against unscrupulous gin owners, cotton merchants, speculators, and other "vermin" (*ohyra*). "We are at the same time surrounded by another type of vermin — Negroes, Mexicans, for what farmers are not delighted to have been blessed by one or two dozen of these cotton pickers?"[12]

Texas voted to join the Confederate States of America in 1861.[13] Texas was both a slave state, of course, and a cotton state, and while there were many who shared Sam Houston's and S.M. Swenson's desire to preserve the Union, by tradition, birth, and economic necessity Texans wished to remain part of the South.

At the outbreak of the Civil War the entire Swedish population in the South did not exceed 750, of whom 153 then resided in Texas.[14] Among these, most were cotton growers, and a few even owned slaves. Thus it is not surprising to discover that these Swedish farmers had divided loyalties: on the one hand, they felt Texas, not the North, to be their new homeland, but on the other, they felt uneasy about not defending Mr. Lincoln and his cause. Politics, naturally, played a great role in their confusion: most Texas Swedes were Democrats, which alienated them from their Northern counterparts, nearly all of whom felt a strong attachment to Lincoln and the Republican party. In spite of this, only a very few Texas Swedes are known to have actually enlisted in the army of the Confederacy, and there is evidence that some even chose to flee to the North to escape conscription.[15]

When the war finally did break out, 3,000 members of the total Swedish population of the United States (then between 18,000 and 20,000, including women, children, and the aged) volunteered to fight for the Union.[16] Illinois and Minnesota alone contributed nearly two-thirds of that total. A number of officers from Sweden (75 to 100) joined the staffs of the Union army to gain valuable combat experience; several were personally appointed by President Lincoln, and a few even won battlefield honors or commissions.

Only about 25 Texas Swedes enlisted or were conscripted into the Southern cause.[17] No leading Confederate officers came from the ranks of the Swedes in the Lone Star State. Texas produced no Lieutenant Colonel Forsberg, no Brigadier General Hansson, no Colonel Hammarsköld, all Confederate officers from other Southern states and all born in Sweden. But Swedish Texans certainly experienced the bitter division of secession, the privations and deprivations of the war itself, and the long and painful process of rebuilding when the hostilities finally ceased, whether they had shared Palm's proslavery ideas or Swenson's antisecessionist point of view before the war. The Nilsson family of Brushy Creek was a typical case in point.

Arvid Nilsson first rented land in Williamson County from S.M. Swenson and began to clear it with oxen and the large wagon that he had brought from Sweden. The following fall (1855) the family purchased 320 acres from Swenson for $1.50 an acre.

Arvid's son Anders Johan bought eight more yoke of oxen and built several new wagons just after the outbreak of the war. All through 1862 he hauled lumber and supplies paid for with Confederate scrip. A year later he expanded his business by hauling cotton from Central Texas to Brownsville for 12½ cents a pound, but now he was paid not in Confederate scrip but in gold, which provided the basis for the postwar family land and cattle fortune.

When the Civil War broke out Arvid was too old and Anders too valuable for normal conscription. But on several occasions Anders was called upon to transport goods (usually cotton) for the Confederate army, for which he was issued special passports to cross military zones.

His younger brother, August, did not fare as well. He and a fellow Swede, Swen Monson, only recently arrived from Sweden, enlisted in the Confederate army early in 1861. August served for two and a half years and saw action in Arkansas. Discharged because of poor health in late 1863, he spent more than a year in recuperation.[18]

Shortly after the war August Nelson was called to testify in a case against a former Union soldier, one C.J. Carlson (also a Swede), in Georgetown. One source says that Carlson was on trial for horse theft, a serious crime indeed. Nelson aroused Carlson's enmity because of his testimony in court, and Carlson swore revenge. On the steps of the courthouse he shot Nelson in the back. August Nelson died on June 14, 1866, leaving a widow, Johanna Augusta Palm, daughter of Johannes Palm (youngest of the three Palm brothers who had come to Palm Valley in 1853), and an infant son, John A. Nelson, born in 1866, just three months before his father's murder.[19] For the Nelson family, the Civil War provided the basis of a fortune and a legacy of personal bitterness as well.

The Palm family, too, was intimately connected both with the development of the Brushy Creek settlements and with involvement in the war. August B. Palm had had some military experience at the State Military College in Reutersville and so enlisted in Fred Moore's Company of Fournay's Regiment (Fournay had been the headmaster at the State Military College). But Palm and his brothers Johannes (now called John), Anders (now Andrew), Carl, and Swen Wilhelm spent most of their time in the ferrying of goods for the Confederate army, and all came home unscathed.[20]

Several other Swedish Texans either enlisted or were impressed into the Confederate army: Johannes, Anders, and Gustaf Monson (as well as their brother Swen who served with August Nelson), and Johan Israelson (an immigrant of 1859, whose father's farm in Sweden bordered on the Swenson farm, Lättarp). Researcher Carl Widén claims that Israelson saw military action in the Confederate cause,[21] but other sources state that he, like Andrew Nelson, transported cotton and sheep to Mexico for Swenson's brother-in-law, W.T. Dyer.[22]

Johannes Christenson (also called "Christiernson" or "Christerson") was an early immigrant of the 1850's, who came from Småland at the behest of the Palm family. Widén lists him, too, as a Confederate soldier, but his biography is conflicting. Another source states that his frail physical condition kept him out of the war. John J. Johnson (also called Johan Johnson), an immigrant of 1859, was born in Barkeryd and worked at Govalle until impressed into the Confederate army as a transport and supply driver. During the Civil War Johnson worked with John Israelson driving cotton and sheep to Mexico.[23]

Swen (Svan) Larson, who came to Palm Valley in 1854 with Arvid Nilsson and his family, is also said to have been impressed into the army.

Carl W. Berryman, originally Bergman, arrived in Texas with his brother, Swen, in the 1850's. After his enforced military experience Carl settled in Austin and became a grocer and a pillar of the Gethsemane congregation, while Swen became a farmer south of Austin.[24] Others who served the Confederacy, and who are not named by Widén, include Samuel Forsgård, one of the Forsgård brothers who came to Texas in 1855. Samuel settled in Waco, while others of his large family (13 siblings) settled in Austin and Houston (e.g., Gustaf Forsgård, S.M. Swenson's agent in the port city). Samuel Forsgård served with Gurley's regiment, commanded by Captain G. Goodrich.[25] Still others could not have actually fought in the war, as Widén claims: August Månson, for example, did not join his elder brothers, Johannes, Anders, and Gustaf, in Texas until 1870.

To round out the list, one researcher has identified someone named Nelson from Kerr County as a fervid anti-Unionist. He has also located anonymous Swedes serving in Company B of the Eighth Texas Regiment and Company A of Captain E.C. Billing's Company, Wane Legion.[26]

Some two dozen Swedish settlers thus served the Confederate cause in Texas, yet very few either enlisted or fought. Most were conscripted or impressed into service and thus took the opportunity (as involuntary military servants) to at least turn a profit or to minimize the deprivations suffered by their families. For some, like Anders Johan Nilsson or, as he called himself by 1866, Andrew John Nelson, the war meant hard work but big profits if one avoided Confederate currency. For others, like Anders's brother, August, the war was an exercise in bloody futility, destroying a way of life as quickly and surely as it destroyed the men and women who fought valiantly and vainly to defend the indefensible.

The Settlers

Mass Migration to Texas, 1867-1880

In the years immediately following the Civil War, the second wave of the great migration from Europe began in earnest. "America fever" was spreading in Sweden, too, as the number of Swedish emigrants rose to 4,000 in 1865, shot up to 32,000 in 1869, and peaked at 46,000 in 1887.[1]

Three important events led to the release of the European and Scandinavian masses, largely pent up for five years by the Civil War. The first was the passing of the Homestead Act in 1862, which offered up to 160 acres of free land to any American citizen or any immigrant who declared his or her intention of becoming a citizen. This was especially opportune in opening the vast areas west of the Mississippi to land-hungry Europeans.

The second factor was a more localized one. Sweden suffered a series of three crop failures, caused largely by drought, between 1866 and 1868. Agricultural conditions had been steadily deteriorating, despite several reforms, since the early 19th century, and this resulted in the first mass migration of 1866-1868, both internally (from the countryside into the cities) and externally (to America and Canada). But the migration would never have been possible on any scale without the third development — the creation of competitive fleets of large Atlantic steamers.[2]

Most migration to America prior to the Civil War had been by comparatively small, slow, and expensive sailing vessels, which carried only a small number of passengers in great discomfort on grueling voyages often lasting three months or longer. The cost, too, was relatively great, compared to the cheap tickets available later in the century. The long journey could cost more than two years' wages for a Swedish farmhand in 1860; travel under sail meant liquidating the family farm and everything on and in it just to pay for the transatlantic crossing. By 1900 the trip cost only about the equivalent of six months' wages, and the possibility of remigration to Sweden became a reality as more and more steamship lines with more and bigger vessels competed strenuously for the vast immigrant market. By the end of the century the dreaded voyage could be made in as few as ten days, in comfort, with decent food and hygienic shelter provided.[3]

How did all this affect the Swedish Texans? S.M. Swenson left Mexico in the summer of 1864 to visit relatives in Sweden. He must also have done some huckstering in Barkeryd, because on June 12, 1867, nearly a hundred men and women, most between 15 and 30 years of age, left the Forserum train station for the long journey to Texas.

Swenson had been aided in his recruitment efforts by Daniel Hörd, his former foreman, who was preparing to remigrate to Texas after nearly a decade in Sweden. A special "emigrant train" had been engaged to take the group to Göteborg. It was the largest single group ever to migrate together to Texas; indeed, it represented (after the Bishop Hill experiment of the 1840's) one of the largest groups ever to leave a single area of Sweden for a single area in America. One member of the group, Johannes Swenson (son of "Johan i Långåsa" and therefore yet another of S.M. Swenson's nephews) wrote a lively account of the journey 50 years later. It has been translated by Carl T. Widén and often reprinted, so a summary here will suffice.[4]

At Göteborg the emigrants boarded the steamer *Hero*, which carried them to Hull in England. From there they moved by rail to Liverpool and finally boarded the *City of Baltimore*. With a crew of 125 and 1,000 passengers, the *City of Baltimore* left Liverpool, docked briefly in Ireland, where more emigrants came aboard, and made for America.

Land was sighted on the 29th of June — just nine days and six hours after leaving Liverpool, the *City of Baltimore* cast anchor in New York harbor, where S.M. Swenson and his friend Olof Hedström, Swedish Methodist preacher from the "Bethel Ship" (see Chapter 12) came on board to greet them. On July 1 the whole company came ashore at Castle Garden, where they were examined by medical officers and pronounced fit. Hedström was helpful during this process, after which the company split up temporarily, some going to boardinghouses, then later to S.M. Swenson's house on Atlantic Street in Brooklyn.

After a few days of seeing the sights in New York (including fireworks and P.T. Barnum's famous midget, General Tom Thumb and his tiny wife), the immigrants headed for Galveston. Their steamboat was manned by a surly crew, and, to make matters worse, during a bad storm it sprang a leak and was barely able to limp into Smithville, North Carolina, for repairs. On the next leg of the journey, to Key West, the Swedes endured poor food, and few of them were prepared for the tropical sun, so they were badly sunburned while swimming.

The poor food continued, and fights broke out among drunken crew members. One full night the ship sailed before the wind, unmanned. Finally, on the 22nd of July, the travelers landed in Galveston, glad to be alive and to be able to quit the awful ship. They were met by Gustaf and Wilhelm Forsgård (formerly of Barkeryd), who saw them to the train, which carried them as far as Brenham, where Swante Palm, John Israelsson, Otto Swenson, and a large wagon met them. While some went to Houston with Forsgård, others continued on toward Austin and Manor.[5]

As the migration brought Swedes in ever-increasing numbers, the limited amount of available land was soon sold, and the newer, more-numerous settlers had to look elsewhere for cheap land. New Sweden, in eastern Travis County, was the first new colony east of Austin (settled in 1873; named in 1877), but it was quickly followed by the settlements at Manor, Lund, Manda, and Kimbro. Williamson County soon sported Swedish colonies at Hutto, Taylor, Georgetown, and Round Rock.

These two areas—some 200 square miles—accommodated 90 percent of the Swedish immigrants to Texas before 1890. However, the geography of the area, and hence the crops that could be grown there, differed greatly. The Williamson County settlements of Round Rock, Palm Valley, and Brushy Creek lay in an area that had soon become the center of intense cotton cultivation, with support services such as the railroad, communal

Manda Community, c. 1898

Adolf Fredrik Anderson Cotton Gin, Knight Ranch (New Sweden), 1880's

cotton gin, and wagon transport to make delivery of the raw product easier and more efficient. The vegetation in this prairie region was mainly high grass, live oak, mesquite, and scrub pine.

Eastern Travis County was more heavily wooded, with stands of live oak giving onto pastureland. Cotton became a staple crop here, too, but cultivation was more diversified, corn being an important crop as well. Some of the stonier ground, near Decker, for example, took more than a decade to clear but was then replanted in corn.[6] These were the primary "target" areas into which Swedish settlement was channeled in the years immediately following the Civil War.

Strangely clad, sweating Swedish immigrants marching down Congress Avenue in Austin had begun to be a newsworthy sight as early as 1866. In the summer of that year the *Daily Austin Republican* reported this novel phenomenon:

> A few emigrants arrived from Sweden yester-
> day evening [June 13], consigned to A.B. Palm. We
> understand there will be many more Swedes coming
> here this summer. Let them come. There is plenty
> of room for all foreigners desirous of homes in our
> state. All hard-working industrious people, of what-
> ever nationality, who will come to this country, are
> now more than welcome.[7]

In 1868 the same newspaper recorded a similar sight, one which, in the intervening time, had become commonplace:

> Last evening [October 25, 1868], we saw a huge
> wagon, heavily loaded with trunks and boxes, fol-
> lowed by ten or twelve men of foreign aspect and
> dress, all good looking and evidently in good health.
> On inquiry, we ascertained that they were Swedes;
> one company among many that have come and are
> moving to Texas under the auspices of Mr. S.M.
> Swenson of New York. The more of this immigra-
> tion, the better. These people bring with them good
> means, sober and industrious habits, and a good
> way of attending faithfully to their own business.
> Success to Mr. Swenson! May he bring all of Swe-
> den into this part of the "Star State!"[8]

A somewhat chillier welcome to Swedish immigrants newly arrived in Texas had appeared in *Svenska-Amerikanaren* (Chicago), warning Swedish readers of some of the vicious propaganda being spread by "carpetbaggers." The author, "H.P. J--n" of Houston, understood those Swedish Texans who had supported the Confederacy since they could not help but "sympathize with those among whom they had lived for a number of years." He went on, however, to state that, though Texas had not suffered the ravages of war directly, the situation was still "anarchic," especially in the northeast parts of the state, where "armed hoards marched pillaging and murdering through the land, committing the worst atrocities in particular against Negroes. . . . Murderers . . . ride in broad daylight on the streets of Clarkesville." One of these murderers, Mr. Guest, had slaughtered three people — all Black — on a single day. General Griffin had to send a squadron of cavalry to Huntsville to restore order.[9] Such reports were hardly likely to encourage migration to Texas from the North.

But "J--n" also noted the recent arrival of the large group of Jönköping Swedes in Texas. "The 25th of July, there arrived here [Houston] 85 Swedes from Jönköping County, Småland. . . . Twenty-one of them stayed here in Houston with a very honorable and respectable fellow countryman who had paid their passage. Last summer, there also came a company of ten Swedes from the same area, under the same man's care."[10] All the rest of the Swedes traveled to Brushy Creek north of Austin.

In a letter to *Jönköpingsbladet* of December 1, 1868, an anonymous Texas Swede warned his fellow *smålänningar* that America was not a land flowing with milk and honey and therefore not a land for the lazy, since "the Americans are the hardest working people on earth, each one working, in one way or another, to get rich." The same correspondent cautioned Swedes that their reputation as an honorable people was beginning to be jeopardized by the growing number of immigrants who refused to fulfill the conditions of that labor contract which had paid for their passage to America.[11] Americans had always distrusted the contract, or indenture, system, feeling it was a not-so-subtle substitute for slavery, however short the period of indenture. Consequently, they were reluctant to enforce the indenture laws, since these laws protected the "slave owners," not the victims. The contract labor laws were gradually phased out in the post-Civil War era, until, with the Foran Act of 1885, it became illegal to bind any immigrant to a prolonged forced-labor contract to repay emigration passage.

But the "prepaid" ticket was still an important method for maintaining the emigration, even after the era of contract labor had ended. Families could send home for other relatives, while those in the Old World were spared the trauma of liquidating their entire estates or becoming indebted themselves before finding gainful employment in America.

Swante Palm himself acted as "passenger agent" for the Liverpool, New York, and Philadelphia Steamship Line as early as May 1869, when he sold tickets for passage from Sweden to Austin for $98, prepaid.[12]

A few years later he was acting as agent for the American Emigrant Co. of Hartford, Connecticut, one of the largest non-Scandinavian emigrant companies, responsible for transporting emigrants from Göteborg (via Hull) to New York and then by rail to Austin ("150 pounds of baggage per person transported free of charge to final destination"). Tickets from Göteborg in 1873 cost between 35 and 42 riksdaler per person, 75 to 85 riksdaler for a family.[13] One riksdaler was then worth about four U.S. dollars.

The Swedish agent for the S.M. Swenson enterprise was Swenson's older brother, Johan Swenson ("Johan i Långåsa"). During the 1870's nearly 1,000 Swedes moved to Texas, to swell the population to 1,293 Swedish-born Texans—four times the number at the beginning of the decade. The Swenson pipeline was obviously operating smoothly and efficiently: the number of Swedish-born Texans doubled each decade up to 1900, when the Great Migration slowly began to taper off as far as Texas was concerned.[14]

At least two groups, as large or even larger than the group emigration of 1867, left the Barkeryd area during the early 1870's, both of them arranged by Johan Swenson in Sweden and Swante Palm in Austin. These immigrants had a few advantages over those who had preceded them on the journey—they could make the trip from New York to Texas completely by rail. Land, on the other hand, had risen steeply in price and was much scarcer in the choice primary colonies. Still, up until the beginning of the 1880's, when migration patterns shifted from Sweden to remigrating Swedes from the northern states (chiefly due to widely publicized land speculation schemes advertised in the

Johan Swenson

Swedish-American press), the pattern of life in Swedish Texas in 1878 was remarkably the same as it had been 30 years before.

The same pattern of land use continued into the 20th century. Swedes were conservative farmers and distrusted innovations (which may explain the failure of their sole cooperative venture, Svenska Lantbruksföreningen af Texas, the Swedish Farmers Association of Texas, in 1898), and they were also rather few, in comparison with, for example, the thousands of Germans to the southwest. Eventually, however, old age and rising land prices caused most of the immigrants to sell their farms and retire to the cities. Although many sons took over from aging fathers, they, too, eventually grew old, and then the farms left their original family owners. Today, only a few farms along Brushy Creek and Cottonwood Creek are still in the hands of the original families. Most of the older generations have gradually sold off the farmland and moved into Austin, Manor, Round Rock, and the other smaller towns, which now serve the needs of the grandchildren and great-grandchildren of the first settlers.

Gottfrid Swenson cultivating cotton, Henning Walfred Swenson farm near Type, 1921

Crops, too, have changed, and cotton is no longer "king." Now fields are increasingly sown with soybeans, milo, and even flax, thanks to modern methods of irrigation and better methods of water recovery. In the coastal colonies such as El Campo, Swedes grew rice and owned large rice warehouses and irrigation systems. Some Swedish farmers cultivated both cotton and rice. But the old gins (often called "gens" by the local Swedes, who built most of them) became part and parcel of the landscape and of the rhythm of life in Central Texas from the 1880's on: here and there, one can still see them, reminders of an earlier and more arduous way of life now almost vanished.

12

Swedish Institutions in Texas

The Swedish Lutheran Church

For most Swedish immigrants to Texas, as with those in the rest of the expanding nation, the church had been the center of their world. At home in Sweden the bells of the village church had marked the hours of their days, their holidays, and the events of their lives: births, baptisms, weddings, funerals. But the hard life on the frontier was usually lived far from any established community, and, at least in the early days, even these few towns were more important as centers for secular nourishment than for spiritual.

A handful of men realized early that the migration to the New World would lead Swedes into an alien environment far from their native spiritual home. They were also concerned that their fellow countrymen would stray off into the bewildering variety of non-Lutheran Christian denominations in America. Thus, they determined to plant the State Church of Sweden — the Swedish Evangelical Lutheran Church — on American soil and to ordain Swedish-American Lutheran pastors in America without waiting for the indifferent bureaucracy of the Church at home to provide them with the men they so desperately needed on the frontier.

Lars Paul Esbjörn (1808-1870) from Delsbo, Hälsingland, was the first Swedish pastor to sail from Sweden specifically to serve the needs of recent Swedish immigrants. By 1860 Esbjörn and his newly arrived colleague, Tuve Nils Hasselquist, had persuaded their Norwegian counterparts to join them in founding a national association of Scandinavian Lutheran congregations. The body so constituted, the Augustana Synod, vowed to found a Theological Seminary for the training of ministers to serve the frontier immigrants. Augustana College and Theological Seminary was duly constituted and opened its doors that same year.

By 1875 Augustana was regularly producing pastors for the rapidly expanding Augustana Synod. Each year new congregations were founded as Swedes poured into the United States in ever-increasing numbers, to Illinois, Iowa, Minnesota, then to Nebraska and Kansas: the numbers of Swedish towns and, inevitably, Lutheran congregations increased rapidly.[1]

Swedish Texans had to wait, first, for the end of the Civil War and then for the return of Daniel Hörd and the 100 immigrants of 1867 before their numbers were large enough to make the dream of a Lutheran congregation even a remote possibility.

By the end of 1868 there were enough Swedes in Central Texas to attract the attention of one of the few ordained itinerant Church of Sweden pastors, Pastor K. Karlén (or Carlén) of Halland in southwestern Sweden. On December 12, 1868, Pastor Karlén held the first Swedish Lutheran worship service in Texas, the historic significance of which was not lost on the communicants.[2] There were now nearly 300 Swedes in the area, and a committee was formed to discuss the possibility of establishing a Lutheran congregation in Texas. Swante Palm was elected *ordförande* (chairman); he later recorded his speech to the committee in the records of what was to become the Gethsemane Lutheran Church. His words have never been fully translated into English, and, with their combination of elegance, pragmatism, and idealism, deserve to be quoted at length:

> We greet Pastor Karlén, who has declared
> himself willing to participate in the creation of a
> Swedish Lutheran congregation here, which we
> hope will become a Swedish Lutheran
> congregation with a church. We bid Pastor
> Karlén welcome among us and call down over

him happiness and God's blessing in this, our noble undertaking. . . .

But my hope is not just that a Swedish Lutheran congregation be founded, but that it be protected against decline. We ought [to build] the church on a high point in the middle of [the town]. . . . Those among us who lack money can make themselves otherwise useful by donating some labor and materials. If a school were to be established, part of the building, if not all of it, should be built of stone, brick, or concrete, and the schoolrooms of wood. Such a building can be built for from $1,000-$4,000. It ought to have a tower in order to be equipped with a place where we might, in the future, install a bell to call us together to worship. We all love song, our solemn Swedish hymns, and it is only for that reason that I mention that we can easily acquire a melodicon or a smaller organ which some member of the congregation can play. There are several among us who can do "organ duty." It is because of our love for the songs that I mention this, for instruments we can get for a small amount of money, if not as a gift. But I do not wish to confine myself to trivialities like this.

My heartfelt hope, which doubtless is shared by most of you both in Austin and from neighboring areas, is not only that a Swedish Lutheran congregation now be founded here but also that it somehow be insured against decline. I am equally anxious that our beautiful Swedish language be preserved and that the memory of our Fatherland (which we all love) plus also by those of us few who are now here and who now want to found a congregation with great personal sacrifices, that all this may not die out. This desire is only natural and not an expression of base vanity. The permanancy of our church demands it. Let us never forget that we are Swedes and that it is important that we not forget the Fatherland of our forefathers' good name and reputation. Countrymen, am I not correct in this? This will come to pass best by living daily not just as honorable Swedes but even more as Christian Swedes. Let us pass this on to our children and posterity as an inheritance, let us seek to retain this memory among those who are going to take our places after us. Many of them are already born here; in the future many other Swedes will probably be living in this country.

It is therefore imperative and well advised to unite a school with the church, where the language can be taught in the same place that the Swedish language is preached: Church and school are twins. No one ought to seek to separate them or tell them apart for he who with profane hands does this, for him it will not go well. So it seems to me.

Palm clearly understood the importance that a Swedish Lutheran congregation would have as the repository for Swedish culture in America: it would be through the church and its schools that the language, music, literature, and customs of the homeland would be preserved and passed on through the generations. Thus, it is not surprising that Palm's committee decided to petition the Swedish state church directly, to plead for an ordained minister to come from Sweden to Austin, Texas, to serve the tiny colony so far from any other Swedish congregation.

It was well into the year 1870 when Pastor D.M. Tillman, a Swedish-speaking Finn, arrived in Austin to organize the congregation. On December 19, 1870, a constitution was drawn up and plans were undertaken to investigate the feasibility of building a church. By 1872 a site had been secured on West 9th Street, and on February 11 the decision to build was made. The church was finished and ready to be dedicated on March 10, 1874, by Pastor O.O. Estrem, a Norwegian minister active among the Bosque County Norwegians.[3]

The congregation's request for a pastor from Sweden had been referred by the archbishop back to the United States, to the Augustana Synod of the Lutheran Church. The synod promised to send an Augustana pastor to Texas as soon as one became available. In the meantime, Pastor S.P.A. Lindahl, an Augustana-trained minister, was attached to the Austin congregation

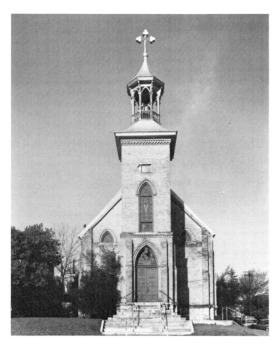

Gethsemane Lutheran Church, Austin, 1960's

in November of 1874, becoming the first American-trained Swedish minister to preach to the Texas Swedes. On February 14, 1875, the congregation was officially named Gethsemane Swedish Lutheran Church of Austin, Texas. At that time, there were 88 communicants and 46 children.[4]

In 1882 the urban Swedes decided to be the first congregation of their nationality to build a permanent church of their own in stone and brick. The old wooden church on West 9th Street was sold for $900, and a new site on Congress Avenue, just two blocks north of the new capitol, was secured. All the aspirations of Swante Palm's speech in 1868 were to be realized in the new building. Although of modest size, the church was optimally located on a small rise to add to its stature. It was built in a pointed Gothic style with pointed window embrasures, a wide nave, and open Gothic bell tower. The walls were built of brick and Texas limestone, much of the latter salvaged from the ruins of the old capitol, which had been destroyed by fire in 1881. The exterior walls were of light brown brick, which contrasted nicely with the light stone of the foundation and the tin roof. The altar, communion rails, and pulpit were of hand-carved

Texas pecan in matching Gothic style. Windows were simple white, or milk, glass, although most have now been replaced — as they were intended to be — by stained-glass memorial windows. All in all, the church was a magnificent achievement for the tiny Swedish-Texan colony. Its cost — $6,500 without the bell tower — was not easily justified, but the Gethsemane congregation was extremely proud of what it had accomplished.[5]

The stone church on Congress Avenue served its congregation for three-quarters of a century. But as Austin grew, absorbing much of the former rural population and early migrants to the Central Texas area, the little church finally proved too small. So, in 1962, a new church was built on Anderson Lane (then the northern limit of the city) in a strikingly modern style using the then-new technique of posttensioning concrete blocks developed in Germany during World War II to save structural steel. A massive stained-glass window nearly 40 feet high fronts the chancel, and an equally large triptych in Italian mosaic graces the entrance to the nave.[6] A further expansion in 1978 added additional classrooms, an auditorium, and a parish hall, making Gethsemane the largest Lutheran congregation in Austin. But the little church on Congress Avenue has not been forgotten. After a hard fight led by Carl T. Widén, son of one of the early pastors of the church, it was declared a National Historic Landmark in 1976.

The other half of the Swedish settlements lay some distance north of Austin, spread out along Brushy Creek in what would someday be called "Palm Valley." It was clear by the early 1870's that two congregations, one urban and one rural, would have to be formed to meet the needs of the two geographical areas in which the Swedes had settled.

Brushy Creek benefited, too, from the expertise of Karlén and D.M. Tillman, who had organized a congregation on the occasion of his first worship service in 1870. The cemetery land, one acre of the more than 20 donated by S.M. Swenson, was consecrated by Tillman on February 10, 1872.[7]

Finally, in July 1876, the long-awaited Augustana pastor assigned to Texas arrived on the scene. He was Martin Noyd, born in 1850 in Hälsingland, Sweden, and he was a man well worth waiting for. Powerfully built with a handsome beard, Noyd settled near Brushy Creek, the second and, with 194 adult mem-

Rev. Martin Noyd and confirmation class, Palm Valley Lutheran Church, 1891

bers, largest of his twin charges. As a man burdened with two
groups of isolated fellow countrymen separated by a day's hard
ride, he had to have considerable skill and plenty of physical
stamina. Many of Noyd's successors complained about the long
wearying rides on horseback, the miserable roads, the mud, the
flies, the unrelenting summer heat, but Noyd was not the sort
to complain. He soon realized that his job would be an enormous
one, with two flocks scattered over a vast area of Central Texas
and only one true house of worship for all of them. The problem
was the first one to be tackled by the freshly ordained young
newcomer, but it was not until April 1894 that a steering committee was formed and a plan for a brick church acceptable to all
was adopted. The cornerstone was laid on June 19, 1894, and
the building was consecrated on April 12, 1896.[8]

The Palm Valley Lutheran Church, as it has been called
since its consecration, is one of the largest and most beautiful
of the Swedish churches in Texas. It is built of pressed Round
Rock brick, paid for by Andrew J. Nelson, a member of the
committee who oversaw the building's construction. The church
itself is built in a simple Gothic style with a tall spire on the

Palm Valley Lutheran Church, 1900's

west side, a barrel-vaulted ceiling, and a dozen fine stained-glass windows, gifts of parishioners over the years. The building is 70 feet long and 40 feet wide and is located on the west side of the land which S.M. Swenson donated to the congregation in 1872 at the behest of his niece Anna Palm, whose son Henning had been buried on the site in 1863.

Over the years the fine old Gothic church has continued to serve the needs of the congregation admirably. Recent restoration has reinforced the bell tower and façade through a thorough repointing of the brickwork. A parish hall and modern parsonage now complement the church, but the beautiful cemetery, almost wholly dominated by Swedish surnames, still exudes an atmosphere of an earlier, hardier era, of the pioneer days on the frontier and of the breaking of the plains by immigrant farmers.

What no one had anticipated in December of 1868 was that the two areas historically associated with Swedish colonization — Austin and Brushy Creek — would largely be settled very soon. Future Swedish settlement would henceforth (throughout the 1870's and 1880's) move decidedly east from Austin into northeast Travis County, into the area created out of Knight's Ranch near Manor which would eventually be known as "New Sweden." This colony grew much faster than had either the Austin or the Brushy Creek settlements, since the pace of Swedish migration to America — and therefore to Texas as well — had also quickened significantly. Within just three years of the opening of land sales in Manor, the Swedes there organized to form their own Lutheran congregation.

At this time (1876), the Austin congregation was only six years old and had moved into its new little wooden church on 9th Street only two years before. The Brushy Creek congregation, although larger, was younger and poorer and still meeting in a wooden schoolhouse. The Manor-area Swedes rightly considered themselves to be a third and distinct geographical entity and either would not or could not make the 40-mile round trip to Austin or Brushy Creek to worship.

The three congregations were linked in a loose and rotating series of double pastorates: initially, Austin and Brushy Creek, then Austin and Manor, finally Manor and Brushy Creek were picked to be served by one pastor, and the "odd congregation out" would have to make do with temporary clergy. Even the seemingly indefatigable Noyd begged to be relieved of his Austin duties in October 1879 to devote himself more fully to his two other widely separated parishes.

Dr. John A. Stamline

John Anderson Stamline was the second Augustana-trained pastor to serve in Texas. Like his predecessor Noyd, Stamline was a man of enormous vitality, endurance, and physical energy. He oversaw the early consolidation of all three Swedish Lutheran congregations, which he also served on a regular rotating basis. He described, in vivid detail, a communion service in the early days of the New Sweden settlement:[9]

In those days, there were no planned roads laid out between the present Palm Valley colony and the Manor, or Knight's Ranch, settlement. Nor was one hindered by fences, but rather one made his way across the prairie as best one could. I had intended to take the most direct route, but went too far to the right and wound up in the German settlement of Pflugerville. Here I was forced to ask about the way, for I noticed that I had become lost. I stopped outside a house which lay by the road east of the old German Lutheran church, and a woman there noticed me. I asked her in English if she could show me the way to Knight's Ranch and if she knew where a number of Swedes lived. The answer came back: "Nicht verstehen," with a number of shakings of the head added for emphasis. Then the German language which I had learned at Augustana College served me in good stead. Through its use, I received satisfactory answers to my questions. She showed me the road to Andrew Sellström's who lived by the school section, one of the first settlers in the area. There I was warmly received and in his house I found both spiritual and physical respite, although the house only had two rooms. I will never forget the two blond-haired little boys John and Carl who were out in the yard playing when I arrived, how they ran to their mother and said "Nu kommer pästen" [lit., "Now the plague is coming"; they meant to say "Nu kommer prästen," "Now the minister is coming" but they could not say the letter "r"]. Sellström and his brother saw to it that a message reached Knight's Ranch and the Swedes who lived near the school, and the surrounding area, that they should come to divine service which would be held at Sellström's the following afternoon. The fastest message one could send in those days was a rider on a Texas pony for we did not have any modern conveniences then such as we have now [1915]. It rained heavily during the night, but nevertheless people came from many miles distant to participate in the service. Some came in wagons, others on horseback. In all its simplicity, this was an unforgettable event, God's word was heard by pious listeners and it later bore fruit, for most of these communicants made up the core of the founders of the New Sweden congregation.

To the southeast, the large influx of Swedes caused rapid growth in the New Sweden congregation. By 1894 enough Swedish settlers lived east of Manor to form a second congregation in Manda, where a small chapel (served by the Manor minister) was built. The parent church became the "New Sweden Evangelical Lutheran Church" of the Augustana Synod in 1887, when the community adopted the name "New Sweden" to distinguish itself from the town of Manor, six miles to the south. Both the main church and the chapel in Manda were in constant use for nearly 30 years. Then, in 1918, it was decided to erect a large new church at a new site midway between the old church and the Manda chapel and to consolidate all activities.

New Sweden Lutheran Church, 1920's

*Dr. Alfred L. Scott and family in front of parsonage, New Sweden Lutheran Church,
c. 1905*

Reverend Alfred L. Scott, pastor of the New Sweden
congregation at that time, and a Swedish-American contractor
named Wesley O. Gustafson drew up plans for a striking cruci-
form church in Gothic Revival style, with a mighty spire well
over 100 feet in height. The southern tower had something of
the Russian "onion-dome" look about it: the church was modeled
after a similar structure in Wakefield, Nebraska.[10] The large
wooden building also boasted a massive portico supported by
a pair of columns surmounted by elaborately carved capitals.
The interior of the church featured a large choir loft, a "mothers'
room," an altar with a large painting of Christ in Gethsemane
by a local artist named N.P. Smith, and a modern organ that
cost more than $4,500. The contractor spent nearly $50,000 on
the construction of this extraordinary structure.

The church (which is still in use) was consecrated on
May 4, 1924, a year and a half after construction had begun.
While it was now some distance from the cemetery, the new
location was unarguably more strategic, elevating the church as
it does and allowing the cross-capped spire to be seen for miles
around from every direction. With the completion of this church,

moreover, rural Swedes had something to be as proud of as their urban counterparts in Austin.[11]

In fact, despite its rural location, New Sweden in its heyday was a thriving community, supported by cotton production. There were two doctors to serve the area (one a Swede named Carlberg), two Swedish-owned drugstores, a "confectionery," a millinery shop, a shoemaker, a hardware store, a telephone exchange, a Swedish photographer, and a blacksmith. The Anderson and Axel gin provided local employment as did a small mattress factory, which also opened its doors to the community for musical performances. English-language services were not held in the church until 1923, and for many years the children of New Sweden attended Swedish-language Bible camps in the summer to learn scripture and Luther's Catechism in the language of their parents and grandparents.

Christmas was a major Swedish-American celebration in New Sweden, with men of the congregation dispatched into the countryside some weeks before the holiday to return with a

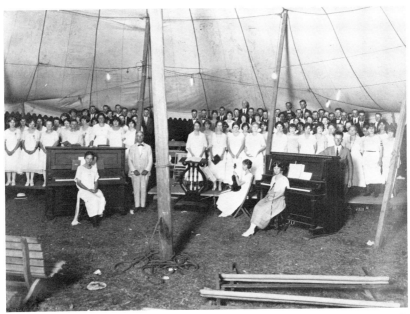

Luther League Bible camp for teenage members of the Augustana Synod in Texas, Round Rock, early 1920's

suitable cedar tree, which was then decorated with lighted candles in the traditional Swedish manner. Julotta was celebrated at six o'clock on Christmas morning, and Swedish hymns such as "Hosanna Davids son" ("Hosanna, Son of David") and "När juldagsmorgon glimmar" ("When Christmas Morn Is Dawning") were sung for nearly a hundred years.[12]

Today the community of New Sweden is little more than a collection of farms, an extraordinary church, and a sign on the highway, but it breathes that same sense of Texas Swedishness that one encounters in Palm Valley: a feeling of peace, endurance, and the humble rewards of honest labor. This, one hopes, will be the last to disappear.

The Swedish Methodists

While the Augustana Synod of the Lutheran Church (the American body of the State Church of Sweden) remained the dominant Swedish religious institution in Texas by a factor of two to one, other denominations gained impressive numbers of adherents. Of these, the largest by far was the Swedish Methodist Episcopal Church, whose oldest and largest congregation was in Austin.

An ethnically Swedish branch of the Methodist Episcopal Church was a result exclusively of the Great Migration from Europe, in which Swedish emigration played a significant role. Its origins in America can be traced back to Olof Hedström, a Swedish sailor who was stranded in New York in 1826, when his ship, the Swedish frigate *af Chapman* was sold. After several years of real hardship in America, he married a devoutly Methodist American woman with whom he attended a Methodist revival in 1835. He was converted and soon took up lay preaching. Within a few years he had decided to concentrate his ministry on the increasing numbers of Scandinavian immigrants arriving almost daily in New York. To accomplish his task, he fitted out a rotting old dismasted bark in the harbor as a floating chapel. Within a few years Hedström's little ship became officially known as the "Bethel Ship," ministering to the physical and spiritual needs of thousands of new immigrants each year, including many who were headed for Texas. (In later years S.M. Swenson, who came to know and admire Hedström and his work, was instrumental in aiding this initial experiment in outreach ministry.) Hedström lived until 1877, by which time the movement which he had done so much to promote had been carried to all parts of Swedish America, frequently by men who had personally served with Hedström in New York or through the handful of Swedish Methodist congregations then being founded in the East and Midwest.[13]

The history of Swedish Methodism in Texas begins almost as early as that of the Swedish Lutheran church. The first lay minister to preach the doctrines of John and Charles Wesley among the Texas Swedes was C.C. Charnquist, a multifaceted man who wore, variously, the hats of entrepreneur, farmer, author, printer, publisher, newspaperman, translator, hymnodist, and musician. He was also an energetic organizer and vigorous religious leader.

According to a brief autobiographical sketch, Charnquist had arrived in Texas from Michigan on October 18, 1871, with his wife and children. It had been a wearying journey, and he and his family lay gratefully in the shade of a giant oak, out of the heat of the unseasonably warm Texas sun. Little did he or his family realize that in just three years he would build the first Swedish Methodist church in Texas on that very spot.[14]

Charnquist had originally come to Austin to serve as organist for the fledgling Swedish Lutheran congregation on West 9th Street. But almost from the beginning he felt compelled to mount the pulpit and give witness to his faith, a demonstration that did not sit well with the congregation, who expected such avowals only from ordained clergymen. Yet, despite his conversion to Methodism back in Sweden in 1863, Charnquist had not intended to break with the adherents of the Church of Sweden. Indeed, even after he had withdrawn from the Gethsemane congregation, Charnquist's first act was to form den lutherska brödraförsamlingen (The Lutheran Brethren), still well within the limits of traditional Swedish Lutheranism.[15]

133

Gradually his preaching obligations became more intense, and Charnquist was forced to spend less time as a stonemason (his principal livelihood) and more time riding the Sunday circuit. The little circle of the Lutheran Brethren expanded rapidly, and the need for an ordained minister to administer the sacraments grew as well. Distribution of the sacraments by a layman met with strong disapproval among the Austin Lutherans, a disapproval strong enough finally to dissuade even the single-minded Charnquist.[16] He decided to form a Methodist congregation in Austin.

His landlord and friend, S.A. Lundell, suggested that Charnquist use Lundell's roomy home for Sabbath meetings, which he did. Six Swedes—Charnquist, Lundell, C.J. Swahn, Mathias Goldstein, Josef Ledin, and Johannes Johnson—and their wives thus formed the first Swedish Methodist congregation in Texas in October 1873.[17]

This small but energetic pioneer band began almost immediately to collect money for a church of their own. For $450 they purchased a site on 15th Street and Red River near what

Swedish Methodist Episcopal Church, Austin, 1890's

would someday be called Svenska kullen, or "Swedish Hill," the area in east Austin where many Swedes first lived, as it lay near S.M. Swenson's Govalle ranch. By Pentecost the next year, the church stood ready. The thrifty Charnquist notes that "the church cost over $1,000, the organ $300, the chandeliers around $40, the bell $65, the adjoining parsonage another $700, the stable $45 and many other things which belonged to the church but which I cannot remember."[18]

The little congregation on Swedish Hill under Charnquist's leadership grew from a dozen to 38 a year later. By the time he left Texas in May 1880, the congregation had grown to 175 and was quickly becoming too large for the church. A glimpse of the hard life even in the city in those early days may be found in Charnquist's ministerial record of his first six years in Texas:[19]

> I have, through the Grace of God, held 1,936 meetings . . . not counting song meetings, of which there were over 1,000. . . .
> I have led five revivals and spoken four times a day at each and the whole congregation has participated in such activities. . . .
> I have missed but one meeting because of illness and that was the toothache.
> I have baptized 128 children. . . .
> I have followed 25 to the grave, both young and old.
> I have united 20 couples in Holy Wedlock.
> I have written 569 songs and published hymnals valued at over $950.
> I have distributed and sold Bibles and diverse religious writings valued at over $1,000.
> I have taken 171 members into the congregation.
> I have trained 13 girls in music.
> I have held Swedish school for children 2-3 months every year. . . .
>
> Austin, Texas   May 12, 1880.
> C. Charnquist

In the fall of 1880 Charnquist's successor, Viktor Witting, arrived in Austin. He was one of the nationally known organizers of the Swedish Methodist Church, and he spent two years in Texas working hard among Swedish Texans. They continued, gradually, to convert to denominations which had, for all practical purposes, been forbidden in the fatherland, until the repeal of the Conventicle Acts in 1858. Witting's most significant ministerial accomplishment was the amalgamation of the Texas Swedish Methodists into the national conference organization. He was also very active outside the city of Austin and was eager to increase the number of Methodist congregations in the other areas opening up to Swedish settlement.

Soon after the founding of the Austin congregation, a rural group of Swedish Methodists had been organized into a small but strong congregation in Decker, eight miles east of Austin. Decker also became the home of an Evangelical Free Church congregation as well. It was thus unusual (though not unique) in being one of the few colonies in Texas without a Lutheran connection or congregation. (Charnquist had held services in homes in the Manor and Decker areas as early as 1872.) A small white wooden church was erected in 1879. A parsonage and cemetery plus nine additional acres of land were all acquired or built by 1884. The Decker congregation was served by the Austin minister until 1883, when it became independent and self-supporting. P.A. Lundberg was the first true resident pastor, an earlier candidate (Peter Newberg) having died of smallpox after preaching but one sermon.[20]

Viktor Witting (later to be publisher of the first Swedish-language newspaper in Texas) departed the state in 1882 and was ultimately succeeded by Dr. O.E. Olander, who became the denomination's Texas leader in 1896. Under Olander, the Swedish Methodist Church entered its second important period. Realizing that the wooden church on Swedish Hill in Austin had reached the limits of its usefulness and that the embryonic congregation could ill afford the massive costs of erecting a new and larger church, Olander began to investigate the possibility of acquiring an already existing church from another congregation. In 1898 his efforts were crowned, rather spectacularly, with success. A large church near the new capitol in downtown Austin came onto the market for $2,500. The massive bell tower was in a poor state of repair as was the interior, but, with $5,000 spent on renovations, it was ready for rededication on May 10, 1898.[21] This fine old edifice served the Swedish congregation until 1964, when a site on Berkman Drive was secured.

By 1923, when the church was ready to celebrate its 50th anniversary, the Swedish Methodist Episcopal Church in Austin alone had more than 360 members, with 160 in Sunday School and 60 in Epworth League, the youth society named for John Wesley's birthplace. The congregation accounted for one-fifth of all Swedish Methodists in Texas, some 1,600 persons in all.[22]

Sanctuary of Swedish Methodist Episcopal Church, Austin, 1890's

The efforts of Charnquist and his successors resulted in some 16 Swedish Methodist congregations across Swedish Texas, most of them rather small, but enough to constitute two districts within the Southern Swedish Mission Conference of the national denomination. Statewide, over 600 Swedish-Texan young people participated in Epworth League activities, and nearly all of the 600 tried to attend annual statewide Epworth League meetings. For more than 30 years the 1,600 Swedish Methodists of Texas even supported their own junior college, Texas Wesleyan College in Austin, which is discussed in Chapter 19.

But, as with the Swedish Lutherans, most of the ethnic identity which once characterized the Swedish Methodist Episcopal Church has gradually vanished with the passing years. Here and there a reminder—the Olander Room of the old Central Swedish Methodist Church in Austin, for example, or the plaque commemorating the former site of Wesleyan Hall (the old Texas Wesleyan College building, razed in 1976) on The University of Texas campus in Austin—testifies to the "Swedishness" of many

Swedish Methodist Episcopal Church, Decker, 1900's

a Methodist church in Texas. In 1973, for example, the wooden church built by Swedish Methodists in 1901 in Decker, once some eight miles east of Austin and now, like so many of the formerly rural Swedish colonies near Austin, absorbed by the city, received an official Texas Historical Marker for the church and community, thanks to the dedication of several members of the community and the Travis County Historical Survey Committee.

The inscription on what is now the United Methodist Church of Decker, but which began life as Svenska Methodist-kyrkan i Decker, reads:[23]

> First settlers in this area on Decker Creek were Swedish immigrants, who attended church in Austin from 1867 to 1870's. Beginning in 1871, the Rev. C.C. Charnquist of Austin preached in homes. With advent of more settlers, a church was erected and dedicated at Pentecost 1879. In 1882 a public school was opened. In 1884 the church was enlarged and parsonage built. In the pastorate (1901-2) of the Rev. C.O. Freeman, the present sanctuary was erected. The large modern wing was added in 1967.

The Swedish Evangelical Free Church

Swedish Lutheran and Methodist congregations tended to be larger and more numerous than any other religious organizations in Texas, but, despite the small size of the overall population, a third denomination made sizeable inroads — the Swedish Evangelical Free Church.

In fact, of all the varieties of Protestantism practiced by the Swedish Texans, the Free Church movement might be called the only truly Swedish-American denomination. Its origins can be traced back to the breakup of the Ansgarius Synod in 1875 in Worcester, Massachusetts. This group of independent Swedish congregations felt unable to join the Augustana Synod, with its strict adherence to the Augsburg Confession, and many of them banded together under the leadership of Peter Paul Waldenström to become the Svenska missionsförbundet (Swedish Mission Society), founded in 1878.

This group evolved into the Swedish Evangelical Mission Covenant Church in 1885, with congregations both in America and in Sweden.[24]

Other members of the former Ansgarius group, however, felt that the proliferating structural organizations of Swedish churches in America—districts, conferences, synods—hindered the true work they were designed to do. These churches joined forces to become the loosely organized Kristnas gemensamma verksamhet (Common Christian Work) in 1884 and later became the Svenska Evangeliska Frikyrkan i Amerika—the Swedish Evangelical Free Church in America. From the beginning this group felt disinclined even to look upon itself as a denomination. Its doctrine tended to be somewhat loosely defined, based on personal experience of grace and a literal and absolute adherence to Scripture. Its primary organ of information was a newspaper called *Chicago-Bladet*, edited by John Mortenson and Professor J.C. Princell, a follower of Waldenström and the intellectual leader of the Free Church movement.[25] One of their early collaborators was the Norwegian-born Nels (or Nils) Saabye, who felt a call to minister to the distant Swedes of Texas.[26]

As early as 1885, four Swedes in Brushy (now Georgetown) had banded together for Bible readings and discussion of Biblical prophecy. In 1888 the first Free Church pastor arrived to work with them, and a year later he was replaced by the national organizer, Nels Saabye. In 1891 the first Swedish Evangelical Free Church in Texas was organized at Brushy, with a charter membership of 23. The first church building was erected in 1892 and enlarged in 1906, and a new and much larger building was erected in 1924. By the time of its 50th anniversary in 1941, the Evangelical Free Church of Georgetown (as it is now known) had nearly 300 members and was the second-largest Swedish Free Church in the state.[27]

The second of the Free Churches to be organized was in Decker, east of Austin, in 1892. That same year a church was built for the congregation's 33 adult members. In nearby Elroy—today, like Decker, a suburb of Austin—a Free Church congregation was organized in 1904, and a little church was built by the 16 charter members. Similar congregations were founded in Kimbro, Melvin, Type, and Kenedy over the next four years.[28]

But soon the flight to, and expansion of, the cities began to affect the smaller rural congregations of all the Swedish religious groups, not least the small Free Churches, and it became clear that survival would necessitate amalgamation. The Elroy and Decker congregations joined and moved to Austin, where a new, large church was erected on the corner of 17th Street and Colorado in 1925. For more than 25 years the Austin Free Church congregation worshipped in this fine brick building. In

Swedish Evangelical Free Church, Austin, August 16, 1925

1952 the ethnic era ended, and the congregation was renamed the First Evangelical Free Church of Austin. Ten years later, it moved for the last time, to a larger site on Red River Street north of the university area. In 1977 a commemorative plaque was erected on the 17th and Colorado site, now absorbed by the expanding state government buildings surrounding the capitol. The inscription reads:

> Site of Swedish Evangelical Free Church Worship services started in 1889 led to founding of Swedish Evangelical Free Church in Decker Community (10 mi. E.) in 1892. A similar Swedish congregation originated in April 1904 at Elroy (20 mi. SE). In 1923, the two congregations merged, relocated in Austin, and in 1925, built a church on this site. Swedish was spoken in the services until the 1930's.

Renamed "First Evangelical Free Church" in 1952, the fellowship erected a new building on Red River Street in 1962, after selling this property to the State of Texas.[29]

In 1896 the tiny Swedish colony of Kimbro, in northeast Travis County, became one of the communities most powerfully affected by what later came to be known as the "Great Revival." It was led by Reverend Gustaf F. Johnson (later to become one of Swedish America's most famous evangelists) and Reverend John Herner, Swedish preachers sent into Texas as missionaries by the Board of Missions of the Evangelical Free Church.

The Kimbro Evangelical Free Church was organized on July 30, 1897, with 37 charter members. Two weeks later, one of them, Nels Torn, donated an acre of land on which to build a church. The "Mission House" was finished in three short months and was dedicated by Reverend Gustaf Johnson. Within a few years membership topped 100.[30]

Kimbro Orchestra, c. 1914

In 1901 A.F. Smith, a graduate of Bethany College in Lindsborg, Kansas, became musical director of the church and turned its five-year-old string ensemble into a fine string orchestra (the Kimbro Orchestra) which trained the young people of Kimbro musically for more than 50 years. The Swedish love of music — especially choral singing — was satisfied by the creation of a Men's Chorus in 1927, which sang both Swedish and English religious and patriotic songs for over 20 years.[31]

The original "Mission House" — a modest one-story wood structure, with a small bell tower — served the community well until it was destroyed by a tornado on May 1, 1944. A new church, similar in design to the old one, soon stood on the same site. It was dedicated in the fall of 1944 by the same Reverend Gustaf Johnson who had dedicated the first building 47 years before.[32] In 1954, with the rapid urbanization of the countryside, the congregation (together with the church) was merged with the tiny Free Church congregation at Type and relocated to nearby Elgin. As was the case with the Austin congregation, the Elgin Evangelical Free Church is no longer ethnically identified as Swedish in any way, although a few of the parishioners are still of Swedish stock.

One of the outstanding tenets of the Swedish Free Church movement was its support of domestic and foreign missions.

Evangelical Free Church at Type decorated for a wedding, 1910's

Despite its small national membership, it carried on missionary work in China, the Belgian Congo, and Japan almost from its inception. (One missionary minister, F.O. Bergström, could preach in English, Swedish, and Japanese.) As early as 1905 the Texas Skandinaviska Fria Missionssällskap (Texas Scandinavian Free Mission Society) had been organized to serve mission fields at home and abroad. The society was especially helpful in aiding the struggling small congregations in rural areas by underwriting the costs of traveling preachers and by augmenting the funds necessary to build mission houses or churches. It continued its activity, with ever-diminishing resources, until the 1940's.[33]

13

Swedish Texans and the Galveston Flood

Most early Swedish immigrants to Texas were familiar with this seaport, as it was in Galveston that their long sea voyages ended. In the days of sailing vessels, the immigrants traveled first to New York or Boston, then, via Key West by coastal steamer, to New Orleans, and finally on to Galveston, and across Galveston Bay to Buffalo Bayou and Houston, where S.M. Swenson's agent Gustaf Forsgård met them and arranged for their further travel inland to Travis and Williamson counties. Some Swedes, however, elected to remain in the growing coastal cities near the Gulf of Mexico, and a number of these families formed the nucleus of coastal urban communities.

The Galveston Flood of September 8, 1900, was the worst natural catastrophe in the history of the United States.[1] On that Saturday evening, hurricane-force winds of more than 100 miles per hour slammed a wall of water into the low-lying island at the entrance to the harbor. Smashing homes, churches, buildings, and virtually everything in its path, the water swept on over the densely inhabited portion of the island.

More than 6,000 people were to die that night or in the following hours in the stinking rubble that had been Texas' greatest seaport. In the next few days, as dazed volunteers began hauling the dead from the wreckage, it became apparent that the bodies could not even be properly buried, much less identified. In desperation the authorities sank bodies by the bargeload far out in the deep waters of the gulf. Even so, without food and water, outbreaks of disease in the devastated city took a heavy toll on an already weakened population. Over 10,000 people were homeless — early estimates had been nearly ten times that — and bands of looters plundered the dead, despite martial law and the threat of being shot on sight.

The small Scandinavian community was as badly hit as any other group, and, almost from the moment they learned of the disaster, their fellow countrymen in other parts of Texas began organizing relief. *Texas-Posten*'s editor, Mauritz Knape, urged his readers to subscribe to a relief drive as early as September 20, only days after the flood. His concerns were threefold: to raise as much money in as short a time as possible; to get the funds into the hands of those most desperately in need; and to distribute the funds "regardless of [to] which sect or religious denomination" the afflicted belonged.[2] To aid in the collection of funds, Knape designated 50 local agents as official representatives of the paper's list of subscriptions. Soon the funds began to arrive, a dollar here, $2.50 there. Within weeks more than $2,000 had been collected and a large contribution made by the newspaper itself, but it was a tiny sum compared to the need. Clara Barton of the Red Cross, who was on the scene for some time, estimated that over a million dollars would be needed simply to bury the dead and destroy the most dangerously damaged buildings. Five million dollars, she estimated, would be needed to restore basic services and reestablish vital distribution networks: food, water, gas, roads, hospitals, police, fire, and schools.

Mathilde Wiel-Öjerholm, the unofficial poetess laureate of the Swedes in Texas, contributed a poem entitled "Änkans skärf" ("The Widow's Mite") written expressly for the fund drive. Published on the front page of the October 11 edition of *Texas-Posten,* the poem urged her fellow countrymen to give as much as they could, remembering the Biblical tale of the widow's mite:

> Vi människor äro så små, så små
> Vår kraft, vår förmåga så ringa . . .
> Vår bibel dock lär oss att alla få
> Sin skärf, såsom hjälpmedel, bringa—
> Blott välment. När änkan sin skärf utaf
> Ett välvilligt hjärta lade,

Oss sagdt är, hon långt mer än andra gaf,
"Emedan hon gaf allt hon hade!"

Så blifve det då vårt heliga värf
Att enhälligt hjälpa i nöden.
Den rike sitt guldmynt, den arme sin skärf,
Låt öka de gåfvornas flöden
Som ämnats att lindra din broder i nöd—
Kanske blir det din tur—den nästa—
Så bringe du hugnad och lindring och stöd!
Och, o, gör ditt allra bästa!

(We human beings are so small, so small
Our power, our ability so puny
Our Bible, though, teaches that we all may
    bring our mite as a means to help,
if only it is well-meant. When the widow gave
    her mite from a well-meaning heart,
It should say to us, that she gave much more
    than others
"Because she gave all she had!")

(So then let it be our sacred duty
To help those in need unanimously.
The rich man his gold coin, the poor man
    his mite
Let them increase the flood of gifts
Which are intended to help your brother
    in need
Perhaps it will be your turn—the next one—
So let you bring consolation and relief
    and support!
Oh, do the very best you can!)

Almost immediately the Augustana Synod went into action to help the Swedes of Galveston. They also organized a relief committee to send funds to Reverend Segerhammer, then pastor of the small Zion congregation in Galveston, which had lost 15 of its members in the disaster. Pastor J.A. Stamline, who had served in Galveston in the 1890's, was also dispatched immediately with $500 from the Kansas Conference Mission funds. In addition, the conference president, G.A. Brandelle, urged the national Augustana Synod's various congregations to aid the relief work by sending money to the Conference Relief Committee in Lindsborg, Kansas.[3]

On October 4, 1900, a memorial service for the Swedish dead of Galveston was held. There was no music, for the organ had been destroyed in the flood. Nor was there any electricity yet, nearly four weeks after the storm. The names of the dead were read, thanks were expressed to all who had helped, and solemn hymns from *Hemlandssånger* were sung.

And yet, just two weeks after the memorial service, D.A. Lofgren of Michigan City, Indiana, a former pastor of the Zion congregation, self-righteously reminisced in *Augustana* about his early days in Galveston, when it was a wild and wicked city, where, even in Swedish homes, "the deck of cards often held the place of honor where the Bible should have been."[4]

During the years after the flood there was a general migration out of Galveston, with little new incoming blood. For more than 15 years the Lutheran congregation was listed as a mission, even though the modest property was soon worth $15,000.[5] The congregation survived, however, and today Zion Lutheran Church has a membership of 125.[6]

Methodist activities in Galveston began even earlier than Lutheran but were cut short even more abruptly by the devastation of September 1900. In the flood all but eight members of Galveston's tiny Swedish Methodist community were drowned. The church and property were almost totally destroyed.[7] But, under Pastor Johan (John) Fredrik Sarner, the tiny remnant rallied and began to rebuild for the future.

Within a year, thanks to the building society, the church was rebuilt at a cost of more than $3,000.[8] Perhaps more importantly, the Scandinavian Seamen's Mission (Skandinaviska sjömansmissionen) was linked with the Methodist Church, so that Pastor Sarner became chaplain of the mission as well. Thus, even during the city's darkest hour, the work with the visiting sailors from Scandinavia went on.[9]

In later years the mission (renamed "Seamen's Bethel") was again made an independent institution, thanks to a $40,000 legacy from the Swedish vice-consul in Galveston, Bertrand Adoue. This remarkable man had served his adopted homeland (he was himself born in Aurignac, France) as vice-consul for over

148

30 years until his death in 1911.[10] Although born a Catholic, he was elected a Knight of the Royal Swedish Order of Vasa, First Class; after his death, his son, Louis Adoue, took over the consular duties for many years. Seamen's Bethel was ultimately renamed "Adoue Seamen's Bethel" in memory of its benefactor, whose generosity helped more than 7,000 seamen every year.[11]

Scandinavian Methodist Episcopal Church with seamen's reading room on ground floor and parsonage on right, Galveston, 1900's

Adoue Seamen's Bethel, Galveston, c. 1917

14

Swedes in the Cities

Austin

The Swedish-born population of Texas reached its zenith in the decade 1910-1920. Of the 4,706 Swedish-born Texans reported in the 1910 census (a figure which swells to 11,598 if one includes the second generation born in America with at least one Swedish-born parent), larger percentages every year moved into the cities. By 1920, then, most of the pioneers were reaching ripe old ages indeed, and most were deciding to settle in the cities.

Good farmland had become scarce and expensive. Laws preventing the kind of contract labor arrangement that had permitted S.M. Swenson to import so many workers on prepaid tickets had been passed in the 1880's. Thus, the influx of laborers who, in turn, became renters, then small-farm owners, had largely ceased by 1900. By that time, too, many Swedes in America could afford to send home for relatives who were restless in Sweden and wished to join their successful families in the New World.

While land agents were still extolling the virtues of land along the Texas coast and in the Panhandle, it was clear that cattle ranching, not farming, would be the agricultural wave of the future. *Texas-Posten*, the newspaper of virtually all the Swedes in Texas, continued to run the agents' large advertisements for many years — indeed, both Otto Knape and Ernest Severin (owner and editor of the newspaper, respectively) were land agents in their own right — but the era of pioneer settlement had largely ended with the outbreak of World War I.

151

Group of Swedish Texans in Austin for the dedication of the State Capitol, May 1888

Migration of Swedes from the northern states — especially from Iowa, Nebraska, and Illinois — was largely confined to the 1890's; by 1910 it had virtually ceased. New arrivals tended to bypass the older, larger, better-established colonies to found satellite colonies near, but independent of, the earlier communities. In time, however, both the direct immigrants and those who came to Texas from the northern states tended to fall back to the cities, leaving the farms in the hands of their children.

As advancing age made the Swedish-born Texans shift their interests more and more to the cities, the rural Swedish-American villages began to lose first their post offices, then their mercantile establishments, their cooperatively owned or run cotton gins, and their telephone and electric companies. Rural electrification and the gradually expanding state and national communications net took over; better roads provided easier access to markets, depots, and gins at greater distances; and rural delivery of mail slowly eliminated the need for local post offices. Schools closed as families continued to drift into Elgin, Manor, Georgetown, Austin, or Round Rock. In most communities — such as Lund, New Sweden, Kimbro, and Palm Valley — only the church and its cemetery filled with Swedish names and phrases remain to mark the boundaries of the former Swedish territories. Sometimes, as with Stockholm, a tiny late community outside Lyford on the Gulf Coast, only the name remains to tell us of the existence of a former Swedish town or colony. Still others, like Decker and Hutto, have been absorbed into the rapid urban expansion of Austin and Round Rock, respectively.

But if the Central Texas farm country declined in importance for Swedish Texans, the cities took on new, vital functions. If businesses disappeared on the prairie, new ones grew up in town supported by an expanding Swedish consumer class.

A glance at *Texas-Posten* in the early 1920's shows a variety of such establishments in downtown Austin. John Palm, treasurer of the State National Bank, actively competed with Carl Widén at the American National Bank for Swedish accounts. Even fiercer competition existed in Williamson County, where August Swenson's Farmers and Merchants State Bank of Hutto struggled with Henry Lundblad of Georgetown's Farmers State Bank for the Swedish trade. One could stroll down the streets of Austin in 1920 and stop in at the Strid Brothers' shoe store and shoe repair, E.E. Wicklund's ("the watchmaker to the Swedes"), Carl Wentland and Sons real estate agent, Johnson Rubber [tire] Co., Hirshfield and Anderson's men's clothiers, Swann's carpet and furniture store, O.L. Krook's jewellers, the Bergstrom Brothers' auto repair, and Christianson's photo studio ("the Swedes' photographer"). Burials could be arranged through Rosengren's funeral parlor (operated by the son of one of the first Swedish settlers in Austin); special Swedish foods could be purchased from one of four Swedish grocery stores; cemetery monuments could be ordered through Julius Seaholm's Marble Works; horses could be shod at Swan Martin's smithy; and Swedish books and newspapers could be purchased — and published — through the Texas-Posten Publishing Company. For years, then, one could grow up in, or retire to, Austin and live almost entirely in a Swedish-speaking enclave.[1]

For legal matters Swedes could call on A.O. Sandbo, who had been born in Norway and had attended Yale University, where he studied theology, and the University of Texas, where he studied law. He was married to Swedish-born Anna Nyberg, who had the distinction of being the first woman ever to receive a law degree from the University of Texas. Together they ran a highly successful law practice known as the "Scandinavian Law Office," which specialized in representing Swedish clients.[2]

In downtown Austin were located most of the Swedish-American churches: the Swedish Free Church at 17th and Colorado; the Swedish Methodist Church just three blocks further south; and Gethsemane Lutheran Church on Congress Avenue, a stone's throw north of the capitol. For some years there was even a fledgling Swedish Baptist congregation at 18th Street and San Jacinto. From 1850 until his departure for the East during the Civil War, S.M. Swenson ran his mercantile operations out of a large, handsome building on Congress Avenue. His Avenue Hotel competed with the Driskill Hotel in catering to the needs of travelers and politicians in Austin on legislative business until it was mostly destroyed by fire in 1918.

One of the other landmark businesses in Swedish Austin was the Lundberg Bakery. Carl, later called Charles, Lundberg emigrated to Texas in 1872 as a journeyman baker. By 1876 his reputation had grown, and he was widely regarded as "the best baker in Austin." That was the year that he built his bakery at 1006 Congress Avenue in the shadow of the capitol. He built it to last, with limestone walls a foot thick, a "damask-design" tin ceiling, and, on the pediment, according to the *Austin Statesman* of March 26, 1876, he placed "a large eagle with outstretched wings, carved out of solid stone by that excellent mechanic Mr. John Didelat." The paper went on to point out that "Mr. Lundberg is sparing no expense in fitting up the most tasty and attractive bakery and confectionary in the South. Children and maids waited with baskets to take home loaves hot from the oven. House specialties were sponge cake, ladyfingers, glazed kisses, and almond-meal macaroons.[3]

Lundberg died in 1895, and for more than a decade the Swiss baker Henry Maerks ran the business. He in turn sold to a German baker, George Sighofer, who operated the business under the name Congress Avenue Bakery. Later, as the American Bakery and Cafe under O.P. Lackhardt, the old Swedish bakery entered a period of renewal, even after its name was changed somewhat inexplicably to the New Orleans Bakery.

But then it underwent a change for the worse, beginning in the 1930's. For a time, it was even used as a nightclub called "The Combo"! Ultimately, however, the structure came into the

Lundberg Bakery, Austin, 1990

Lundberg Bakery (lower left), *1880's*

hands of the Heritage Society of Austin, a branch of the National Trust for Historic Preservation, which now uses the building as a tourist information center. Under the aegis of the Society the old Swedish bakery, with its proud stone eagle and the name "Lundberg" at the roofline, has been restored to something like its former state and function.[4]

The Swedish residential district, at least before the turn of the century, was a well-defined section called Svenska kullen, "Swedish Hill." There seems some confusion today, however, as to exactly where its boundaries once were. The most likely determination is an area stretching from Waller Creek on the west and east to East Avenue and bounded by 14th Street on the south and 17th on the north. After the construction of the first Methodist church in 1874, however, and the availability of the former Govalle ranch lands for purchase, the Swedish population seems to have shifted decidedly to the east. By 1900 Swedish Hill was bounded on the west by East Avenue and on the east by Navasota, while its northern boundary lay at 15th Street. The southern edge of the Swedish enclave was still 14th Street East.[5]

Looking northeast from State Capitol with "Swedish Hill" beyond church, Austin, 1880's

The area had gradually grown from some 18 families in 1874 to nearly 40 in 1900, but it is clear that the latter figure represented but a fraction of the Swedish residents of Austin; by 1900 Swedes were living in all parts of the city and, indeed, all parts of the state. Their businesses, churches, schools — the Swedish Methodist Texas Wesleyan College was located on College Hill off Red River Street from 1906 to 1934 — burgeoned with the influx of new population. And, as the aging pioneers retired to what had become the Swedish capital of Texas, Swedish culture in the Lone Star State reached its zenith.

Georgetown

Georgetown was not as closely connected with the Swedish colonization of Williamson County as were the older rural settlements along Brushy Creek. But, like Austin, it served as a center for urban remigration as the pioneer generation left the countryside for comfortable city homes in the 1880's and 1890's. Georgetown was also a large commercial center for mercantile and financial activity, much of which centered on the expanding economic base established by the Swedish community.

As early as 1871, the peripatetic Carl C. Charnquist had visited the Brushy Creek settlement to hold Methodist worship services in local homes. His successors, Viktor Witting and P.A. Juhlin, continued Charnquist's work, and by 1882 they had formed a rural Methodist congregation in direct competition with the older Palm Valley Lutheran Church.[6] But the fluid nature of the demographics of the area soon went against them, and the church the year-old congregation had built in 1883 at a cost of $2,200 soon proved to be far away from the new resettlement in the Georgetown area. What had been a conveniently located rural church when it was built was, only 20 years later, far away from the Swedish community, which continued to drift eastward and northward. So, during the ministry of O.F. Linstrum, a decision was reached to buy a lot on University Avenue, the main thoroughfare in downtown Georgetown. Monies were collected for the erection of a new and grander church, one which was to take four years to build and cost nearly $15,000.[7] Apparently the decision was a wise one, for the country congregation that numbered 97 in 1882 had grown to more than 300 by 1918.

Clearly, urban congregations would continue to absorb rural ones as the process of urbanization, the so-called "flight from the farm," continued in the 1930's and '40's. In fact, for some years the Georgetown Methodist Church added more members than the older Austin congregation, to become the largest Swedish Methodist Church in Texas.

St. John's Swedish Methodist Episcopal Church, Georgetown, 1910's

But it was the presence of so many Scandinavian merchants that gave Georgetown its Swedish flavor. In the 25th anniversary booklet of the Georgetown Swedish Methodist Church, for example, one could find advertisements for the Forsberg and

Anderson Grocery Store; Lindell, Peterson and Hamilton Hardware; Strömberg-Hoffman Co.; S.A. Heard (Hörd) Groceries; the Post Office Drug Store; (Svenskarnes apotek — "the Swedes' Drug Store"); First National Bank of Georgetown (with O.A. and C.A. Nelson on the board of directors); Mrs. C.H. Swenson, Millinery; Miss Gertie Stromberg, certified piano teacher; P.J. Anderson and Wm. Sandgren, blacksmiths; and Oscar Berkman, shoemaker. The town boasted a rather famous Swedish-Texan physician in the person of Doctor Henschen, the "Swedish Doctor."[8] Dr. Gustave Esaias Henschen was the son of Dr. William Henschen, a leading Methodist organizer and for many years the publisher of the weekly Methodist national newsletter *Sändebudet* ("The Messenger"). Dr. G.E. Henschen served with distinction in the medical corps in France during World War I, as did more than a dozen others from Georgetown, including three young Swedish-Texan nurses. (In fact, Georgetown seems to have had more of its sons and daughters in uniform than any other Swedish community in Texas.)[9]

And, for a few months in 1908-1909, Georgetown was the home of *Texas-Bladet*, the second Swedish-language newspaper in Texas and the only serious rival that the Austin-based *Texas-Posten* ever entertained.

Wagons loaded with Andrew J. Nelson's cotton crop in front of Williamson County courthouse, Georgetown, c. early 1890's

Main Street, Round Rock, c. 1908

Round Rock

Until its rapid growth during the last few years, Round Rock in Williamson County was a typical sleepy little Central Texas town. Yet appearances were a bit deceptive, for while the stores along Main Street may have looked like their counterparts in hundreds of similar towns around the state, there was one significant difference: in Round Rock, many of the names above the stores were Swedish. In fact, Round Rock, even more than Georgetown, was the mercantile center for the Williamson County Swedes. It was here that the immigrants who had settled in Brushy Creek and Palm Valley came to sell their cotton, buy provisions, visit the doctor, and do their banking.

Round Rock was the center of the mercantile empire built by Anders Johan Nilsson, better known as "Rike" (Rich Man) Andrew John Nelson, an immigrant of 1854. Like the other Texas Swede known as "Rike" —S.M. Swenson— Nelson's great wealth was based on land. Beginning in the 1870's, he and his family began purchasing land in south Williamson County, renting or selling it to incoming Swedish immigrants for cotton production. Soon he had become one of the largest landowners in the county with more than 8,000 acres. He began diversifying his interests in much the same way that Swenson had done a decade or so before him.[10]

Much of the expansion of the Nelson family businesses was due to the skill of Nelson's sons, Carl, Walter, Oscar, and particularly Thomas. Born in 1888, Thomas E. Nelson had a thoroughly Swedish-American education at Bethany College in Lindsborg, Kansas, and the University of Texas at Austin.[11] He became a banker in Round Rock, and in 1928, with his brother Carl, he started the Round Rock Cheese Factory, which, at its peak, produced more than 325,000 pounds of cheese annually from the Nelson-owned herd of 300 dairy cattle. Thomas was a founder of the Farmers State Bank of Round Rock and president for many years.[12]

Thomas Nelson's cousin John A. Nelson built a large hardware store in Round Rock in 1892, a lumber company in 1895, and, five years later, John A. Nelson and Company, Bankers. He owned the largest dry goods store in Round Rock and was part-owner of a local broom factory. Trinity College (see Chapter 19) was built on land donated by Nelson, and he was

John A. Nelson Store, Round Rock

Residence of Mrs. Andrew John Nelson, Round Rock, 1900's

also responsible for raising nearly $7,000 to get construction of the school under way.

It should be emphasized that all these enterprises — banks, broom and cheese factories, hardware and dry goods stores — were Swedish-owned and -operated. Most of the workers, clerks, and stockholders were either immigrants or second-generation Swedish Texans. Nor were the Nelsons the only Swedish entrepreneurs in town (although they were by far the wealthiest). The local drug store was owned and operated for more than 50 years by the Quick sisters, daughters of pioneers from Barkeryd in Småland. There were two Swedish grocery stores and four Swedish blacksmiths and wheelwrights, a Swedish shoemaker, a contractor, and even a Swedish insurance company. The J.A. Nelson and Co. Hardware dominated the west end of Main Street (as the building still does) and housed both Nelson's large hardware business and his bank. At the other end of town Trinity Lutheran College of Round Rock, the most ambitious experiment in higher education undertaken by the Swedes of Texas, conducted classes from 1906 to 1929; since then, the college buildings have housed a Lutheran home for the aged. The Swedish Ginning Company operated just outside town and was one of the largest in the area for many years. On Main Street a Swedish farmer could do his banking, shop, order repairs to his buggy or his barn, and even purchase steamship tickets for himself or for relatives still in Sweden—all without having to speak a word of English![13]

At the end of town was the magnificent mansion built by Mrs. Andrew John Nelson. It was erected between 1895 and 1900 and was designed and built by the Page Brothers, highly regarded Austin architects. Thomas Nelson and his wife, according to the Texas Historic Landmark plaque set up in 1973, had the façade of the house redesigned from its original Victorian style to its present Classical look in 1931. In 1960 Eugene and Jean Crier Goodrich, renovated the house and renamed it Woodbine. It is undoubtedly the finest example of domestic architecture built by Swedish Texans extant and still graces the main thoroughfare of Round Rock.

Lund

The community of Lund—and its eastern satellite Type— marked the extreme eastern edge of Swedish settlement in Central Texas. Just as New Sweden was a younger offshoot of the Brushy Creek settlements, so was Lund largely settled by farmers from New Sweden.

The land around Lund was quite similar to the "black waxy" prairie near Brushy Creek. In eastern Travis County the land was higher and drier with denser vegetation, such as prickly pear cactus. One of the first to try to tame it was Per Sjöholm, later Seaholm, born in Munkarp, Skåne, in 1828. Seaholm had emigrated in 1883 after a distinguished military career as a corporal in the Royal Skåne Hussars. His son, Gustaf Seaholm, had arrived in America the previous year and had made his way to the mill town of Bridgeport, Connecticut, where he met and married Emma Person from Värmland. Per Seaholm headed south and settled first in New Sweden, Texas, in 1887.[14]

His son joined him that same year, and for a time they rented land from Pastor J.A. Stamline in New Sweden. But talk of Lund (or rather the area that was to become Lund) must have been in the air, because old Corporal Seaholm purchased land and settled there within two years of his arrival in Texas. His son joined him, and soon a dozen families moved into the area, with more arriving all the time.

Among them were Carl and Fred Bergman and their friend August Thornquist. The three had become friends in Bridgeport, Connecticut, in the early 1880's. They might have heard of the rich land to be had cheaply in Texas from Johan Westling, whose son and brother were already farming in New Sweden. At any rate, the Bergman brothers and August Thornquist came to Manor in 1884 and bought their own land in Lund five years later.[15]

The soil was rich, but the heavy layer of ground cover made plowing difficult. The brutally hot summers also took their toll, as the letters home to Sweden written by the Bergmans so graphically attest. But despite the initial hardships, the Lund colony flourished as few of the other smaller satellite settlements were to do.

One of the reasons for its success was the large number of experienced farmers who came to the area. Most of the Lund Swedes had spent some years in Texas and now knew the vagaries of cotton production and the Texas climate. (The coastal colonies — Olivia and El Campo, for instance — were settled largely by immigrants who were familiar with the American crops grown in the northern and midwestern states: corn, wheat, and rye.) Lund was also bordered on the west by the New Sweden colony, which, in turn, bordered the eastern fringe of the Brushy Creek or Palm Valley settlements. Thus, there was available a continuity of experience on which the Lund pioneers could draw.

The first cotton gin was constructed, as usual, by the Swedes themselves, in this case, August Thornquist and Gustaf Seaholm. These two pioneers joined forces with the Bergman brothers to link Lund to Elgin by telephone as early as 1899.[16] A general store was opened in 1890 by Nels Ankarstolpe, who also built the town's first blacksmith shop. A post office had been opened in 1895, at which time Gustaf Seaholm suggested that the town be named "Lund" after the famous cathedral and university town in his home province of Skåne.[17]

Nels Ankarstolpe Blacksmith Shop, Lund, late 1890's

Since the Bergman letters survive, we know more about the mercantile business in Lund than any other area of Swedish Texas. An American, J.E. Rivers, had opened a general store in the Lund area in 1894. With the coming of the post office, Rivers automatically became postmaster as well, since he had the only building in town in which to house the post office. The Bergmans bought the building (and thus also the post office) in October 1897 for the sum of $5,400. They had to borrow against their land to raise the money.

Carl Bergman, therefore, became Lund's second postmaster, in which capacity he served until his death in 1903. Fred Bergman then ran the store (and his own farm, while serving as postmaster as well) for a further two years. At that time, the store was sold to a fellow Swede, Gustaf Carlson, who in turn sold it three years later to a pair of Swedish brothers, Claes and Victor Bengtsson, owners of a similar store in Elgin. A year later it was purchased by Gustaf Robert Axell, born of Swedish parents in New Sweden in 1886, and Gustaf Seaholm. The latter pulled out after four years, leaving Axell sole proprietor for the next 30 years. The business was shut down for good in 1944 and the building torn down the same year. Since then there has been

General Store, Lund, 1930's

no general store in Lund, but for its entire 50-year existence the Lund store was Swedish-owned and -operated.[18]

In March 1899 Carl Bergman wrote to his sister Sofie in Linköping a bit about the business he and his brother ran:[19]

> We deal in groceries, hardware, cloth goods, odds and ends, as well as men's clothes and footwear. A country store has to be supplied with everything—we even have medicines on hand. Our inventory was worth $4,462 when we took over the store and the buildings were worth $1,066. We paid $3,162 in cash and borrowed the rest. Last year, we repaid $1,200. Our sales amounted to $11,200, whereof we have debts of $1,500 outstanding as a result of a bad harvest and a low price on cotton. It has to be sold on credit and, if the price is not right, there are many who will not be able to repay their debts.

Reverend J.A. Stamline—the veteran of the early days who had organized almost all the original Lutheran congregations in Texas—now came out to organize the new congregation at Lund. This took place on January 16, 1897, in the Lund Public School. Carl Bergman served as secretary and later as church organist. At the initial meeting were nearly 50 men, women, and children.[20]

The church was finished in the fall of 1899, and the first service was held there on Thanksgiving Day. Fortunately, the building was large, for in less than 20 years membership rose to more than 200. Stamline served as pastor for nearly a decade until he was called to be the first president of Trinity College in Round Rock.[21]

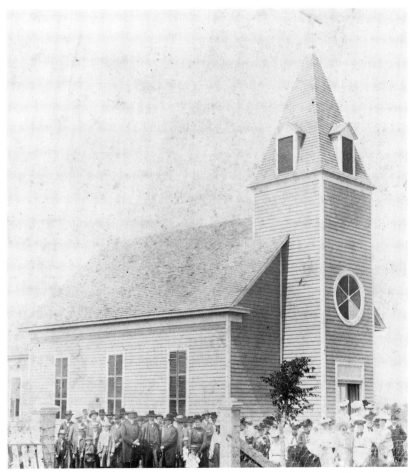

Bethlehem Lutheran Church, Lund

Altar painting by Olof Grafström, Bethlehem Lutheran Church, Lund, 1900's

In 1902, on Good Friday, an altar painting of the Cruci-
fixion was unveiled and dedicated by Pastor Stamline. The picture—some seven feet high by three wide—had been commissioned by the recently formed Young People's Society (Ungdoms-
föreningen). They had contracted the work from Professor Olof
Grafström, chairman of the Department of Art at Augustana
College in Rock Island, Illinois. Grafström was, at that time,
one of Swedish America's outstanding artists. He supplemented
his academic income by painting altarpieces for Swedish Lutheran churches. In his long career Grafström painted some 200,
perhaps as many as 300, altar paintings, but only one is known
to have been commissioned by a Swedish-Texan congregation—
Bethlehem Lutheran Church in Lund.

Stamline and the church council were so enthusiastic over
the new painting that they sent a "testimonial" letter to Grafström
which, with their permission, the artist later reprinted in the
brochure he sent to prospective clients. As it is one of the few
public documents from the early days of the Swedish-Texan
colonies, it deserves to be quoted *in extenso*:[22]

The altar painting in the Swedish Evangelical Lutheran Church in Lund, Texas, painted by the artist O. Grafström at Augustana College, Rock Island, Ill., and commissioned by the Young People's League, is not just a masterpiece of artistic talent and beautiful art and taste, but also a beautiful and worthy adornment to the altar, and as such it provides general satisfaction and contentment. For all who enter the church, it is a sermon about "The Crucified" and as such it inspires the heart to holy deliberation and reverence. It also provides the visitors to this temple with a sense of hope, that they may be near to Him, who has died for our sins and risen for our return to righteousness. Certified by members of the church council, Swedish Evangelical Lutheran Bethlehem Congregation, Lund, Texas, Sept. 21, 1901.
(signed) J.A. Stamline, Pastor, P.V. Nelson, Gust. Peterson, Andrew Berkman

Augustana, the newspaper of the Augustana Synod, reported the dedication of the painting in its pages, an article which was also reprinted in Grafström's brochure:[23]

Good Friday was a day of celebration within this congregation [Lund, Texas]. A perfectly beautiful and eloquent altar painting by our talented artist Olof Grafström in Rock Island was unveiled. The work represents Christ on the cross with a repentant woman on her knees at the foot of the cross. She seems to be sunk in holy reverie and prayer and about to demonstrate the last service of true love to the body of Christ by preparing it for burial by anointment, which the alabaster plank beside her signifies. The woman seems to have come to the cross at sundown. The picture, as well as the ceremonies in connection with its unveiling, made a deep and lasting impression on the many people who were here assembled. Pastor C.P. Rydholm [then pastor at New Sweden] held an excellent talk on the subject and the text, "Behold, the Lamb of

God." The choir sang several songs suitable to the occasion and a number of suitable psalms were declaimed, chosen from the psalms of the Passion in the Swedish hymn book. This painting is a beautiful and noble gift by the Youth League.

The painting cost a total of $156.70 and was paid for entirely by the Young People's Society. It has, to date, hung in three different buildings and survived both tornado and fire intact. It is now in the third church to stand on the same spot and has the central place of honor behind the altar.[24]

The first church building was moved to the present site in 1916, but by 1924 it had become too small, and a new and larger church (similar in design to the original structure) was built on the same site.[25] This church withstood the test of time very well until April 5, 1980, when it was badly damaged by a tornado. It was deemed that, since the structure had been moved off its foundation, it would be too difficult to repair, and a decision to build a new church was undertaken. This new structure, built of brick with a bell tower and parish hall, was finished and dedicated in the fall of the next year, an impressive achievement for a congregation of just over 100.[26]

The Lund congregation was also somewhat unusual in the range and variety of its cultural (as well as spiritual) interests. Within five years of the founding of the church, Stamline and his helpers had established the following special interest organizations: Sunday Church School (Söndagsskolan), Luther League (Lutherförbundet), Sewing Bee (Syföreningen), Ladies Aid Society (Fruntimmerföreningen), Forget-me-not (Förgät-mig-ej, a continuation of the Linnéas, an association for young women named for Carolus Linnaeus, the Swedish "flower king"), and the men's and women's choirs. Perhaps the most significant step toward the preservation of Swedish culture in Texas was the establishment of a regular Swedish summer school as early as 1899, which was sometimes held at two or more different times to accommodate all those who wished to participate. The school lasted six weeks each year and was taught by teachers elected at annual church council meetings. The curriculum emphasized the Catechism, Bible history, and reading and composition in Swedish. The Summer Swedish School continued until 1923.[27]

The Swedish language was retained longer at Lund than almost anywhere else in Texas. Reverend Rodeen began preaching in English in 1929. Between 1945 and 1951 one Swedish sermon a month was preached, and from 1957 to 1960 Swedish services were still held at Lund and New Sweden on Sunday afternoons, with two additional services in Swedish held every spring and every fall.[28]

Ericksdahl and the Development of the S.M.S. Ranches

As mentioned in Chapter 6, S.M. Swenson moved his business ventures to New York in 1866, liquidating all of his Texas properties including his Austin home, Govalle. In New York he and his partner from New Orleans, William Perkins, opened the Swenson Perkins Company on Wall Street, soon to become a wholly Swenson operation as the S.M. Swenson and Sons banking house. Swenson also ran a clearinghouse for Texas-produced items such as tallow, hides, beef, etc., that needed storage in New York before being shipped for export.[29]

Swenson held vast areas of idle land in Texas which he had acquired before the Civil War with railroad scrip. According to Gail Swenson,[30] the State of Texas had begun to make land grants for the railroads as early as 1852. S.M. Swenson had settled permanently in Austin only two years before, but, realizing the importance of the railroads in opening up the interior of the state, he began acquiring land certificates issued by the Buffalo Bayou, Brazos and Colorado Railway. He secured scrip for 100,000 acres, which could be located in any unclaimed territory in the northern or western areas of Texas. The land was located on alternate sections in parts of what would someday become Jones, Throckmorton, Shackelford, Haskell, and Stonewall counties, leaving alternate sections for school land. Later these alternate school sections were acquired when Swenson purchased some of the original grants given to soldiers who had fought in the Mexican War. Swenson's sons, Eric Pierson and Swen Albin — his partners on Wall Street — urged their father to begin to use the several hundred thousand acres of land they had acquired and on some of which they were beginning to have to pay taxes. In 1882 the three came west to examine their vast acreage, with an eye to establishing ranches there.[31]

It is now clear that the areas he had acquired in North and West Texas were all part of S.M. Swenson's grand design for colonizing the Lone Star State with Swedes from his home province, Småland. A dozen years before he leased the Ericsdale, Throckmorton, and Flat Top ranches to his sons, he had stationed one of his many nephews, John Swenson, in Jones County on land that would later become part of the Ellerslie ranch, under the aegis of the Swenson Land and Cattle Company. John was the son of Swenson's brother-in-law Daniel Swenson and his sister Amalie and had been born on the family farm, Lättarp, near Barkeryd, where Swen Magnus himself had spent his youth.[32] Swenson urged his nephew to come to Texas, and so young John began scientific herd production in Jones County in the 1870's. To help him, Swenson obtained the services of four Swedish "cowboys," all from the Barkeryd area: C.G. Seth, "Judge" Joe Erickson, August "Dippe" Holmberg, and the latter's brother Mage.[33]

S.M. Swenson had decided to build three great ranches, each to be named for one of the three surviving Swenson children. The "Eleanora" Ranch (named for the youngest daughter, Mary Eleanora) was located near Throckmorton in the county of the same name and eventually came to be known as the Throckmorton Ranch. "Ericsdale," named for Eric Pierson Swenson, was located nine miles east of the city of Stamford in Jones County and was initially a ranch of some 90,000 acres. The "Mount Albin" Ranch, named for Swen Albin, covered a similar area of Jones, Stonewall, and Haskell counties and soon became known as the "Flat Top" ranch after its most prominent geographical feature, a flat-topped hill. S.M. Swenson leased the land to his sons, who were to operate the ranches themselves, borrowing from their father at 5 percent interest to pay the huge costs of starting up such a far-flung business venture.[34]

The early years saw only meager results, and expenditures soared to more than $200,000. The brothers hired their cousin Alfred Dyer (son of Anna Swenson Dyer, their father's sister) as their foreman. At the time, Dyer had become one of the most knowledgeable cattlemen in the state. Under his leader-

ship as manager, the brothers kept purchasing land: the 79,000-acre Tongue River property and 5,700 acres which became the Ellerslie Ranch were acquired in 1898.[35]

The town of Stamford was laid out on land donated by the Swensons to entice the Texas Central Railroad into the Swenson territories. The brothers later bought back the land to develop Stamford along their own designs. By 1901 the town had a population of 3,000, and Swedish immigrants were buying land to ranch or grow cotton in record numbers.[36]

Ericksdahl, on the other hand, was created out of the original 50,000-acre ranch that the Swensons organized in 1882. The brothers' plan was to attract Swedish immigrants into the area, where they could then settle, establish small farms or ranches of their own, or work as hands on the nearby S.M.S. ranches, as they now called the Swenson properties. (The parent company was the Swenson Brothers Cattle Company, which became the Swenson Land and Cattle Company in 1926. The new name, by which the company is still known, reflected the double interests of the family—land development and ranching.)[37]

The man put in charge of the Ericksdahl development was Anders Johan (or Andrew John) Swenson, another of S.M. Swenson's myriad nephews. A.J. was the son of Johan i Långåsa, S.M.'s brother and emigrant agent in Barkeryd. He was born at Långåsa in 1863 and met his uncle Swen Magnus in 1881 on one of the latter's visits home. The elder Swenson convinced the young man to emigrate, promising him work in Louisiana or Texas on one of his sugar plantations or cattle ranches.

173

Andrew John Swenson

A.J. Swenson emigrated that same year and worked for a time on his uncle's property in St. Mary's Parish in Louisiana, but he found the muggy weather oppressive. By January 1882 he had made his way to Brushy Creek, where his aunt, Anna Dyer, and sister, the second wife of Reverend J.A. Stamline, were living. From his brother-in-law, Swenson learned of his uncle's vast undertaking in North Texas, and soon he found himself in Jones County working on the earliest of the S.M.S. ranches.[38]

His career with the Swenson company was to last well over half a century, which was not, however, unusual for highly placed Swenson managers. He began as a ranch hand and was gradually entrusted with greater responsibilities, culminating in his becoming general manager for all the Swenson holdings in Texas—more than 400,000 acres. In addition, he was chosen to oversee the partition of the Ericsdale ranch and the creation of a Swedish community, "Ericksdahl" or "Ericsdale," in its place. (The latter seems to have been used rather freely to describe the area created from the original ranch lands: the actual community of "Ericksdahl" included the settlements of Avoca, Lueders, and Stamford, and the Bethel congregation of the Lutheran Church near Avoca, which served them all.)

Andrew John Swenson (center, facing camera) *at chuck wagon*

His English still a bit shaky, A.J. Swenson enlisted the aid of his brother-in-law, Pastor Stamline, to boost the sales of Ericksdahl land. The Swenson brothers donated 80 acres of land for a church and offered to pay a minister $300 a year if and when a Lutheran congregation was organized. Stamline asked his colleague Pastor L.J. Sundquist — then the minister at Gethsemane Church in Austin — to help him, and together they persuaded some 50 Swedish families to relocate to Ericksdahl. The land was then selling for $10 to $16 an acre, and by 1908 all of it had been sold. (By comparison, land in the Georgetown area was then selling for $50 to $70 an acre.)[39]

Stamline organized the Bethel congregation in Ericksdahl on January 25, 1906, with services held around the A. J. Swenson chuck wagon and in various homes until the wooden church was finished in the fall of 1907.[40]

This "little white church on the hill," as it was known, served the congregation well for some years. But in 1919 the Reverend Hugo Haterius arrived in Avoca, and things in Ericksdahl were never again quite the same. Haterius had been born in Nebraska in 1886, the nephew of C. J.E. Haterius, the driving force behind the Olivia experiment in land sales to Swedish immigrants (see page 181). Hugo spent a brief part of his youth in Olivia, and after his ordination at Rock Island, Illinois, in 1916, he came south in 1917, moving to Ericksdahl two years after that.[41]

Haterius was a tireless civic booster as well as a zealous churchman, and under his guidance a number of community projects were conceived and carried out. He spearheaded a rural electrification program, for instance, which ultimately brought electricity to Ericksdahl and surrounding communities. He also led a drive for a water cooperative, so that the ravages of the 1928-1930 drought would never again be repeated. He convinced the county to build a paved road from Stamford to his church and oversaw the construction of the "Swede Dam" on California Creek, which also served as a bridge for the country road.[42]

But the Reverend Hugo Haterius's most memorable public act was in persuading the congregation to drill for oil on church property.

Oil was first discovered at 3,235 feet on the Carl Olander farm, one mile south of Bethel Church, in 1937. Soon Reverend Haterius found oil on two of his own farms, on property belonging to four other members of the congregation, and finally on the church property itself. The drilling on the church land began on April 2, 1938, and had reached a depth of 3,250 feet when oil was discovered on April 14. The initial flow, however, was only 475 barrels in six hours—hardly the "gusher" they had hoped for! Still, the steady flow of "black gold" augured well for the future of Ericksdahl, especially after the very bleak years of the Great Depression.[43]

Reverend Haterius decided to put the unanticipated windfall from the oil discovery to good use. By 1939 the old wood church was showing its age. It was also proving too small for the growing congregation. Haterius decided to build a truly impressive house of worship, built of native stone in a monumental style and size. Construction began in November 1939.

The rock was quarried right on the site, dressed, and hauled by horse and mule teams into position. The new church occupied the same site as the old wooden one. Its double rock walls were more than 100 feet long and 60 feet wide, with a crenellated Gothic bell tower capped with a cross-tipped spire over 100 feet tall. The new church could hold almost 500 people, considerably more than the congregation at the time. The value of the church was initially $42,000 (the actual cost, $25,000 with donated materials and labor), but because of the nearly two years

Bethel Lutheran Church, Ericksdahl, 1980's

it took to complete the structure, the final value (and also cost) was actually somewhat greater.[44]

The new church in Ericksdahl is undoubtedly the boldest architectural statement ever made by the Swedish Texans. Its sheer size and magnificence — excessive even in 1940 — constitute a testament to the permanence of this small ethnic group on the vast plains of northern Texas. To build in stone meant they had come to stay, and even though membership had declined somewhat, as rural congregations inevitably do, Haterius's dream of "a Taj Mahal on the prairie," as one visitor put it, remains a bright symbol of faith, labor, and prosperity.[45]

While A.J. Swenson was occupied in selling off Ericsdale Ranch to build an immigrant community, the Swenson brothers were busy building their empire. The three ranches they fenced in 1884 were among the first in the state to be so enclosed. Their willingness to experiment and innovate often meant success to the S.M.S. brand in difficult times. Frank Hastings, for example, who managed the Swenson concerns for 20 years until his death in 1922, was the first person to introduce "mail-order" cattle. So stable and uniform was the S.M.S. brand that customers were confident of satisfaction without the bother and expense of an on-site purchase.[46]

Perhaps the most dramatic event in the long and colorful history of the Swenson Land and Cattle Company occurred in 1904 when the Swensons acquired the Espuela Ranch, one of the most famous of the foreign-owned Texas properties. The Espuela ranch — some 437,000 acres supporting 40,000 head of cattle — had been acquired cheaply by a London syndicate in 1885 because terrible blizzards the previous year had killed nearly 7,000 cattle. But the equally cold winter the following year decimated the herds by another thousand head. Profits slipped alarmingly as expenditures skyrocketed to replenish the stock. Water was inadequate, and long treks between watering tanks and shelters caused the cattle to lose weight. Soon the British were eager to sell.

Eric Swenson offered the Espuela Land and Cattle Company, Ltd., of London, exactly $5 an acre for the huge ranch, a thrifty Swedish price which would include land, cattle, horses, and all equipment. After strenuous negotiations the British gave in on September 6, 1906, and the Spur Ranch (translating the Spanish word *espuela*) became part of the Swenson empire.[47]

The new manager of the Spur was to be "Judge" Joe Erickson, one of the four Swedes imported from Barkeryd in

Joe Erickson

1884 to help A.J. Swenson on the undeveloped Swenson land in Jones County. He was succeeded by the second of those cowboys, August Holmberg. Again, one of the prime reasons for acquiring the huge Spur lands was to turn some of them into farms and small ranches at a very handsome profit. The first 36,000 acres were on sale by August of 1908, just when the last of the land composing the former Ericsdale Ranch was sold. Within 20 years 1,145 parcels of land totaling 231,147 acres (at nearly $14 an acre) had been sold. Ten years later the entire Spur Ranch had disappeared, except for 60,000 acres which stayed in the Swenson family until 1970, when they too were sold. The new towns of Spur and Gerard, linked by the Stamford and Northern Texas Railway with Stamford and Ericksdahl, prospered for many years on large-scale cattle and cotton production.

As a Swedish community, Ericksdahl is unique in several ways. Most obvious is the fact that it is still here. Unlike most of the outlying communities of Travis and Williamson counties, where only a church and perhaps a cemetery mark the existence of former Swedish colonies, the presence of the S.M.S ranches

Running the SMS brand on a calf

has granted the Ericksdahl area a still-viable economic base. While the huge Bethel church may rarely be as full as it once was, it is still the focus of a community, not just an isolated rural church. And, finally, making it unique in all the world, this is the place where the Swedish cowboys worked. Nowhere else, even in Texas, were Swedish immigrants so intimately connected with a large cattle ranch on such a scale. And nowhere else was a single Swedish-owned land company so directly responsible for literally creating whole towns where once only the wind had blown. Nowhere else in the world did Swedes from Småland tend the chuck wagons, brand the cattle, and roam the range tending fences or rounding up strays. The history of Ericksdahl has provided a unique chapter in the annals of Swedish Americans and Swedish Texans.

15

Swedish Place-Names in Texas

Ahandful of colonies were settled almost exclusively by Swedes, pioneer settlers who left permanent signs of their passing in the names they left behind. The change of Brushy Creek to Palm Valley was one of the very few occasions in Texas when the population shift was almost completely from American to Swedish. And, while Elgin and Manor at one time came close to being "Swedish towns," there never developed quite strong enough a sense of unity among the urban Swedes actually to affect the names of these communities.

Manda was named in 1893 for Amanda Bengtson Gustafson, Swedish-born sister of the village's first postmaster.

Kimbro was the third name of a small settlement in east Travis County first named Cottonwood. It was called Smiths rote after the first Swedish settler, William Smith, born Gustafsson, until 1900. The Swedish word *rote* denoted an administrative district that supported a single soldier in case of war. In 1900 the settlement was renamed Kimbro in honor of Lemul Kimbro, who had purchased the land in 1853.[1]

Olivia was named for Olivia Olson Haterius, wife of Lutheran minister C.J.E. Haterius, who developed the community. Reverend Haterius hoped to attract Swedish farmers to the community he called Paradiset (Paradise) on Wolf's Point near Port Lavaca on Matagorda Bay. Olivia Haterius was born in New Sweden, Iowa, in 1859 and died in Kansas in 1949.[2]

Chesterville was a small community founded by a Swede in Colorado County in South Texas. Born Nils Nilsson in Källsjön, Ockelbo parish, Gästrikland, in 1838, he changed his name several times (to Kjellstedt and Kjellster) before he emigrated at the age of 19. He had a colorful career in America as a gold miner, sailor, farmer, and entrepreneur before becoming a prosperous merchant in Illinois in the 1870's. Nelson Chester, as he called himself in America, headed for Texas in 1893 to develop a tract of land in a town he built and named for himself. He devoted most of the last decade of his life (he died in 1903) to the development of Chesterville. His daughter, Alvinia, became the first postmistress in 1895, and the post office itself survived until 1950.[3]

Palm Valley officially received its present name in 1894, when the brick church was dedicated. It was not Swante Palm but his industrious sister-in-law whose memory is perpetuated here. Newly widowed, Anna Palm settled on Brushy Creek, alone except for her six small sons, in 1854 and remained there for the rest of her long life. Her sons grew up to manage large farms along Brushy Creek.

Nelson was once a railway station in the middle of the Nelson cotton lands for the loading and unloading of crops and materials. Named for Andrew John Nelson (Anders Johan Nilsson from Öggestorp) and his sons. The Nelson properties were, and still are, vast.[4]

Lund was named by a native of the province of Skåne in southern Sweden, Gustaf Seaholm, who was one of the first settlers in the area of New Sweden in the 1880's. He suggested the name of Lund (site of Sweden's oldest cathedral and second-oldest university) for the post office in 1895.[5]

New Sweden is the most obvious Swedish place-name still on the map in Texas. For many years it was a community that lay north of, but identified with, the town of Manor. With the creation of a "New Sweden" Lutheran congregation in 1877, the Swedish community found a sense of ethnic identity, and both church and community changed their names to New Sweden in 1893.[6]

East Sweden and **West Sweden** lie on either side of the Brady railhead in McCulloch County; nowadays, however, these are only vaguely defined farming areas.

Ericksdahl, or **Ericsdale**, was named for the ranch of the same name created by S.M. Swenson in the 1880's. The ranch, which was divided and sold as individual farms, was one of three such holdings, named for each of the three Swenson children. The whole Swenson clan is commemorated in the tiny hamlet of **Swenson** near the headquarters of S.M.S. Ranch industries in Stonewall County.

Swensondale in Stephens County was named for Nels Swenson and his younger brother, Peter, born in Husensjö, Sweden, near Hälsingborg. In 1917 oil was discovered on the family land. Almost overnight a small community grew up around the 12 massive oil rigs on the ranch, and it quickly came to be called Swensondale. The surviving members of the Swenson family (Nels died in 1918) formed the Swensondale Oil Company with a capital stock of $1,000,000, almost all held by the family. Twelve years later the oil had been exploited, the rigs departed, and Swensondale vanished from the map. The company broke up in 1928, six years before Peter Swenson died, at home and alone in Swensondale at the age of 93.[7]

Swedonia in Fisher County in North Central Texas was a typical secondary colony, founded by 16 remigrating Swedish families from Travis and Williamson counties.

But year after year too little rain fell in Swedonia, and within 20 years all the settlers save two families had moved away. Swedonia proved to be one of the few areas in the state not suitable for cotton, despite fertile soil and a favorable climate.

Then, in 1921, oil was discovered. After nearly 50 years of hard living, J.A. Young and his family—the last inhabitants of Swedonia—became wealthier than almost any of their fellow countrymen. But by then the colony of Swedonia—which once boasted a church, a school, two stores, and a blacksmith's shop— had long since disappeared from any maps of Texas.[8]

Stockholm was a subcolony of the small town of **Lyford**, the southernmost Swedish colony in Texas. Lyford had been founded by Swedish immigrants who had purchased land in Cameron County near Brownsville. By 1914 some 130 Swedes had purchased more than 13,000 acres of land. In addition to the usual cotton and corn, Lyford was one of the few Swedish colonies in Texas to develop a thriving dairy industry.[9] The only Swedish Mission Covenant congregation in the entire state of Texas was founded in Lyford in 1912. West of Lyford and Brownsville, and only 22 miles from the Mexican border, eight families built a community called Stockholm after the capital of their homeland. They began planting cotton, corn, and vegetables in the spring of 1911. They were plagued from the beginning by rattlesnakes, heat, and Mexican bandits. Stockholm had a school (until 1928, when the district was merged with Lyford), a Swedish-owned and -operated general store, and a cotton gin. Now nothing but the name remains to remind travelers of the existence of the proudly named but ephemeral Stockholm, Texas.[10]

The most recent Swedish place name in Texas does not belong to a town, village, or ghost town, but to a U.S. Air Force base near Austin. Captain John August Earle Bergstrom had the unfortunate distinction of being the first Austinite to be killed in battle in World War II. He died in a Japanese bombing raid while serving in the Philippines, only three days after the bombing of Pearl Harbor. Bergstrom was the maternal grandson of August Swenson, the venerable patriarch of the Palm Valley community. The dedication of **Bergstrom Air Force Base** took place in 1942.[11]

16

The Swedish Language in Texas

I n 1964 Texas was the primary goal of an expedition from the Institute of Dialect and Folklore Research of the University of Uppsala, Sweden. A previous recording tour of the United States in 1962 had, naturally enough, concentrated on the northern and midwestern states with the largest Swedish immigrant populations. But in 1963 the leader of the team, Professor Folke Hedblom, received a letter from Carl Widén of Austin, inviting the scholars to record the speech of Swedish Texans.

Widén had reported that Gethsemane Lutheran Church in Austin and several other Swedish congregations in other cities still celebrated julotta, the traditional Swedish Christmas service. Hymns in Swedish were still sung, and Pastor Herbert Johnson, a second-generation Swedish American, preached in the language of the Old Country. Swedish ambassador to the U.S. Gunnar Jarring, confirmed Widén's enthusiasm concerning Swedes in Texas, and Hedblom's second expedition, which arrived in the spring of 1964, began in Austin.[1] Hedblom and his team recorded a number of Swedish-born settlers who had lived in Texas ever since their arrival in America. John Swensson, for example, was more than 90 years old in 1964 and still spoke Swedish fluently. He had come to Austin in 1896 and worked as a laborer on the railway until he was able to find work with his uncle at the cotton gin ("bomulls-jen") near Austin.

185

There he "räntade land" (*arrenderade* is the usual Swedish term) and worked for a time on the "rällråd" (*järnväg* in standard Swedish). On his farm he planted cotton and "karn" (corn; the Swedish word is *majs*) on land he later purchased for $50 "äckern" (per acre). While plowing was relatively easy, the removal of stumps, especially those of "moskit-buskarna" (mesquite bushes), was arduous labor. Many years later Swensson, now an old man, contracted a mild case of the Spanish flu. He was advised by his doctor to return to Småland's clean, cold air. There he was to take long walks, sit in the snow, and draw the air deep into his lungs. "Dä ä dä som killar gömsa," he said ("It is that which kills the germs": in standard Swedish, *döda bakterierna*). American expressions had thus crept into Swensson's otherwise excellent Swedish. These terms were, almost without exception, expressions for which there were no Swedish equivalents, at least not when he learned the language as a boy. Many of them had to do with life on the Texas prairies: "ränta" land, "genna" cotton, buy goods at a "ståre," fish in a "kricka," hire "mexare" as laborers, and so on.[2] The team from Uppsala was most amazed by the Texas Swedes' stubborn refusal to acclimatize completely to American ways. One of Hedblom's informants said that the reason most young Swedish-Texan men married women from within the ethnic group was that American girls couldn't "koka," or prepare food.

Hedblom was impressed by the fact that, in all essentials, the Swedes of Texas lived much as Swedish farmers always had, in ways that were often quite different from their American neighbors. Swedes helped one another "i filen" (in the field) with corn, wheat, oats, sugar cane, and, most important, cotton. Girls milked the cows, made cheese and butter, and sold dairy products to augment farm income. Pigs were slaughtered in the fall and before Christmas, and the meat was then either salted or smoked over oak bark, so that it would be preserved until summer. Many families joined "köttklubbar" (meat clubs), in which they butchered animals weekly in a certain order, each family receiving particular portions in a rotating cycle. Much of the daily fare was Swedish as well: salted herring (salt sill) was still a staple, as was blood pudding ("paltbröd") and Småland cheesecake ("ostkaka"). Even the interiors of Swedish houses were more Swedish than American (however much they resembled one another on the outside): Swedish houses had more pictures on the wall and never had an American fireplace.[3]

And, while relations between Swedes and Blacks, on the one hand, and Swedes and Mexicans, on the other, were by no means egalitarian, Swedes were at least used to working cotton fields alongside other minorities and were therefore perhaps more sensitive to their own sense of differentness, real or imagined. (An informant revealed that as a child he could speak Swedish and "spanjor" —Spanish—when he went to school but not a word of English. "It seems probable," Hedblom surmised, "that it was considered 'finer' to be a Swede in Texas than in the northern states."[4]) Hedblom knew that men like John Swensson and his generation represented the last of the old-timers who retained their native language. Already in the 1920's the move to English in the churches was well under way.

But Hedblom was surprised at the persistence of Swedish over such a long period, especially considering the small number of native speakers to begin with. And, while some Texas congregations (such as Gethsemanc or New Sweden) held out much longer (well into the 1940's) than their northern counterparts, they all eventually had to bow to the inevitable. Swedish-language summer schools and Bible camps taught young Swedish Texans the language of their parents and grandparents, but, one by one, communities switched to the language of the New World, until only a julotta service once a year gave testimony of the language they had lost.

Then, in 1971, Professor Sture Ureland of the University of Umeå in northern Sweden undertook a recording expedition of his own to Texas. He had eagerly read Hedblom's articles as well as those of Professor Carl Rosenquist of the University of Texas at Austin, who had studied Texas Swedes in the 1930's. Rosenquist had written that Swedes of the second generation

> manifest contempt for Swedish, partly because of their desire to sever connections with a group occupying an inferior social position and partly because they recognize in the speech of their parents only a peasant dialect. They do not wish to speak a language which identifies them with a lower class in both the old world and the new.[5]

187

Dancing around the Christmas tree; SVEA of Texas, Houston, 1989

Forty years later Ureland disagreed vigorously. "No contempt of Swedish has been found on the part of any of the 50 representatives of the Texas Swedes interviewed. Their linguistic attitudes are quite the contrary of Rosenquist's assertions."[6] Moreover, Ureland found that he and Hedblom (both trained linguists) also disagreed with Rosenquist's description of Texan Swedish as a "peasant dialect." On the contrary, wrote Ureland, Texas Swedish shows "an extensive leveling of dialect characteristics toward Standard Swedish."[7] He found this a "remarkable trend" in American Swedish. He also found remarkable trends (at least when comparing the forms of Swedish in America with those of Standard Swedish) in aspects of inversion rules, gender agreement, number agreement, passivization, relative imbedding, and negative placement.[8] And he noted a number of the same kind of translations that Hedblom had found in 1964, but Ureland distinguishes between loan translations ("keepa böckerna," keep the books; "i sommartiden," in the summertime), direct loans ("vi lyssnar på *reidion*," we listen to the radio; "jag var inte *disappointed*," I was not disappointed), and loans adapted to Swedish rules ("han som blev *killad* i kriget," he who was killed in the war; "*gasolinen* kommer från Corpus Christi i *piper* till

Austin," the gasoline comes from Corpus Christi in pipes to Austin). Ureland concluded:

> In light of the discovery of changes in the syntactic rule system and the lexicon of Texas Swedish, a special brand of Swedish exists in the state of Texas, that of Texas Swedish.[9]

Carl Rosenquist's declaration in the 1930's—"Today Swedish is a dead language. The triumph of English is all but complete"[10]—was clearly premature. But with the passing of the aged immigrants, the loss of Swedish in the churches, and the closing of the summer language camps, Swedish died out almost completely after Ureland returned to Sweden. The demise of the venerable *Texas-Posten* in 1982 was a major blow, since, right up to its final issue, the weekly newspaper published a full page of news in Swedish.

Yet there are a few hopeful signs which may give the Swedish language in Texas a new lease on life. The oil boom of the 1970's brought a large number of Swedish businessmen and women and their families to the Lone Star State. While they did not intentionally immigrate, their more or less permanent status in Texas has created a set of conditions that force them, in retrospect, to confront the fact that their children may very well grow up in America, not Sweden, with all the cultural ramifications that such an upbringing entails. Their children speak English almost exclusively, read American books, and watch American television.

So, in 1980, a group of women in Houston started SVEA of Texas, an organization of Swedish and Swedish-speaking women founded to keep contacts with Sweden, to stimulate and preserve the Swedish language and traditions, and to serve as a source of information about Swedish cultural events. Within a year they had nearly 70 members in Houston alone, and five years later membership in the state had almost doubled. SVEA of Texas sponsors social and cultural events (readings by visiting poets and novelists, for example, and film retrospectives) to which spouses are also invited. The most significant contribution SVEA of Texas has made to the preservation of the Swedish language in Texas, however, is the publication of "SVEA Nytt."[11]

This modest newsletter first came out in the spring of 1980 under the editorship of Kicki Mazur and at the urging of

the founder of SVEA of Texas, Gudrun Wallgren-Merrill. Designed, of course, as a vehicle to inform SVEA members of organization activities, it soon became much more — a cultural organ,
in Swedish, for the "new" Swedish Texans. It was, in fact, the
first new Swedish-language publication in Texas in more than
50 years. It contains tips on dealing with Swedish and American
bureaucracies (IRS, Immigration, Swedish voting procedures,
and the Ministry of Education are most frequently mentioned),
advice on moving and resettling, places to eat, shops that stock
Swedish items all across the state, recipes both Swedish and
Texan, and more. But "SVEA Nytt" also functions as a true
newspaper, printing stories of interest to newly arrived Swedes
about Texas and Swedish Texas. Occasionally it even prints
poetry in Swedish, the only publication in the state to do so.[12]
Thus, the end of *Texas-Posten* was *not* the end of Swedish in Texas;
as long as "SVEA Nytt" is published, the Swedish language in
Texas isn't completely dead.

SVEA of Texas display of Swedish handicrafts, Houston, 1989

The Swedish-Language Press in Texas

Södra Vecko-Posten (1882)

The first of the three Swedish-language newspapers published in Texas was called *Södra Vecko-Posten*, and its editor was the leader of the Swedish Methodists in Texas. Thus, the aim of the paper was primarily, but not exclusively, a religious one of explaining the Methodist doctrines to Swedish Texans. But its secondary purpose was blatantly propagandistic: to clarify conditions in Texas to those in the North and in Sweden who might harbor lingering doubts about Texas' participation in the Civil War. *Södra Vecko-Posten* (or *Southern Weekly Post*) intended to attract Swedes to "this rich and healthy state, whose millions upon millions of acres of fertile land merely await the hand of the farmer to fill the cultivators' barns with their golden fruit."[1]

The author of this optimistic prose was *Södra Vecko-Posten's* publisher and editor, the Reverend Viktor Witting, one of the founders of the Swedish Methodist Church in America. He had been born in Malmö in 1825, the son of an artillery captain from Finland. He received a good education in Sweden and began his life of adventure as an apothecary's assistant. He soon tired of this mundane career and went to sea in 1843. During this time he came to America and, in 1847, decided to remain. He made his way to Bishop Hill, Illinois, where he stayed until 1849. After another stint in a druggist's shop in Galesburg, Illinois,

Viktor Witting

he headed west to the California goldfields. He was, like almost every other Swede, singularly unsuccessful in his search and so returned to Illinois in 1852.[2]

Witting was converted to Methodism in Peoria in 1854 and began his preaching career in Andover a year later. He soon recognized his abilities as a journalist and served as editor of the Methodist newspaper *Sändebudet* (*The Messenger*) from the year after its founding in 1862 until 1867. He was then sent to Sweden for nearly 12 years, during which time he organized congregations in his homeland into a regular annual conference.

Witting returned to America in 1879 and within a year had made his way to Texas. He remained there for two years, during which time he published *Södra Vecko-Posten*. Following his departure from the Lone Star State, he returned to the editorship of *Sändebudet*, a post he then held for six years. In 1889 he was sent to Quinsigamond, Massachusetts, as pastor of the Swedish Methodist congregation there. At the same time, he edited a Christmas annual entitled *Bethlehemstjernan* (*The Star of Bethlehem*). He even started a local weekly newspaper called *Österns Sändebud* (*Eastern Messenger*) — all at the age of 70![3]

He edited and translated more hymns than any other Swedish-American Methodist. He was himself a skillful hymnodist and contributed to many of the early Swedish-American Methodist hymnals. His two-volume autobiography—*Minnen från mitt lif som sjöman, immigrant och predikant* (*Memories from My Life as a Sailor, Immigrant and Preacher*)—was published in 1901, five years before his death in Quincy, Massachusetts, on July 2, 1906. His writings fill in many gaps in our knowledge of the early days of the pioneer church in Swedish America. They also provide some further information on the two years in Texas, which include the publication of *Södra Vecko-Posten*.[4]

During the entire time he stayed in Texas, constantly on the move across the length and breadth of the state, organizing, preaching, and building, Witting somehow found time for continued editorial work—the work, aside from his preaching, which had already made him such a valuable asset to his denomination. The first, or trial, number of *Södra Vecko-Posten* appeared on February 9, 1881, just a few weeks after Witting had dramatically confronted Elder William Smith of the Swedish Methodist congregation in Austin over the question of whether or not to unite with the northern Swedish Methodist Church. Nowhere in this issue is there a hint of Methodist discord—Witting was already moving to unite the divided parties—but he may have alienated some of his own people with his rather high-handed treatment of Elder Smith, who soon left Austin and settled in Smiths rote, later called Kimbro.

In print, Witting evinced a strong desire to satisfy the Swedes' natural craving for news of the Old World and of other Swedish settlements in the northern states as well as in Texas. American news of great import was especially significant, as was a need to set the record straight about events in Texas because "the general opinion concerning Texas in the American, as well as in the Scandinavian, North is not the best."[5]

His own position on religious questions seems rather dogmatic, but he promised "to show complete impartiality in church-related issues. . . . These efforts will be exerted to demonstrate the same Christian spirit to all parties and notices of church activities of all denominations will be printed free." He promised to keep gossip out of the paper, to maintain a high moral tone, and to write in a style that would "in some degree, spread sunshine, joy and happiness in our readers' homes." Stories would deal with uplifting family matters "for usefulness with satisfaction." He also published the weekly stock and grain prices, the arrivals and departures of Scandinavian ships from Galveston, and recent changes in the price of cotton.[6]

Witting soon had the help of his sons in his printing shop in the Hancock Building on West Pecan Street in Austin. He had purchased Swedish type fonts and was thus prepared to publish newspapers and books in both Swedish and English. Subscriptions to *Södra Vecko-Posten* cost $1.50 per year in the United States, $2.00 if sent to Sweden. It appeared on the first Wednesday of every month for 16 issues.

Although he claimed political impartiality—even political indifference—Witting editorialized strongly for the temperance movement, an issue dear to the hearts of most Swedes of all political and religious persuasions. He also worked diligently, in almost every issue, to increase Swedish immigration to the cotton lands of Texas. (In this he may have had a less-than-impartial motive, for Witting was a part-time agent for the National Line, an emigration line specializing in the transport of Scandinavians to the New World.)

He also provided specific and, presumably, reasonably accurate information for prospective immigrants to Texas. Farmhands, for example, could expect to earn from $15 to $25 a month for outdoor labor, a woman $330 to $600 a year for housework, and an "ordinary worker" from $1 to $3 a day. "Swedish servant girls," he wrote, "are very much in demand and can be assured of securing a good position. The wages are from $10 to $20 a month." Children from nine to ten years picked 100 pounds of cotton regularly, week in and week out, for 75 cents to $1 per 100 pounds. All people worked from the age of eight—after 12 years of age, they could pick nearly 200 pounds, and as adults, even 250 pounds a week.[7]

But readership remained small. The Swedes in the North, on whom Witting had counted to read of conditions in Texas, were unaware of the paper's very existence. It was clear to Witting by the end of May 1881 that *Södra Vecko-Posten* was in severe financial trouble. He admitted that, because of a lack of subscribers, he was paying out $10 more a week than he was taking in. Only 10 percent of the Swedish population in Texas (in 1881 about 1,000 in all) had subscribed, and "there are enough Swedes here in Texas to support this [newspaper]. . . . Shall it live or die, that is the question?"[8] He needed the impossible figure of 300 new subscribers immediately, so he delayed publication of what was to be the last issue of the paper until July 6, 1881. He boosted advertising (including that for the H.P.N. Gammel Book Store, which sold Swedish as well as Norwegian and Danish books and Bibles). He even reduced the price of subscriptions from $1.50 to $1.00, but such efforts were not enough. With the 16th issue, *Södra Vecko-Posten* ceased publication, and all outstanding subscriptions were generously prorated and returned. It had been a noble and high-spirited enterprise, but perhaps Witting's close Methodist connections and zeal branded him suspect to the still largely Lutheran Swedish Texans, and the experiment had to fail.[9]

Witting was not a man easily daunted, however. Despite his public bitterness over the demise of his newspaper, he set to work immediately to publish another periodical using his expensive Swedish type — this one to be closer to his religious skills and temperament. This was the second in a series of three volumes called *Stilla stunder: Christligt månadsmagasin för härd och hem* (*Quiet Moments: A Christian Monthly Magazine for Hearth and Home*), which Witting had initially brought out in Chicago[10] and which he was to resume publishing after his move to Worcester, Massachusetts. Twelve issues, some 480 pages, were published in Texas. The content was almost exclusively revivalistic in nature, consisting largely of hymns and translations from the English of John Wesley and sermons written by Witting himself. Nevertheless, it *was* in Swedish, and it was published in Austin, Texas.

Not until the spring of 1896 did another Swedish journal appear in Texas. But when it did, it came to stay.

Texas-Posten (1896-1982)

The true voice of the Swedish Texans was the long-lived weekly newspaper, "their" newspaper — *Texas-Posten*. For 85 years it kept track of church meetings, births, marriages, deaths, and the other important events in the lives of Texans of Swedish descent in every Swedish colony in the state. It reported local news, carried local advertising, reported on crops and climate. *Texas-Posten*, however, fulfilled an even more important cultural role:

TEXAS ★ POSTEN.

LIBERAL POLITISK NYHETS-TIDNING FÖR SVENSKARNE I AMERIKA.

4de Årg. Löp. No. 176. Austin, Texas, Torsdagen den 29 Juni 1899. Vol. IV. No. 26

Den, som vinner.

Den, som vinner, vill han gifva
Äta af det dolda mannat,
Han ett himmelskt namn vill skrifva
På den saliggjordes panna.
Den, som genom jordens öden
Varit trofast intill döden,
Skall, där Salems harpor tona,
Evigt bära lifvets krona.

Ho är den för Herren träder
Vid den stora morgonväkten
I de hvita bröllopskläder,
I den skimmerljusa dräkten?
Det är den, som korset tagit,
Den, som sina kläder tvagit
Med det helga blod, i hvilket
Blir beredt det rätta sliket.

Den, som vinner, skall få blicka
Evigt in i fridens rike,
Skall för intet där få dricka
Lifvets vatten utan like,
Ingen natt skall vara mera,
Sol och måne ej regera:
Ljuset, som det templet hyser,
Blott från Gud och lammet lyser.

Sälle de, som sorgedräken
Bytt mot kronor ut och palmer,
Hvilkas namn han skref i boken
Och som sjunga segerpsalmer!
Slut är tvifvel, slut är fara,
Ingen död skall mera vara,
Hvad vi mist skall återvinnas,
Där ej tid skall längre finnas.

Den, som vinner, skall han kalla
Till den nattvard han bereder.
Ett Jerusalem skall falla
Strålande ur skyar neder,
Där vid Herrens helgedom är
Lifvets träd för evigt blommar.
Intet törne mera sårar,
Herren torkar alla tårar.

"Se, jag kommer!" Gif mig skruden,
Red mig Herre, till ditt möte!
Anden säger "kom", och bruden
Hastar till sin brudgums sköte.
"Se, jag kommer!"– Åren ila,
Sekel efter sekel skrida,
Bli de flere, bli de färre
Bruden väntar. Kom, o Herre!

C. D. af Wirsen.

Krönika.

För Texas Posten.

I förra numret påpekades eller påyrkades, att svenskarne borde vara litet mera politiska af sig. De, som ej vore det, skulle försöka att litet mera sätta sig in i de politiska lärobegreppen, så kunde svenskarne vinna en smula mera uppmärksamhet af amerikanerna. Frågan är nu, huru man skall gå tillväga för att blifva en framstående politikus, och jag tror mig i all korthet kunna redogöra därför och till och med visa huru detta kan gå för sig utan att precis ge sig till att studera politisk ekonomi och andra konstiga arbeten.

För att blifva eller åtminstone anses för en god republikan—jag menar icke den sorts republikaner som i forntiden funnos i Österlandet, hvarom den goda boken talar; ehuru de kanske voro likaså goda som vår tids republikaner—behöfs icke så fasligt mycket hufvudbry. Först och främst bör man påyrka "gold standard" och säga, att det är enda sättet att kunna bibehålla penningarnes köpvärde. Utan sådan få vi ingenting för våra pengar. Äfvenså bör man för att vinna republikanskt anseende orda om tullarnes förträfflighet, huru de skydda landet från att öfversvämmas af billiga utländska varor, hvilka skulle komma att nedsätta lönerna för våra nu väl lönade arbetare. Likaledes bör man, då det passar sig, påpeka huru G. O. P., detta storartade gamla parti, kämpade för slafveriets upphäfvande; dock bör man ej ofta uppvisa den gamla blodiga skjortan. Ej heller bör man förglömma att uppräkna namnen på de store amerikanska presidenter, som voro republikaner, såväl som publikaner och fråga, om vi väl äro bättre och förståndigare än de voro. Det gör ofta stor effekt. Dessutom bör man så långt man är i stånd till tala nedsättande om de andra politiska partierna, synnerligast det demokratiska, som gynnar krogen och vill föra landet till finansiel ruin. Isynnerhet bör man lägga an på att förlöjliga Bryan och hans teori samt slå sig i backen på att han icke heller nästa år blir vald till president, huru mycket han än må arbeta därför. Tala om huru välstånd åter kommit i landet, sedan republikanerna kommit i makten, och om någon säger emot, så svara: res från de södra demokratiska staterna upp till de norra, och där skolen I få se på annat. Icke heller bör man förglömma att berömmande tala om nuvarande regerings utrikespolitik, huru förträffligt att vi fått tag uti Filippinerna, hvilken uppblomstring vår handel därigenom skall gå till mötes och så hvilken välsignelse för infödingarne denna annektering skall medföra. Detta är det hufvudsakligaste just nu, och om du därtill talar litet om hvilken vis, lugn och sansad president McKinley är, skall ingen kunna säga utan att du är en fullfjädrad republikan.

Anser du däremot mera i öfverensstämmelse med dina intressen att slå dig tillsammans med det demokratiska partiet, så går du ungefär alldeles motsatt tillväga. Då blir det ditt göra att tala om hurusom "frisilfver" är penningefrågans enda lösning, 16 till 1 är det rätta förhållandet mellan silfver och guld; det är den enda utsigten för den fattige att kunna få några slantar. Orda om den odödlige Jeffersons läror, äfven om du icke vet hvad han lärde; det skall gifva dig stort anseende som demokrat. Dessutom skall du göra så mycket gäck du kan af "The G. O. P.", som du bör likna vid en gammal utlefvad gumma. Tala om, att republikanernas tariff har blifvit landets ruin och säg med en mr Havemeyer, att tullarne, eller beständare, Dingley-billen är moder till alla trusts; ty just emedan utländska varor och fabrikat utstängdes genom höga tullar, kan ingen medtäflare här i landet uppträda emot fabrikanter och korporationer, som därför kunna slå sig tillsammans och sätta hvad pris de vilja på sina artiklar. Folket måste köpa dessa nödvändighetsartiklar till hvad pris som helst, ty de kunna ju ej få några från utlandet på grund af de höga tullarne. Glöm ej heller påpeka, att det var demokraterna som började med anti-trustlagar, äfven om republikanerna för syns skull börjat sjunga på samma visa. Icke heller bör du, om du vill anses såsom en god demokrat, förgäta att klandra den pågående annekteringspolitiken. Påpeka huru infödingarne på Filippinerna blifva nedskjutna för det de kämpa för samma frihet som För. Stat. sökte, då de slogo sig lösa från Englands öfvervälde och förtryck, hvilket deras historia så berömmande omtalar. En god demokrat sätter sig emot all vidare utvidgning af landets gränser genom upptagandet af så aflägset liggande länder som Filippinerna, hvilket innebär nödvändigheten af en mångdubbelt större armée och flotta, hvilka icke kunna anskaffas utan att öka skatterna för det amerikanska folket. Och som de rise alltid veta huru att svänga sig undan, blir det de fattige som få bära bördan. Några vinkar om att det republikanska partiet egentligen ledes af landets ... McKinley icke har följt den väg han utstakade och lofvade följa vid krigets utbrott, hjälper äfven mycket till att göra en person demokratisk, förutom mycket annat, som så godt som följer af sig självt.

Prohibitionisterna och folkpartiet ha just ej så många anhängare att det lönar mödan lära någon huru man skall bli en utaf dem. Anföraren för folkpartiet i Södern, den beryktade Cyklon-Davis, tyckes verkligen ha blåst bort. Annars hörde jag honom en gång hålla ett fördrag, därvid han använde en mängd stora böcker för att läsa ur och därigenom så mycket bättre öfvertyga folket. Han sade, att folkpartiet trodde och antog den store odödlige Jeffersons lärosatser, hvilka nu och då citerades; men det förkastade en hel del annat; ty det trodde på en regering för folket, af folket och genom folket; icke genom penningemän, korporationer och särskildta bossar. Folket, allmänheten, du och jag var det som skulle styra och regera hvarandra, hvarigenom riket kunde besparas ofantliga summor, på samma gång som icke bara några utvalde få med sina gynnare kommo i åtnjutande af ämbetena och deras goda inkomster.

Hvad prohibitionspartiet angår, säger sjelfva titeln, att en anhängare af det partiet måste vara en nykterhetsvän. De ha skrifvit på sin fana: "Ned med krogarne, bort med bränvinet!" En god prohibitionist glömmer därför aldrig omtala hvilka krog- och krögarevänner både republikaner och demokrater äro. I självfva verket supa de ur samma glas, d. v. s. äro båda lika gynsamt stämda emot tillverkare och försäljare af rusdrycker. Sedan har man ett rikt och anslående ämne framför sig. Man talar om hvad mycket ondt krogen gjort, huru många både gamla och unga, som förderfvats genom densamma och huru många som kunnat bevaras, om ej dessa frestelsens nästen funnos. Men krogen kunde ej utrotas utan genom regeringens lagstiftning. Därför borde alla landets tjänstemän, från presidenten och ned igenom, vara prohibitionister. Deras höga exempel såväl som lagstiftning skulle blifva en oskattbar välsignelse för både palats och koja. Tänk om intet bränvin funnes! O, sådana besparingar såväl för staten som den enskilde! Det vore enda vägen att komma till allmänt välstånd här i landet. Då, och endast då blir det "prosperity" för alla.

Ungefär så där går det till att bli politikus, och det är ju icke någonting så förfärligt svårt att lära sig. Har man bara tagen i sig en smula och så begriper åt hvad håll det lutar, bör litet hvar af svenskarne kunna bli framstående på politikens område. Huruvida man vill bli republikan, demokrat, prohibitionist, mugwump, etc., det lemnas åt en hvars eget afgörande. I det stycket får man följa sitt samvetes öfvertygelse. Hufvudsaken är, att man väljer ett af partien, håller med det samt därjämte strafvar att på bästa (eller värsta) sätt tilltvåla de andra partien. Så går det till i krig och politik.

KRONIKÖR.

MINNESRUNA.

Helt oförmodadt spred sig förliden torsdags morgon, den 22 ds, underrättelsen om att svensk-norske konsuln hr Swante Palm under natten aflidit. Föregående dag var han som vanligt ute och språkade med sina vänner, och innan han vid 11 tiden på onsdagskvällen gick till hvila, hade han suttit en lång stund och samtalat med sina slägtingar, som bodde i samma hus, tydligtvis lika rask och kry som vanligt. Men då man på torsdagsmorgonen kom in i hans sängkammare för att servera honom en kopp kaffe, fann man ut att den gamle somnat in i den sista sömnen, hvarur han ej mer kunde väckas. Tillkallade läkare voro af den öfvertygelsen att han dött mellan kl. 12 och 2 på natten af hjärtslag eller ålderdomssvaghet.

Konsul Swante Palm var född i Besthult, Sverige, den 31 jan. 1815, hvadan han vid sitt frånfälle var 84 år, 4 mån. och 21 dagar gammal. Han ankom till Texas 1844, då han landsteg i Galveston. År 1849 reste han till Panamanäset, men återvände redan nästa år och slog sig ned i Austin, där han sedan bodde till sin död. Han var i början köpman, men under de sista årtiondena sysselsatte han sig ej med annat än de göromål som stodo i förbindelse med hans befattning såsom vice konsul. Under president Grants första termin blef hr

Aflidne svensk-norske vice konsul Swante Palm.

Palm af honom utnämd till postmästare i Austin, hvilken syssla han skötte till allas belåtenhet. Hr Palm, som fått en god uppfostran i Sverige och till och med en tid var med om utgifvandet af en tidning i Kalmar, sysselsatte sig på sina lediga stunder att samla böcker och studera. Också hade han tills några år före sin död ett af de största privata bibliotek i staten om icke i Amerika. Det bestod af omkring 30,000 band, värderade till $100,000. För några år sedan skänkte han största delen af denna boksamling till statsuniversitetet här i staden, och hedrades med att bli utnämd såsom universitetets bibliotekarie. Studenterna hafva också i vår samlat medel till uppsättandet af hans byst i universitetet.

Konsul Palm ingick i äktenskap år 1851, men hans hustru dog redan för 19 år sedan. Under sin vistelse här i staten har han tvänne gånger besökt det gamla fosterlandet, näml. år 1873 och 1884. Före sin död talade han flere gånger om att han önskade återvända till Sverige och få sin graf redd där, en önskan som dock icke gick i fullbordan.

Om något var konsul Palm i själ och hjärta svensk. Svensk literatur, svenska språket och svenska folket lågo honom ömt om hjärtat. Medlem af härvarande luterska församling var han äfvenså luterska läran varmt tillgifven. Af läroverket i Lindsborg, Kans., hade han hedrats med filosofie doktorsgraden och konungen af Sverige hade gjort honom till riddare af Vasa orden.

Begrafningen egde rum från statsuniversitetet på fredags e. m. kl. 5. En kör sjöng ett par utvalda sånger, hvarefter pastor G. A. Dorf, biträdd af pastorerna dr Smoot och dr Lee ledde sorgegudstjänsten. Efter gudstjänstens slut sjöngs ännu en sång, hvarpå den ovanligt stora processionen tågade till grafgården, där jordfästningen egde rum. Hela universitetets fakulteten förutom slägtingar och många vänner och bekanta till den aflidne deltogo i processionen.

TEXAS.

SKIDMORE.

Öfver 70 järnvägsvagnar, lastade med vattenmeloner, äro utskeppade härifrån sedan säsongens början. Huru många flera som komma att följa hädanefter är ännu obekant.

SEALY.

Flera åkerbrukare häromkring rapportera att de hafva fått bollvivel i deras bomull, men inga spår af ohyran har förmärkts på prairie-land. Så många som kunna vara med samla de affallna "squaren" och bränna dem, antingen de finna något märke efter denna pest eller icke, för att vara så mycket säkrare att omintetgöra masken. Annars är utsigten för en god skörd ganska lofvande. Blandat åkerdruk vinner mer och mer anseende, och många jordbrukare försöka sig nu på odling af grönsaker, som betala sig bättre än bomull till 4 cents pundet.

HUTTO.

Hutto & Brushy allmänna svenska lägermöte kommer att hållas i den för alla väl kända platsen uti Nelsons beteshage. Mötet tager sin början måndagen den 17 juli och varar tills öfver påföljande söndag. Alla distriktets svenska predikanter äro inbjudna och förväntas vara närvarande. Låt alla Guds barn bereda sig och mangrant komma ut. F. A. Lundberg.

—Den svenska luterska församlingen i Hutto håller sin söndagsskolutflykt fredagen den 7 juli i mr A. Swensons beteshage, på samma plats som förlidet år. På förmiddagen blir det sång, tal och musik och på eftermeddagen syauktion. Alla äro hjärtligt inbjudna att komma dit.

DECKER.

Svensk småbarnsskola påbörjas i härvarande skolhus måndagen den 3 juli af skollärar C. A. Peterson. Glömmen ej att sända edra barn dit att lära det svenska modersmålet.

—Manor musikkår hade en månskenspiknik uti mr Andrew Sponbergs beteshage förliden lördagskväll, hvari deltogo såväl äldre som yngre. Där bjöds på musik, ice cream och cake i riklig mykenhet och alla njöto däraf med stor förtjusning. Emellanåt roade man sig med åtskilliga slags lekar. Musikkårens medlemmar önska att särskildt tacka de unga damerna så mycket för deras kraftiga biträde till att få denna månskenspiknik till stånd och så vällyckad och hoppas, att alla som voro närvarande gingo hem med tillfredsställelse i hjärtat.

—Den fria missionens vänner hade förliden söndags eftermiddag dopförrättning i Gilden Creek, därvid tillsammans 14 personer läto döpa sig.

ATHENS.

Rättegången mot den mobb, som lynchade de tre Humpereys, tog sin början i måndags. Tio personer äro arresterade och anklagade för delaktighet i det hemska dådet. Tre af dem hafva bekänt att det var en af en viss Joe Wilkinson uppgjord plan att rödja de tre Humphreys ur vägen. W, anklagade dem hos grannarne att hafva stulit hans svin, och sedan han ej inför lagen kunde bevisa sitt påstående, uppäggade han i förargelsen grannarne emot dem. Äfven beskylde han de tre hängde för att hafva gömt mördaren af konstapel Rhodes, samt att de ha-

it kept the immigrants' language alive for 50 years after most of the other cultural institutions (primarily the churches) had abandoned it. And finally, right down to the last number of January 14, 1982, *Texas-Posten* faithfully reported news of Sweden to her sons and daughters thousands of miles, and four generations, away.

When *Texas-Posten* began publication in April 1896, it joined the ranks of Swedish-language newspapers and other periodicals published in America, which would one day number 1,500. When it ceased publication in 1982, only three were still alive. Its history thus paralleled that of the Swedish-American press in general, and its gradual decline matched that of the other, much larger papers, almost all of which *Texas-Posten* outlived. Thus, the history of this paper is, in essence, the history of the Swedish Texans, the record of their daily activities in detail over the last nine decades.

The decision to start another Swedish-language newspaper in Texas — *Södra Vecko-Posten* had folded in 1881 — was made in a park near Gelleland Creek just outside of Manor in 1896. The actual founder of *Texas-Posten* was Richard Johnson, who chose Philip Engström as his editor. However, both Johnson and Engström stayed with the paper only a few months after the first issue appeared April 18, 1896.[11]

Johnson sold *Texas-Posten* to two cousins, Carl and Mauritz Knape of Austin, in 1897; from then on, for 80 years, the Knape family was responsible for the production of *Texas-Posten*. Mauritz Knape had nine brothers, and one of them, Hjalmar, was much more interested in *Texas-Posten* than was cousin Carl, so the latter was happy to sell his share to Hjalmar.[12]

Hjalmar Knape proved to be a conscientious and enthusiastic newspaperman and a diligent eliminator of obstacles to the paper's success. But in 1910 he became tired of the hard work and retired to land he had purchased in Brady to farm. For some years agriculture, not newsprint, was his livelihood, but in 1915 his older brother, Otto, returned to Austin from Kenedy, where he had been busy selling farmland to Swedes. The land sales were now able to support themselves without Otto's constant attention, and he wanted to get back into the newspaper business. (He had worked for *Texas-Posten* almost from the beginning. For 12 years he had been an agent for the paper, a job which took

Ernest Severin (left)*, Otto Anderson, and John M. Öjerholm in* Texas-Posten *office, Austin, 1912*

him from colony to colony across Swedish Texas. Only the prospect of booming land sales in Karnes and Bee counties diverted him temporarily from his favorite career.) Hjalmar, too, seems to have needed little persuasion to return to the capital to go into business with his brothers. Accordingly, the two became partners with Mauritz, Otto initially serving as subscription editor and travel agent.[13]

With Hjalmar Knape as business manager and the peripatetic Otto in charge of subscriptions, the economic base for *Texas-Posten* was well laid. From the beginning to the end, moreover, it declared itself to be a "liberal political news journal for Swedes in America," which meant that it would be religiously independent, giving all denominations equal space and respect. But it also meant that the editorial page was political and would serve as the Knape sounding board on issues affecting Swedes and Texans alike.[14]

The Knapes retained as editor one of the ablest men ever associated with *Texas-Posten*, John M. Öjerholm, who always maintained a complete tolerance in religious matters despite his personal affiliation with the Swedish Methodist church, in which he was a minister. Öjerholm edited the paper from September 1897 until 1935; he contributed an enormous amount of material—poetry, essays, editorials, even music—to its pages himself. He was born in Nyköping, Sweden, in 1858 and came to Texas in 1887, after serving as a Methodist pastor in congregations in Rockford, Illinois, Rhode Island, Kansas, and Nebraska. Initially he continued his pastoral duties, serving Texas congregations in Waco, Fort Worth, Georgetown, Swedonia, Hutto, and Decker, before assuming the editorship of *Texas-Posten*.[15]

Öjerholm had received a relatively good education in Sweden, and this was reflected in the many psalms, hymns, poems, and essays he later wrote for the paper. He also contributed a weekly column called "Krönika" ("Chronicle"), which listed and evaluated events of the week in a tolerant, or at least amused, style. The front pages were always reserved for "Nyheter från Sverige" ("News from Sweden"), arranged alphabetically by province or by city. "Texas Nyheter" ("Texas News") was the largest section of the paper (next to advertising) and the most highly developed, along lines set up by Otto Knape. (For some years, "Texas Nyheter" even appeared on the front page.)

Each Swedish settlement outside Austin had a regular correspondent who sent weekly reports to Öjerholm in Austin. Some of them seem to have received small stipends, at least up until the Great Depression, but all were carefully chosen by Otto Knape (who visited each of them regularly) for their proven zeal in supporting "their" newspaper. Many of these correspondents' children and grandchildren in turn continued to supply news in the last decades of *Texas-Posten*'s long run, providing information about social, religious, and personal events—in later years, usually illnesses and deaths—throughout the vast state anywhere Swedes were to be found. This became especially important as the smaller settlements, one by one, dropped from view, their congregations either disbanded or consolidated, the members of the communities dispersed.

The advertisements were the financial life's blood that enabled the paper to survive at a minimal subscription rate. While most of the advertisers were Swedish, many were not but recognized the marketing potential in advertising in a medium that probably reached the hands of more than 90 percent of the Swedish population in Austin, if not in the entire state.

In the summer of 1928 the Swedish population in Texas was at its zenith. Neither old age nor the depression had begun to erode the structures they had built, and Swedish-American culture was in its brightest summer bloom. It was July 5, 1928, and this was the news in *Texas-Posten*.[16]

On the first page appeared Swedish news or international news of interest to Swedish readers. Svenska sångarförbundet (The Swedish Union of Singers), for example, rounded off their highly successful American tour with a performance of American, Swedish, English, and Italian vocal music in Los Angeles.

On the religious front, two professors at North Park College in Chicago (the Seminary of the Mission Covenant Church) had been dismissed from the theology department, one for advocating the doctrine of evolution and the other for having "diversive views" about the Resurrection. Their accuser was Gustaf F. Johnson, an evangelist at the Texas Wesleyan College tabernacle in Austin and a leader of regular revivals among Swedes in Texas.

Readers were kept abreast of famous Swedish explorer Sven Hedin's latest expedition into Tibet. (Despite a confrontation with pirates, Hedin had launched several hundred helium-filled weather balloons over the Himalayas.) Other front-page news was the scandal resulting from a huge postal theft from the American liner *Leviathan*. The largest private motor yacht in Swedish maritime history was being built for George Jepson, a Swedish-American industrialist from Worcester, Massachusetts. (The ship was to be 5 meters wide, 25 meters long, and able to make 14 knots.)

On the editorial page that week Editor Öjerholm provided an unsigned list of candidates endorsed by *Texas-Posten* for the Democratic primary to be held on July 28. News of a social nature (visits to and from friends and relatives, illnesses, etc.) was reported from Decker, New Sweden, Georgetown, Fort Worth, Brushy, Coupland, Kenedy, Waco, Hutto, El Campo, Jonah, Elgin, and Austin. Twelve churches in Central Texas reported in that week, including three in Austin.

A "Swedish Evening," presented by the Scandinavian Society (Skandinaviska sällskapet) at the University of Texas in Austin, had been a great success. Swedish songs (and a few Norwegian numbers too) had been performed by a mixed quartet; Miss Tilly Gustafson sang folk songs. From the university's gymnastic department eight girls under Hilda Moleworth's guidance performed Swedish folk dances from Värmland and Dalarna. Students from the Swedish Summer School sang two songs "with perfect Swedish pronunciation." June Knape read a poem entitled "The Steerman" by Swedish-Texan poet John Sjolander. Pastor C.W. Bergquist of Gethsemane showed a series of slides of Sweden and provided "an explanatory commentary." The program had been arranged by Miss Hilda Widén.

Many children in the Swedish Summer School wrote to "*T-P*" that summer. The school had 28 students in three classes and was sponsored by Svenska Klubben, the Swedish Club of Austin. A typical letter (from Mildred Peterson, vice-president of Svenska Klubben) reads: "*Vi har bara en vecka kvar till att gå till svenska skolan. Vi har lärt oss mycket i Svenska Skolan. Om fredag Kväll skall vi ha ett avslutningsprogram av Svenska Skolan och ni äro välkomna.*" ("We have only one week left to go to the Swedish School. We have learned a great deal in the Swedish School. On Friday night we will have the final program in the Swedish School, and you are all welcome.")

Entrance to Swedish American Publishing Company and offices of the Texas-Posten, *Austin, c. 1910*

The final item of news from this issue of *Texas-Posten* concerned the birthday the previous week of one of the last of the original pioneers. On June 30 the venerable August Swenson of Hutto had celebrated his 93rd birthday. He was one of the group of 100 who had emigrated from Forserum in 1867. He had worked as a cabinetmaker in Austin, then had bought land in Hutto, Williamson County, and become one of the most successful farmers in that area. He retired to Austin in 1920 after serving as president of the Swedish-owned Farmers and Merchants State Bank of Hutto. He donated the church bell and the beautiful high altar to Austin's Gethsemane Lutheran church; to the Hutto Lutheran church he had donated a pipe organ. August Swenson died in 1930, after enjoying relatively good health in his last years.

Announcements and advertisements aimed at Swedish-American consumers took up the largest amount of space in *Texas-Posten*, thanks to Hjalmar Knape's skill in attracting clients. The ads of the turn of the century—when sales of land, farm equipment, and patent medicines predominated—gave way in the 1930's to investment opportunities (from no less than five banks on one page), travel opportunities (back to Sweden on the Scandinavian-American and Swedish-American lines), "high-class" jewelers, haberdashers, builders, and, more ominously, funeral parlors and embalmers. Only one land agent was still trying to sell land to Swedes; most who had earlier purchased land were, by the late 1920's, leaving it to their sons, and even Mr. Howerton, the last of the Swedish land agents, only advertised for a "possible" Swedish colony in Moore County near Dumas. (Nothing ever came of it.) And the Farmers Supply of Austin used its largest type to sell TRUCKS and the smallest type for row binders, hay presses, combines, harvesters, etc.

Quite clearly, the merchants who purchased advertisements and space in *Texas-Posten* were hoping to reach an aging, affluent, urbanized Swedish clientele. These consumers were not pioneers but city-dwellers who had left or sold their farms and had liquid capital—sometimes a considerable amount—to invest in bank plans, stocks (the Swedish-American Line offered its stock share through Nielsen and Lundbeck in New York), or property of a more permanent kind, such as in the Austin Memorial Park then being developed.

The Great Depression devastated many Swedish cotton farmers and businessmen alike, and it was hard on *Texas-Posten*, but, by keeping subscription rates low ($2.50 a year in 1935), Knape and Öjerholm held on to all but the most destitute subscribers. The hardest toll was taken on the newspaper's publishers. No longer a young man, Hjalmar Knape sold his interests to Otto in 1933, making him sole owner of the paper. His son, Gerald, came in at that time as director of advertising to help Otto; he was to become editor-publisher after World War II.

Gerald Knape had to oversee the decline of *Texas-Posten*, which slowly began to lose readership as the native speakers of Swedish grew old and died without having passed the language on to the next generation. Bowing to the inevitable, he introduced more and more English into the paper and sought out less specifically ethnic advertisements and advertisers, which probably enhanced the paper's readership. In fact, so much of an Austin weekly paper did it become that *Texas-Posten* actually absorbed the *Austin News* and *South Austin News* in 1949.[17] Knape also reduced the size of the paper itself, from the 16-page, 12-column giant in the heady days of 1911 to a more modest six pages by 1950. Still, a handsome typeface, excellently reproduced photographs, and eye-pleasing graphics characterized *Texas-Posten* even in its twilight years. By the 1960's the paper had shrunk to a four-page format, which it maintained for its final two decades. But Knape refused to raise the subscription rate above $3.00 annually ($3.50 to Sweden), until the brutal inflation of the 1970's forced him to charge $5.00 for 50 weekly issues in 1976, perhaps one of the last great newspaper bargains in America.

Even in the 1940's Swedish businesses accounted for less and less of the advertising revenue and space, and Knape had to look farther and farther afield to find clients. The Texas Press Association bought handsome ads (all in English), as did a number of the older financial institutions still grateful for Swedish business, but more and more the copy was for patent medicines and razor blades; only occasionally did the Swedish-American Line or Scandinavian Airline System offer Christmas trips home to the Old World.

Yet every week Knape managed to produce his paper, providing Swedish Texans (and former Swedish Texans such as Reverend T.J. Westerberg, who continued to subscribe to *Texas-*

Posten for 30 years after he had moved to Chicago)[18] with news of Sweden and the world and of social and religious events. "Kyrko-notiser" ("Church Notices") now appeared more often in English than in Swedish, but still they appeared. And every year Pioneer Days was celebrated, and, for every year it survived, *Texas-Posten* set records of longevity for a Swedish-American newspaper with such a limited circulation.

In 1980 Gerald Knape sold *Texas-Posten* to Lissa Bengtsson, a recent graduate of the University of Texas. Bengtsson was a Swedish Texan and had majored in Swedish and journalism at the university, a perfect combination, she felt, to renew *Texas-Posten*. She switched to a bolder type font and composed articles herself, instead of relying almost exclusively on wire-service news items. She conducted interviews, did photo essays, and commissioned articles such as David Carlson's nine-part history of Texas Wesleyan College. But, like her predecessor, she had a great deal of trouble finding suitable advertisers, even at the modest prices she charged. Nor did she wish to raise the subscription rate above that established during Knape's period. Being owner/managing editor of *Texas-Posten* became an unmanageable financial burden, and in the spring of 1981 Lissa Bengtsson was forced to return the paper to Gerald Knape, who then sold it to Marilyn Berglund Samuelson and her husband, David Samuelson, of Lund.[19]

Marilyn Samuelson did yeoman's service in trying to keep *Texas-Posten* alive. From her first issue in February 1981 she focused on the history of Swedish-American churches in Central Texas, a rich source of information for local history. She retained the paper's modern look and contributed essays and photos of her own. She actively sought out stories and reminiscences from older readers and encouraged new readers to write in with colorful information as well. She kept the full page of news of Sweden in Swedish largely as Lissa Bengtsson had laid it out: to the very end, at least a quarter of the copy in *Texas-Posten* was in Swedish. She tried to revive the old "correspondents'" network across the state, with some success. From time to time she even published Swedish recipes adapted for the American kitchen.

Meanwhile, David Samuelson, a former Travis County Commissioner from the First Precinct, became the chief architect of the paper's editorial page, writing of the demise of the family farm, skyrocketing interest rates (and what to do about them), and other political issues dear to his heart. He advocated nuclear energy, the free enterprise system, accelerated defense spending, and a return to the high moral tone of the Swedish immigrants. (On September 3, 1981, the word "liberal" disappeared from the banner.) The Samuelsons reprinted a long series of articles (in English) about the life and times of modern Swedes. They also printed articles on Swedish towns and villages (Lessebo, Jönköping, Malmö) taken largely from the *Wasa Star*. They were forced to raise the annual subscription rate to $8.00 in October 1981, however, and had to appeal publicly for new advertisers. Despite all the reforms, *Texas-Posten*'s days were numbered.

The paper published a gala Christmas issue with a long article on the history of Christmas celebrations in Austin over a century and a half, including the "Lut Fisk" [*sic*] introduced to an unsuspecting population by the Swedes. Two issues into January, however, were all the Samuelsons were able to manage. David Samuelson's editorial of January 14, 1982, was the last ever to appear in a Swedish-American newspaper in Texas.[20]

Today marks the last issue Marilyn and I will publish [of] the *Texas-Posten*. This past year has been an inspiration to us, [?] the many people who have helped in so many ways.

The potential for the paper to become self-sustaining is there. However, it will take more time and resources. The resources we simply do not have.

The history of our people and the part they have played in building this country is tremendous. We are all proud of our heritage. The paper is a symbol of that.

The Scandinavians have all been builders and producers. The communities where they settled were progressive communities. The farms, businesses and factories were avenues of advancement for their families to attain a better life. Food, clothing and shelter came first, and after that, the higher things in life were provided.

Today, we can look at our educational systems, libraries, art, etc., and recognize the input our forefathers gave.

It is with a great deal of sadness that we terminate our effort with the paper. But we are happy and thankful for the enjoyment and fellowship with so many that came through our contact with the paper. We thank one and all!

Texas-Bladet (1900-1909)

During its 85-year existence the Swedes of Texas remained faithful to "their" newspaper, *Texas-Posten*. But it is an indicator of the inherent vitality of the small Swedish population in the state that, for nearly a decade, *Texas-Posten* had a serious rival — from 1900 to 1909 the weekly newspaper called *Texas-Bladet*. It began as a monthly Christian paper published in Hutto by the multitalented C.C. Charnquist, who was better known as the founder of the Swedish Methodist Church in Texas. He had left the state in 1880 after nine active years as a pioneer preacher. He continued his religious work among the Swedish settlers in Kansas for 11 years; then in 1891 he returned to Texas, which he now considered his permanent home. Still active in the Methodist Church he had founded, he settled in Manda, where he operated a small religious printing house. It was there that he wrote and published, on his own press, his autobiography, *Minnen och sjelfbiografiska anteckningar* (*Memories and Autobiographical Notes*). In Manda he also conceived of the plan to publish a monthly Christian newspaper in Swedish. Using his own Swedish fonts, and with the help of his son, Philip, he began publishing *Texas-Bladet* in the nearby village of Hutto in April 1900.

For seven years Charnquist printed his monthly paper in a tiny rural Swedish settlement in Williamson County, but in 1907 he was nearing 70 and finding the job more work than he and his son together could manage. So, in an extraordinarily daring move, he decided to move the offices of the paper to Elgin because "in recent years, Elgin has become something of a city of Swedes." Philip Charnquist, with J.O. Smith and Per C. Carlson, decided to go to a weekly format and thus go into direct competition with *Texas-Posten*, both for readership and for adver-

God Jul   Godt Nytt-år

Texas Bladet.

NYHETS-TIDNING FÖR SVENSKARNA I TEXAS.

6:te Arg.   Elgin, Texas, Onsdagen den 25 December, 1907.   Nummer 36

En Julafton.

HAFVET, brusade och fräste. Vågorna kastade sitt salta skum högt upp på de kala östränderna. En hård vestan hade bildat i flera dagar, och en på julaftonen hade den om möjligt mera tilltagit i styrka.

På det lilla fiskläget fröde man också julafton. Det lyste klart från hvartenda stuga, under det invånarne, obekymrade om stormen der ute, sutto i sina lugna boningar.

Inne hos Lots Anders var det dock riga glädje. Gamla Anders själf satt framme vid det omaka bordet, med hufvudet stadt i hand, förnärkt i djupa tankar, under det hustrun och dottern, den tjuguåriga Tilda, voro sysselsatta med att tillaga qvällsmåltiden.

Det var en lång strut tyst, så sade mor Gerda, halfhögt, liksom hon vara rädd för sina tankar.

"Undrar nur Sven har det i qväll?"

"Jag tänkte just derpå, jag ock," svarade mannen långsamt. "Han är väl i England nu," inföll Tilda.

...

—Halfdan Rune.

HERRENS TRÄD.

När de vackra julträden glittra och prunka i ett prakt på den sju-nde julaftonen, hänfördt...

Den Heliga Natten.

Det sväfvar ett stilla, domnande sus
Kring slumrande öfverms sängar.
Och silfrade dimmors villande ljus
Nu darrar på Betlehems ängar.
Det höra vi ena salta
Ett hviskande ord
Men herdarne vakna
En hetande hjord,
Det hvilar en skrud af snöhvit färg
På vågiga kullar och fjärran berg.

Du kommer i natt, o heliga fröjd,
Att glans ur läge och ringe.
Ett änglar fröjd himlens saliga höjd
Står mira med strålande ringe.
I arme, oj rådrens!
Han kommit, er vän!
O fröjdens och glädjens,
I vallarenan!
Vår Gud vare ära, på jorden frid.
Åt mänskor en vilja barnhärtig blid!

Vi skynda väl, säg, vi ska väl med?
Med herdarne vi oss glädja!
Vi hasta till krubban, helja oss ned
För barnet, det milda, det späda.
O ljuset går opp
Ur villande dimma
För häljande hopp!
I världen vårt lif var så sorgetungt;
Du, heliga barn, gör det ljust och lugnt.

C. D. af Wirsén

Kyrkliga meddelanden.

Denna afdelning innehåller meddelanden om möten, julfester och andra sammankomster under jul och nyårs-helgen.

AUSTIN.

Metodist kyrkan. — Julotta firas juldags morgon kl. 5.

Lutherska kyrkan. — ...

ELROY.

Lutherska kyrkan. — Julotta hålles i härvarande svenska lutherska kyrka klockan half 6 på julda gs-morgonen.

Baptist kyrkan. — Julfest kom mer att hållas...

LUND.

Lutherska kyrkan. — Söndags ligt firas julotta på juldags mor gonen kl. 5.

NEW SWEDEN.

Lutherska kyrkan. — ...

KIMBRO.

Missionshuset. — ...

STAMFORD.

Lutherska kyrkan. — Ottesång firas kl. 5.30 f. m. på juldags-morgonen.

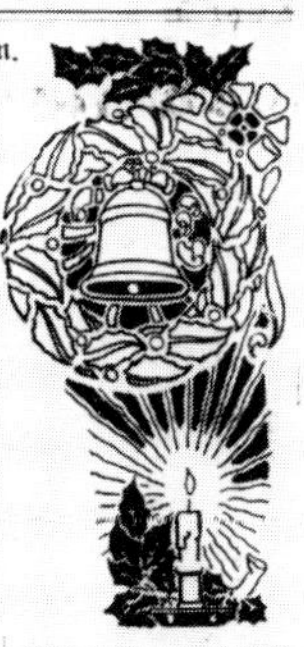

PALM VALLEY.

Lutherska kyrkan. — Julotta hålles...

HUTTO.

Lutherska kyrkan. — ...

DALLAS.

Lutherska kyrkan. — ...

EL CAMPO.

Metodist kyrkan. — ...

MANDA.

Metodist kyrkan. — ...

MANOR.

Lutherska kyrkan. — ...

DECKER.

Metodist kyrkan. — ...

tising. *Texas-Bladet* would appear every Wednesday (a day before *Texas-Posten*) and would comprise some four to eight pages. Its motto was "Svenskarnes framåtskridande" ("To the Progress of the Swedes"), and it would report the news of area churches as well as any and all local and national news of interest. *Texas-Bladet* claimed to have 75 paid correspondents across Texas. And, while the paper itself advocated prohibition, it insisted that it was *not* a single-issue organ for any group or faction.[21]

Yet there must have been some internal dissension, for Smith soon resigned and was replaced by Oscar Zahr. *Texas-Posten* immediately began an attack to drive *Texas-Bladet* out of business by falsely accusing that paper of being owned and operated by the Merchants and Farmers Bank of Elgin ("the Swedes' Bank").

Actually, the ensuing feud that caused such a shake-up in the editorial offices of *Texas-Bladet* seems to have been largely an imagined affair. *Texas-Posten* even wished the new weekly paper well on at least two occasions, albeit in *very* small print. The editors were beginning to realize, as were so many Swedish-American newspaper publishers just like them, that the small number of Swedes in any one geographical region put an absolute ceiling on how many entrepreneurial ventures the people could realistically be expected to support. As a monthly Methodist paper, *Texas-Bladet* might have had a small chance, but in direct competition with an already-established institution like *Texas-Posten*, the fight was going to be a fierce one indeed.

As if to underscore their competitive determination, a decision was made in May 1908 to move *Texas-Bladet* into the capital, where competition with *Texas-Posten* would become even fiercer. The new offices were located at 608 Brazos Street, in a building, ironically, once occupied by *Texas-Posten*. Like its rival, *Texas-Bladet* began offering book premiums to new subscribers, since their headquarters could now include a large stockroom for book storage. New subscribers to *Texas-Bladet*, for example, received copies of *Oskar II och Hans Folk* (*King Oskar II and His People*), while *Texas-Posten* offered *Gustaf III och Smålänningen* (*King Gustaf III and the Man from Småland*).[22]

But, despite the move to Austin, the newspaper did not flourish. In November it was relocated for a third time, this time to Georgetown. On November 11 Per Carl Carlson resigned, and the editors bowed to the inevitable. On April 24, 1909, after less than half a year in Georgetown, *Texas-Bladet* was sold to *Texas-Posten*. The cost of the deal—which included all of *Texas-Bladet's* machinery—was $3,150, and subscribers to *Texas-Bladet* would now receive *Texas-Posten* instead.

In layout and format Charnquist's paper was every bit as professional as Öjerholm's, including the front-page "Krönika" ("Chronicle") supplied by both editors. *Texas-Bladet* tried hard to cover local news of interest to Swedes that might not have gotten onto the pages of *Texas-Posten*. A year before its demise, for example, *Texas-Bladet* reported the construction of a wholly Swedish-owned and -financed cotton gin and cotton-oil plant in Elgin. Carl Carlsson, P.A. Sandahl, Claes Bengtsson, and others had raised $20,000 for the venture, one of the largest of its kind to date in the area. The event was apparently missed by *Texas-Posten*. But the format of *Texas-Bladet*, by accident or design, was too similar to that of its rival, and the Swedes of Texas stayed loyal to *Texas-Posten*.

Swedes are, and have always been, voracious readers. The national success of the first Swedish-American newspaper, T.N. Hasselquist's *Hemlandet: Det Gamla och Det Nya*, published in Galesburg, Illinois, beginning in 1855, is adequate testimony to Swedes' hunger for news and entertainment, especially of an uplifting kind. Witting's limited experiment with *Södra Vecko-Posten* and Charnquist's failure with *Texas-Bladet* notwithstanding, some Swedish authors and printers in Texas remained convinced that there was a market for locally produced reading material in the Swedish language. Thanks to diligent compilers such as Ernst Skarstedt, E. Walfred Erickson, and Alfred Söderström, we at least know the names and titles of some of the Swedish-language publications printed in Texas, even when no copies are known to have survived.

Georgetown served as the last home of *Texas-Bladet* but was also the place of publication of *Sanningens och Fredens Baner* (*The Banner of Truth and Peace*). The journal had begun publication in New Windsor, Illinois, in May of 1908 and had moved to Georgetown in November of the same year. The monthly journal, a "non-sectarian edification magazine," appeared for at least two years, but no copies seem to have survived. The editor's name is unknown.[23]

Equally enigmatic was the fate of *Söndagsskolklockan* (*The Sunday School Bell*), a Methodist magazine which was published in Austin sometime in the 1920's. It came out in several numbers, but no issue has survived, and virtually nothing else is known of it,[24] although it was advertised in the pages of *Texas-Posten*.

Texas Missionsblad, a "Monthly Journal for the Evangelical Lutheran Church and Mission," was edited by one Professor N.A. Melin between November 1909 and at least May of 1910 and was published in Austin. It contained "brief religious articles and mission news," but, again, no copies have survived to give us any further information about Melin or his activities.[25]

Swedish Writers in Texas

C.C. Charnquist

C redit for being the first Swede to publish a book in Swedish in Texas must go to the indefatigable C.C. Charnquist. In addition to his frenetic activities on behalf of the Swedish Methodist congregations which he had founded in Austin, Decker, Brushy Creek, and Hutto, he found time to translate more than 200 hymns into Swedish. In 1877 he published them in a modest volume entitled *Den Ljufwa Rösten* (*The Lovely Voice*) and subtitled "A Selection of P.P. Bliss' and Ira D. Sankey's *Evangelical Songs* no. 1 and no. 2 sung at the Great Revival Meetings held by MOODY and SANKEY in Europe and America, together with a selection of songs by other authors. Collected and reworked with a little addition, newly edited by C.C. -----q---t." The printer was Eugen von Boedman, a German in Austin who was able to deal with Swedish diacritical marks. At about the same time Charnquist brought out a second collection of similar translations called *Den Ljufwa Rösten, andra samlingen* (second collection, "selected, translated, edited and published by C.C. -----q.") This volume contains 13 hymns which do not appear in any of the Bliss-Sankey collaborations and so are considered to be among Charnquist's own compositions.

After his return to Texas in 1891, Charnquist resumed his work as a Methodist preacher, serving new congregations in Waco, Brushy Creek, Georgetown, Hutto, and Manda. While living in Manda, he began publication of *Texas-Bladet* and also sold pianos and organs out of his shop in Hutto. He even found time to pen his autobiography — *Minnen och sjelfbiografiska anteckningar*, a book of nearly 350 pages — in 1900. It is the only book known to bear the imprint "Manda, Texas" and was printed there by Charnquist himself. Copies have recently sold for as much as $400 to collectors of Texana.[1]

Ernest Severin

Ernest Severin

The printers of *Texas-Posten* began diversifying into other printing ventures at the *Texas-Posten* Publishing House founded in 1900. Ernest Severin became director of the publishing house after some years and eventually was considered the foremost Swedish publisher in Texas. He was born in Råda parish, Värmland, son of an architect and master builder, in 1871. At the age of 21 he immigrated to Chicago and found a job at the West Pullman works. After his conversion to Methodism he attended the Swedish Methodist Theological Seminary in Evanston, Illinois, for one year. But his health was delicate, and he soon migrated to Texas to begin work as a Methodist minister. In 1896 he moved to Fort Worth, where he served three years while attending college. After brief stays in Hutto and Taylor he took up farming in Brady, McCulloch County. He returned briefly to his old congregation in Fort Worth, and finally, in 1911, he moved to Austin. He soon became a part-owner of *Texas-Posten* with Mauritz and Hjalmar Knape and also ran the other, non-newspaper side of the business, printing almost anything and everything, in English and/or Swedish, that Austinites desired.[2]

Severin was a bold and idealistic thinker. It was his idea to publish the massive, comprehensive work that, in 1918, became the two-volume *Svenskarne i Texas i ord och bild* (*The Swedes of Texas in Words and Pictures*). But this huge work—over 1,200 pages in length—was miniscule compared to his grand scheme. According to a flyer mailed out in 1920, he contemplated nothing less than a series of volumes (one for each state) that would tell "the story of the Swedes in America." Congregational histories would play a major role in the work, and Severin offered to publish them for free.

Needless to say, the grand dreams of "The Ernest Severin Publishing Company," as he now called it, came to naught. *Three Centuries in America* (Severin planned to spend 18 years on his great work to have it ready for the tercentenary of the New Sweden colony on the Delaware in 1938) was too huge and diverse an undertaking—not to mention expensive—to sell as a concept. Nor was the income from *Svenskarne i Texas* very comforting: while Volume One sold quite well, the subscribers for the second volume were few. Severin never recovered the losses he suffered on the massive work, and 60 years later *Texas-Posten* was still offering mint copies of Volume Two at cost.

After completion of the *Svenskarne i Texas* project, Severin moved his offices to Lindsborg, Kansas, where he persuaded local intelligentsia to become editors and associates for *Three Centuries in America*—men like Birger Sandzén (Swedish America's most famous painter), G.N. Malm (leading Swedish-American novelist), and Dr. G.A. Dorf (former pastor of Austin's Gethsemane Lutheran Church).

Despite his dreams, and even with the larger Swedish population base in Kansas, Severin's hopes were dashed, and his great project never came to fruition. But at least he managed to get into print *Svenskarne i Texas i ord och bild*, the largest record of Swedish-American biography and history of any state save Illinois or Minnesota, the two areas in America with the largest Swedish populations. In 1918, the year of the publication of *Svenskarne i Texas*, with the Swedish population of the state at its maximum, Texas ranked 26th in the nation in the number of Swedish-born inhabitants.

Mathilde Wiel-Öjerholm

One of the two books known to have appeared under the "*Texas-Posten* Publishing House" imprint was *Vildblomster*, a volume of poems by Mathilde Wiel-Öjerholm, published posthumously in 1911. Wife of J.M. Öjerholm, editor of *Texas-Posten*, she had died in 1903. She is the only Swedish woman to have her works published in her mother tongue in Texas; indeed, hers is the only known volume of Swedish verse ever to have been published in Texas. Among her fellow-countrymen she was regarded as an informal poetess laureate, who could be counted upon to deliver occasional verses for the more serious of their communal events. Evaluations of her skill as a poet may not rate her very highly today, but her unique position in the history of the literature of the Texas Swedes and the extraordinary circumstances of her unusual life deserve mention.[3]

She was born December 12, 1858, the eleventh of 13 children, in Lundestad, Norway, near Fredrikshald. Her father was a wealthy farmer from an old Norwegian family. When Mathilde was nearly ten, the family moved to Säffle in Värmland across the border in Sweden, but she and her sister Otillia often spent summers and holidays with relatives in Fredrikshald.

During the winter of 1875 Mathilde and Otillia visited their cousins in Norway, whose parents had both recently and suddenly died. While they were at the house, a servant girl named Sofie, cross with Otillia and finding Mathilde "bothersome," began to slip arsenic into Mathilde's porridge. Mathilde became violently ill but, unsuspecting, continued to eat the food that Sofie prepared, food which contained larger and larger doses of the poison. Mathilde's condition worsened, but she did not die, since her system had gradually developed a limited tolerance for the arsenic. For some time Mathilde resisted the poison, but she became so weak that she was nearly paralyzed. At a propitious moment, Sophie started a fire, hoping that the invalid would expire either in the flames or in the cold night air. But, despite her weak condition, Mathilde survived. Autopsies on the bodies of Mathilde's recently deceased uncle and aunt, in whose household Sophie had been a servant for many years, disclosed massive amounts of arsenic in the hair and nails. Sophie was arrested for attempted murder, tried, and condemned to death. On February 20, 1876, Sophie Johansdotter was beheaded — the last woman ever to be executed in Norway.

This attempt on her life left Mathilde's health more or less permanently shattered and her arms and legs badly crippled for a number of years (although she eventually recovered to a large degree) but with her faith in God greatly strengthened. On crutches, she had visited Sophie in prison and had prayed with her.

Slowly feeling and flexibility returned to Mathilde's limbs, and in 1882 she married J.M. Öjerholm, a Methodist minister, whom she met a year after she had immigrated to America. After some years in congregations in Providence, Rhode Island; Lindsborg, Kansas; Stromsburg, Nebraska; and Rockford, Illinois, Mathilde's health, never robust, began to fail again, and she and her husband sought out the warmer climate of Texas in 1887. She supported his religious work actively, as much as she was able. She organized a fund drive to send food to famine-stricken northern Sweden in 1902. The Central Disaster Relief Committee in Texas (Centrala nödhjälpskommitéen i Texas), organized by Mathilde and her husband and heavily advertised in *Texas-Posten*, held a huge rally on February 7, 1902, at which more than $1,600 was raised. A month later, on March 15, so ill that she had to be carried to the podium, Mathilde Wiel-Öjerholm read her poem "Kan han förgäta?" ("Can he forget?") to a huge Swedish-American crowd, presided over by Baptist, Lutheran, and Methodist clerics.[4] The poem was sold for hunger relief, and a further sum raised from its publication in the 1902 issue of *Prärieblomman*, the national Swedish-American literary annual of the Augustana Synod. Mathilde died only a few months later, on August 19, 1903.

At her funeral on August 21, Pastor C.G. Widén read a poem of his own composition (reprinted in *Vildblomster*) in which he calls Mathilde the one who:[5]

> nyss . . . eldat oss till kärleksifver,
> då det gällde att till Norrland sända
> Bröd åt dem som uti hunger klagat
> Och hvars nödrop nått vårt nya hemland . . .
> Därför sorgdok vi i dag anlägga

Ty på båren hvilar vår skaldinna
Hon, hvars sångmö mången gång har ljudit
Uti Austins svenska hem och kyrkor.

(recently fired us to a fever pitch of love
when it was a question of sending to
northern Sweden bread to those who cried out
        from hunger
and whose cries reached us in our new
        homeland;
for that reason, we put on the veil of sorrow,
on the bier our poetess is lying,
she, whose muse so often did sound
in the Swedish homes and churches of Austin.)

J.M. Öjerholm, in addition to the weekly "Krönika" he
wrote for *Texas-Posten*, was also a poet of modest skills. As it did
with Widén, Mathilde's death seems to have inspired her husband's muse. He wrote a number of religious poems on the
themes of death and resurrection and published them in the supplement to *Vildblomster*.

Mathilde's verse is typical of much immigrant poetry.
There are some nature poems, a number of sentimental works
about the Old Country, childhood memories, and Christmas,
and quite a few religious poems about her conversion and subsequent joy. Some attempts at the Värmland dialect she used later
in life are humorous, and there are even a few poems in Norwegian, the language of her earliest childhood. But a few of her
Swedish poems reveal the profound effect that the immensity
of the American, and specifically the Texan, landscape made
on her European sensibilities. The restless currents of America's
mightiest port are seen as awesome but also something to be
feared in "New York":

Bullrande, jäktande jämnt,
Lik väldiga strömmen du ilar
Framåt i ohäjdad fart,
Aldrig fanns hvila en stund;
Förande allt hvad du möter
Med dig i brusande hvirfvel.
Mäktig du är i din oro;
Likväl förfärlig och grym.[6]

(Rumbling, constantly bustling,
Like the mighty river you hasten
Forward at an unchecked speed,
Never is there a moment of rest;
Carrying everything that you meet
with you in a roaring eddy.
You are mighty in your restlessness
But you are also terrible and grim.)

And, in a poem like "Hemlängtan," the strangeness and danger lurking in the untamed Texas wilderness — much like the energy of New York — cause her to think fondly of the safe homeland that she and so many others have left behind forever:

Visst mera djupblått här sig spänner
    himlens tält
Utöfver skog och dal med saftfullt
    frodig grönska
Och visst nog öfvergå de tusen blomsterfält
I färgers rikedom, hvad skönast man kan önska.
Men ack! osynligt stoft, ett giftigt sjukdomsfrö,
Här ifrån blommors fält med
    sommarvinden flyger;
Och under rödast ros, som hvitast lijlas snö,
Taranteln lurar, gömd, och giftig
    huggorm smyger.[7]

(Indeed the heavens' tent here spreads itself
    more deep blue
Over forest and valley with sap-filled,
    luxuriant green
And indeed the thousands of fields of
    flowers attain
A richness of color more beautiful than
    one could wish for.
But, alas! invisible dust, a poisonous seed
    of disease,
Flies from here on the summer wind from the
    fields of flowers
And, under the reddest rose, like the whitest
    lily's snow,
The tarantula lurks, hidden, and the
    poisonous rattlesnake crawls.)

218

August Anderson and family, c. 1916

August Anderson, "Quartus"

August Anderson was the author of *Hyphenated, The Life Story of S.M. Swenson* (1916), the second book known to have been published by the *Texas-Posten* Publishing Company. He also contributed greatly to the literary quality of the biographies in *Svenskarne i Texas*. According to his own autobiographical entry there, "Q-r-" was born in Saxtorp parish, Skåne, in 1869. His father, Nels Anderson, immigrated to America in 1882. Anderson's mother joined her husband in Texas in 1885, while Anderson himself, though only 16, seems to have made the journey alone. Ten years later he settled in Travis County near Decker with his new bride, Emma Elizabeth Bengtsson. They had seven children—three boys and four girls. Life in Texas for an amateur writer was somewhat unusual. As he himself put it in 1918:[8]

> With precarious health for the past seventeen
> years, my life has been a patchwork of farmer,
> preacher, author, and a bit of a jack of all
> trades, in which my love of study and historical

219

research has occasionally threatened to take over, to the detriment of our economy. Still, it has been thrilling to be part of this extraordinary period in history which we, of all people, have been privileged to experience.

Anderson's reputation, unfortunately, rests primarily on his so-called "biography" of S.M. Swenson, which generations of researchers have innocently cited, unaware of the fact that it is primarily a work of fiction. While he certainly had access to some of the people who had actually known Swenson firsthand, he had no qualms whatsoever about embellishing his text, inventing conversations and meetings, or even rearranging historical events when it suited his narrative fancy. *Hyphenated*, while an entertaining tale written in excellent English — although with some appallingly racist attempts at humor in "Negro dialect" — should by now be reclassified under "fiction" or, at least, "fictionalized biography." That was definitely the opinion of Jeanette Dyer Davis, daughter of S.M. Swenson's sister, Anna Kristina, and William Dyer, overseer at Swenson's plantation in Fort Bend County. Mrs. Davis was in a position to know the facts firsthand as one of the pioneering generation's eyewitnesses. So upset was she with Anderson's version of her uncle's life that she wrote a personal correction to it entitled "*Hyphenated* Refuted," which unfortunately has never been published.[9]

As a historian of his people in Texas, "Q-r-" fared little better, since he died in 1921 at the age of 52, before he was able to realize his larger plans. His collaboration with Severin, Scott, Westerberg, and Öjerholm on *Svenskarne i Texas* seems to have been limited to rewriting the family biographies (which are, on the whole, excellent) and the history of the Pioneer Days (Banbrytaredagen), which he abstracted from his own history of the Texas Swedish Pioneers published the previous year (*Ett Femtioårs Minne 1867-1917*).[10]

Nevertheless, "Q-r-" was one of only a handful of Swedish pioneers in Texas who yearned for a literary career. His *Hyphenated*, inadequate as it is as biography, has been read with pleasure by more people than any other Swedish literary work published in Texas. His history of the pioneers was conceived as a record for the future. Virtually every living immigrant from the large group of 1867 was interviewed or identified. Stories and jokes were recorded for posterity, photographs taken, memories jogged, and family histories (including the Swedish parishes from which Swedes had emigrated) plotted. All in all, then, the literary career of "Q-r-" was by no means a failure, even if it did not attain the heights to which he had once aspired.

John Peter Sjolander — "The Tolstoi of Texas"

This extraordinary sobriquet was bestowed on John Peter Sjolander by Richard Spillane, a correspondent for the *St. Louis Globe-Democrat* in 1898. Other writers, only slightly less extravagant in their praise, regularly referred to Sjolander as "the Sage of Cedar Bayou."[11] The object of such unusual attention was a popular Swedish-born farmer/sailor/poet, who lived in splendid isolation at the head of Cedar Bayou near Galveston.[12]

Sjolander's life before he arrived in Texas was certainly fascinating. He was born Jonas Petter Sjölander in Hudiksvall, Sweden, on March 25, 1851, the second of three sons. His father was the owner and captain of a small merchant ship, who became a religious dissenter from the (Lutheran) State Church of Sweden. As a result of his refusal to submit his son to the normal Lutheran baptism, Olof Sjölander was fined and threatened with a prison sentence. And, even though Olof later relented, young Jonas Petter was unable to attend school, a fact which eventually embittered him. Olof Sjölander drowned in a shipwreck when the boy was only five years old, and what little education Jonas Petter had was provided by his mother.[13]

When he was 15, Sjölander went to work for an English lumber exporter in Hudiksvall and became close friends with the Englishman's son, who was his own age. In 1866 Sjölander accompanied the family to Liverpool and, later, to Trinity College, Dublin. There, although not formally enrolled, he spent his time reading and writing in the library of the university and traveling in Great Britain. He studied English and quickly came

John Peter Sjölander

to love the poems of Robert Burns, who was to remain a lifelong model and inspiration.

In 1870 Sjölander's friend was killed in an accident, and the grief-stricken young man returned briefly to Sweden, a country for which, because of his own and his father's bitter experiences, however, he no longer felt any real affection. He soon took papers and worked his passage back to Great Britain, where he ran into his brother, Erik, in Cardiff. There they found a ship loaded with iron rails destined for Galveston, and both brothers enthusiastically signed on for the voyage. The captain was replaced by a "tyrannical master" just before they were to sail, however, so the Sjölander brothers jumped ship in Galveston harbor and escaped up Cedar Bayou to avoid the patrols that would have sent them back to England in irons.[14]

John Sjolander (as he now signed himself) and his brother were soon earning a living building and sailing boats up and down the rivers and harbors of Texas, occupations which kept them busy for more than five years. From their arrival in 1871, according to the *National Encyclopedia of American Biography*,[15] John and Erik worked in brickyards and did odd jobs when they were not hauling cargo around Galveston Bay. But by the mid-1870's their economic future was sound, if not rosy, so John and Erik bought a farm in Cedar Bayou and went back to Sweden to bring their mother over to Texas.[16]

This was to be John's home for more than 50 years, the source of his inspiration and his pride. Sjolander the poet was entranced by the subtropical beauty of the bayou, with its meandering waterways and lush vegetation. Here he settled on a small farm, where, in 1878, he married Caroline Busch, with whom he had five sons and a daughter. For some years Sjolander and his brother, Erik, operated a ferry service between Cedar Bayou, Houston, and Galveston. But after 1900, when his sons had taken over the shipping business, Sjolander turned his hand more and more to farming and poetry.[17]

Ultimately, his poems appeared in such diverse publications as the *St. Louis Globe Democrat, Boston Transcript, New York Sun, Philadelphia Times*, and virtually all the larger Texas newspapers. He was a master of the occasional verse and contributed literally hundreds of birthday, patriotic, memorial, and congratulatory poems to almost anyone who asked. They were, in the main, simple, heartfelt, sentimental verses, often dealing positively with the cyclical world of life on the land, in harmony with nature and the elements. Many of his verses dealt with animals, plants, and birds that lived or grew in Cedar Bayou, where Sjolander patiently and lovingly observed them. Others were about Texas itself, both its history ("San Jacinto") and its flora and fauna ("The Blue Bonnet of Texas" and "The Song of the Texas Corn"). Between 1919 and 1929 he even published an occasional translation of his poetry into Swedish in *Texas-Posten* and *Svenska Tribunen-Nyheter* (Chicago) under the pennames "Hudik" or "Jotte von Hudik."[18] His unswerving faith in the stalwart, independent farmer whose fierce love of freedom had made foreign domination unthinkable was as Swedish an idea as it was American. Sjolander was not often politically inclined, but he did indulge in a bit of jingoistic boasting during the Spanish-American War. He also, infrequently, wrote prose and had known and entertained O. Henry (William S. Porter) at Cedar Bayou.

In his poetry Sjolander used a number of conventional verse forms (sonnet, ballad, elegy) and a rather simple vocabulary, which sometimes lends an undeserved feeling of monotony to his work, robbing it of its usual freshness, exuberance, and positive attitude towards life. A brief flirtation with blank verse under the influence of Walt Whitman was quickly abandoned for conventional rhyme. Sometimes, as in "The Dusk" (one of his personal favorites), Sjolander strikes a note uncannily reminiscent of Stephen Vincent Benét in "John Brown's Body," though Sjolander's "South" was Texas, not Georgia:[19]

> The dusk of the South comes fleetly,
>   And fleetly it takes to flight;
> But its song is a song sung sweetly,
> And it gathers earth's cares completely,
>   For God to keep in the night.

One of the many poems originally written in English which Sjolander reworked in Swedish for the ethnic-language press was "The Proof," published in the fall of 1919. A comparison of the texts shows that, while he was still a master of his native language, Sjolander's muse had actually become more eloquent in English than in Swedish. Even the Swedish title shows a bit of slippage: "Profvet" is better translated as "The Test." Still, it is clear even from this short example that "Jotte von Hudik" was at least as good a poet as most of his Swedish-American contemporaries and better than many, and that the life-affirming philosophy that endeared his verse to English readers is just as sunny in Swedish:

Profvet

> En gubbe stod och log åt lifvet
>   Och glad han syntes med sin lott
> Jag sporde, "Gamling, hvad är lifvet?"
>   Hans svar blef—"Gott."
>
> En stund han tycktes granska vägen
>   Som rak han gjort med dagligt knog,
> Men snart han såg med blick benägen
>   På mig och log:
>
> "Jo, Godt, blir lifvets summa skrifven
>   Och ingen makt kan ändra den,
> När äldsta grannen din är blifven
>   Din äldsta vän."[20]

The Proof

An old man, smiling, watched the strife;
    And seeing how serene he stood,
I asked: "What is the sum of life?"
    He answered: "Good."

Musing he stood a little while,
    And thought back on the toilsome way,
Then turned and told me with a smile
    Bright as May:

"Yes, you will find life's test is this:
    The sum is good if at the end
You find your oldest neighbor is
    Your oldest friend." [21]

Sjolander actually published only one book of verse — *Salt of the Earth and Sea* in 1928. It is a small but representative sample of the hundreds of poems he composed in his 60-year career in Texas. His simple, sentimental verses speak of the things he loved the most: the waterways and wildlife of coastal Texas; the freedom of the sea, wind, and waves; and the deep, almost mystical reverence for the soil and the abundance that Nature heaps on the "poor" tiller of the soil. Only a few of his poems, however, deal with his Swedish past. One of these few — "Lapland Lullaby" — was enthusiastically praised by Eugene Field (author of many childrens' poems, including "Wynken, Blynken and Nod"), who introduced and published it in the *Chicago News*.

John Peter Sjolander died on June 15, 1939, at Cedar Bayou in his 88th year. He was recognized as the "Dean of Texas Poets," and his very existence was a source of pride to his fellow Swedish Texans, who were avid readers of his poetry in English and in Swedish. Although Sjolander is little read today, one of his poems, "The Blue Bonnet of Texas," was once quite popular and found its way into many Texas schoolbooks: [22]

The Blue Bonnet of Texas

It blooms upon our prairies wide
    And smiles within our valleys,
A Texas flower and Texas' pride, —
    Around it honor rallies;
And every heart beneath the blue
    Transparent sky above it,

In Texan-wise, forever true,
    Shall fold and hold and love it.

The winds that softly round it blow
    Breathe out in song and story
The fame of bloody Alamo
    And San Jacinto's glory;
And everywhere beneath the sky
    That lovingly bends o'er it,
With glowing heart and kindling eye,
    All Texans true adore it.

It blossoms free in homes and fields
    Made by love's labor royal;
To Fleur-de-lys or Rose none yields
    Allegiance more loyal!
And to the world its fame shall go
    And tell the Lone Star's splendor —
Of hearths and homes that gleam and glow,
    Of loving hearts and tender.

'Tis Texan in its beauty rare
    To honest hearts appealing;
And can there be a fame more fair,
    Or deeper depth of feeling?
For Texas hearts, in Texan-wise,
    Are true to the Blue Bonnet,
And love it as the bright blue skies
    That pour their blessings on it.[23]

19

Two Swedish-Texan Colleges

Trinity College of Round Rock, Texas

S wedish immigrants, like members of other small ethnic groups in the United States, were anxious to ensure that some kind of cultural continuity from the Old World should prevail in the new. For most of them, this meant an orthodox spiritual continuity, to preserve an unbroken link with religious institutions in the mother country. The most visible sign of such a link would be the supply of native-born (not American) ministers of the State Church of Sweden. But if that body seemed reluctant to assume the responsibility of training pastors for the scattered flocks of the faithful in America (as was the case with the Swedish church), the training of properly accredited ministers would become the responsibility of the immigrants themselves. This shift was also indicative of the growing sense of independence, of separateness, that the immigrants began to manifest after the Civil War. They had cast their lot with the American republic and had been bloodied in the defense of the Union: they could make their own way and were quickly maturing as a new people—Swedish Americans.[1]

Augustana College and Theological Seminary in Chicago was founded in 1860 as a "mother school" to see to the training

Trinity College, Round Rock, 1906

of Swedish Lutheran pastors for the foreseeable future and to represent a vital—perhaps the most important—link between Swedes in America and their kinsmen in Europe.

But the more clearly American ideal of education for its own sake quickly manifested itself in the Swedish community. The need for secondary schoolteachers was seen as acute, and the "daughter" colleges spun off from Augustana—Bethany in Lindsborg, Kansas; Gustavus Adolphus in St. Peter, Minnesota; Upsala in East Orange, New Jersey—were all founded in the 1880's and 1890's. Other denominations of Swedes felt similar needs: the Methodists had Wesley Academy and Seminary in Evanston, and the Swedish Baptists founded their college and seminary, Bethel, in St. Paul in 1913. It is against their background that we should see the Swedish Texans' experiment in higher education, Trinity College in Round Rock.

From its very inception, the college was steeped in idealism. More than the modest Wesleyan Academy founded in Austin by the Swedish Methodists along almost wholly American lines, Trinity College in Round Rock was to be a full-fledged, accredited Swedish-American junior college modeled on Augustana College in Illinois and Bethany College in Kansas. Its cur-

228

riculum was patterned after these larger institutions, both of which were able to draw from the vast number of Swedish Americans in the Midwest and Plains states.

Discussions centering on the possibility of founding a college for Swedish Texans had begun as early as the turn of the century and became earnest in 1904.[2] The enormous distance to Lindsborg—most southerly and nearest of the Swedish-American schools—had made attendance there hard for Swedish Texans.[3] The Kansas Conference of the Lutheran Augustana Synod had suggested that the Swedish community in Texas should consider the possibility of establishing and funding a school of its own, although the conference also refused any money to the projected institution.[4] It was agreed, however, that the annual gift to Bethany College could remain in Texas, to go to a school maintained by the Swedish Lutheran congregations of the state.

John A. Nelson had pledged $7,000 and four city blocks of land for a building site, if the school could be located in Round Rock. He also promised to drill a well. The International and Great Northern Railroad offered to refund half the cost of hauling building materials to the site, which was located on the eastern edge of the city of Round Rock.[5] So, at a meeting in Austin in January 1905, the steering committee decided that it had enough money to begin construction of the first major building on the newly acquired site.

In March the designs of C.H. Page for a two-story building of white limestone, in Texas mission style, were accepted. The structure was to be equipped with a cellar under the southern wing (unusual for Texas). The building was to be 147 feet long and 60 feet wide. In addition to six large classrooms, an auditorium, 20 student rooms, two offices, four bathrooms, a library, music practice room, kitchen, and dining room were planned. Spacious corridors would run the length and breadth of the building.[6]

Work began in earnest immediately, but a lack of materials slowed construction, so that the main floor was not finished until January 1906. The school's charter, under the name "The Evangelical Lutheran Trinity College of Round Rock, Texas," was granted on March 22, 1906, and two months later construction was complete. The school was to be owned and operated wholly by the Austin and El Campo districts of the Kansas (later, Texas) Conference of the Augustana Synod of the Swedish Lutheran Church. Thus, Trinity College was, exactly as its founders had wished it to be, completely and exclusively the child of Swedish Texans. Funds for the school's operating expenses were to be raised wholly within the state and the Swedish community.[7] It was a daring undertaking, given the limited number of households which could be expected to support such an enterprise. Many families belonging to free churches or Methodist congregations, for example, could hardly be expected to support a Swedish Lutheran college, yet many did so out of a sense of community responsibility. Trinity quickly became the Texas-Swedish colonies' hostage to fortune, and its daily events became the stuff of innumerable newspaper accounts.

On the first day of classes, in October of 1906, Trinity College had enrolled 59 students in three academic divisions — the Academy, the School of Business and Phonography, and the School of Music. (By the end of the year, total enrollment had risen to 96.) President Stamline taught Christianity and Swedish; Mr. Arthur Wald taught Latin and Mathematics (in addition to operating the Music Store and the Book Store); and Mr. J.L. Larson taught Natural Sciences, History, and English Language and Literature. The single teacher in the Business School, Mr. C.E. Johnson, taught Banking, Commercial Law, Bookkeeping, Arithmetic, "Phonography," and Typewriting, while Anna Latitia Palm directed the School of Music alone.[8]

The "academic" four-year program comprised six courses (Christianity, Swedish, English, Arithmetic, Geography, U.S. History, and Penmanship) each semester. In the senior year, German, Advanced Latin, and Plane Geometry replaced History, Geography, and U.S. History; Civics, Medieval History (fall), Physics, Botany, and Modern History (spring) were added. It was a rigorous academic regime.[9]

The School of Business offered two primary courses of study — Bookkeeping and Typewriting — "for a practical business training . . . under Christian influence." Again, the normal academic load was six courses (plus Penmanship): Bookkeeping, Arithmetic and Rapid Calculation, Business Law, Grammar, Spelling, and Business Correspondence (in the Bookkeeping course), and Shorthand, Typewriting, Grammar, Spelling, Correspondence, Practical Office Work, and the inevitable Penmanship in the Typewriting course.[10]

The School of Music (with a faculty of one, like the School of Business) considered itself a conservatory and offered four levels of piano instruction (advanced students received private instruction) and one level of voice.[11]

In the beginning, the school's modest library had only 200 volumes, but the Augustana Book Concern in Rock Island, Illinois, sent books to the fledgling college, which doubled its holdings by 1912. Tuition was $45 annually in the Academy, $55 in the School of Business, and $18 to $27 in the School of Music. Room rent was $27 a year, and board was $90 a year or $2.50 per week. There were two literary societies, the Philomothian, conducted in English, and the Svea, in Swedish. The Bailey Debating Club discussed burning issues of the day. The True Culture Club offered young ladies a chance to explore the right-thinking ways championed by the college, while boys were signing up for the Anti-Cigarette League. Chapel was held every morning and divine worship each Sunday, alternating English and Swedish services. On Saturday nights, students' prayer meeting was held. Musical groups consisted of a mixed chorus (in the strong Swedish choral tradition) and "mandolin orchestra."[12]

Chapel attendance was mandatory for all students, as was a section of Bible Study and Swedish. No elective courses were permitted except those approved by the faculty, nor was any student allowed off campus for any reason after six p.m. without permission.[13] Events of importance to the campus and community were published in *Väktaren*, a monthly periodical in Swedish, which appeared from 1913 to 1920.[14]

Within a few years, the faculty grew from four to seven, and the student body from 96 to 112. The School of Business quickly became the School of Commerce (1909), and soon an Athletic Association was formed as well. As the student body grew, so too did the college. New departments (Geology, Biology, Botany, Zoology, and Violin) were added as the need for them arose. Curfew was extended to 7:30 p.m., but, on the other hand, daily room inspections at 8:00 p.m. were made mandatory. New laboratory space was built with endowment money for the geological and biological sciences, and a "Base Ball" team was organized in 1911.[15] The Oratorio Society—a sine qua non in Swed-

Trinity College students, c. 1915

ish-American institutions of higher education — was organized in 1912 and performed Gabriel's *King of Israel* and Gaul's *Holy City* at the end of each fall and spring term. The debt, however, had also grown to $2,500 by 1910, while enrollment slipped to 85 as the novelty of the school's existence wore off.[16]

These were, in fact, the boom years for Trinity College of Round Rock. Never again would enrollment top the 85 students of 1913-1915. Moreover, during 1915, the college's debt rose to an alarming $8,600, despite the $2,000 Halvorson Endowment, a donation from C.B. Halvorson, a Norwegian-born pioneer who had settled in Austin. Attempts to raise the endowment were met with failure, since the college was maximizing the financial resources of the Swedish-American community of the whole state — the colonies and churches were already giving all they could afford.

The last president of Trinity College, Reverend Harry C. Alden, tried valiantly to stem the tide of decreasing enrollment and growing debt. Under his leadership the college's actual worth rose to nearly $60,000, and by the end of the 1927-1928 term all outstanding loans had been repaid. The library's holdings had risen from 200 volumes in 1907 to more than 3,500 in 1928-1929.[17] While only 48 students were enrolled that last year, they were taught by a staff of 8 — an enviable 6 to 1 student-teacher ratio. The school took in revenues of over $17,000 that year and could boast a total of nearly 250 graduates from the Academy and other departments (Commerce, Music, etc.) between 1907 and 1929. In fact, in March 1926 Trinity College had changed its name to the more accurate Trinity Junior College and was almost immediately accredited by the State of Texas.[18]

But, even then, forces were at work that would end the 20 years of service the college had provided its community. In the annual report to the Augustana Synod for 1927, for example, it was revealed that, despite $7,000 in endowments, donations of $3,000, and appropriations of $2,300 ($1 from every Swedish Lutheran communicant in Texas), the college was still $5,000 in debt. Per capita costs for Trinity students were $183, the highest in the entire Augustana Synod. A year later the Texas Conference petitioned the synod for $5,000 "as aid in carrying on the school work in Texas." These funds were, in fact, granted, with two provisos: (1) that the Texas Conference would vote to continue the educational work of the college and (2) that the college would not assume any debts or donations that would prevent or endanger either future merger with some other Lutheran body or a smooth dissolution. The final blow came from the Texas Conference itself, meeting in El Campo in March 1928.[19]

The board of the college, acknowledging the $5,000 offer from the national synod and the pertinent restrictions, polled the 16 congregations of the Texas Conference to ask for their continued support. After a sometimes acrimonious confrontation, the votes were tallied: seven congregations were for continuing Trinity, eight were against further expenditures, with one congregation (New Sweden) hopelessly deadlocked. President Alden notified the synod in Rock Island, the $5,000 was not sent, and Trinity Junior College decided to close its doors at the end of the 1928-1929 academic year.[20]

The contents of the college were sold at auction after the last commencement on June 16, 1929.[21] With the help of the Lutheran Aid and Orphans' Society, the property was purchased by the United Lutheran Church in America (the oldest German Lutheran synod in America). Within a few months, renamed Trinity Lutheran Orphans' and Old Folks' Home, the former college began a new period of service. Despite some initial bitterness that the college had been "ripped from our Swedish hands and thrust into German ones," the two groups were soon inextricably mingled, both as clients in the home and as administrators.[22] In fact, in deference to the Swedish heritage of the place, the ULCA ran the home on an "intersynodical" basis: Swedish members of the Augustana congregations sat with German members of the ULCA on the home's Board of Directors. In 1931 the State Lutheran Mission Society even began publishing a bimonthly newsletter, the "Texas Inner Mission News," which was largely devoted to the doings at the Trinity Home.[23] The composition of the board itself, despite the synodical differences, may even have been a bit top-heavy in favor of the Scandinavians. And, while some people lamented the fact that "it seems as if it is hard to retain that which the old pioneers had acquired,"[24] most would probably have agreed with the chairman of the Association of Charities of the Texas Conference:

> The College . . . had its days of sunshine and
> its days of clouds. It met its days of success
> with joy and with thanks, and . . . its days of
> hardship with hope and courage. That the sun
> now sets, as it were, in a dark cloud, ought not
> to discourage us, but rather make us await a
> new and greater day.[25]

Today Trinity Home is still serving the needs of the German and Swedish Lutherans of Central Texas. The old Trinity College main building is gone now, but a historical marker was placed there in 1972 by the State of Texas to commemorate the home's former status.[26]

Texas Wesleyan College

The evident success of Trinity College in Round Rock, built by Swedish-Texan Lutherans, caused the second-largest Swedish religious group, the Swedish Methodists, to wonder if they might profitably establish a similar institute of higher education in Texas.[27]

The first problem was that of location: where should (or could) they build a school most advantageously? El Campo

Texas Wesleyan College, Austin

and Georgetown both wanted it, but Austin was felt to be the better site. In February of 1909 a 21-acre site between 24th and 26th streets and between Red River Street and Waller Creek had been secured, the asking price of $6,300 to be paid "by the businessmen of the city of Austin" if a school were to be built on the site. Over $5,000 in subscriptions toward the construction of the school had also been raised by that time.

The school was to be called the "Texas Wesleyan College," and in the summer of 1911 construction began. By the beginning of 1912 the school was ready to open with a total enrollment of 14 students. The college was housed in a single building, built of brick with a tile roof in a modified Texas Mission style. The ground floor contained the chapel, classrooms, library, president's office, dining hall, and kitchen. The second and third floors were used as dormitories for women. In 1929 a men's building, including dormitories and showers, was built on the campus, next to a laboratory and science building. The year before, a large tabernacle had been built on campus, in what came to be known as Wesleyan Park. Here the Union Swedish Revival was held annually, attended by thousands.

Enrollment more than doubled in the 1914-1915 school year. Financially the school was hard-pressed until the Chicago-based Methodist Board of Education donated $2,500 for the day-

235

Students on Texas Wesleyan campus, c. 1915

to-day operations of the school, and President O.E. Olander donated his $800-a-year salary toward operating expenses.

Texas Wesleyan operated the Sunny Brook Dairy, which employed students as workers and turned a tidy $600 annual profit. Cows were pastured on the school grounds near Waller Creek, where the University of Texas Law School now stands. Many students were able to pay their modest tuition through this early "work-study" program.

Calling the institution a college had been, in fact, a mistake. From its opening, Texas Wesleyan had accepted students with seven years of elementary school, beginning the eighth grade. Graduation requirements were a bit tougher (by one credit) than the minimum entrance requirement for the neighboring University of Texas. The college was, in reality, an "academy" from the beginning.

Courses consisted of 170 "class recitations" and were divided into Academic and Commercial departments. In the former one studied English, mathematics, history, science, and the Bible, adding language (Spanish or Swedish) and social sciences in the second, third, and fourth years. The Commercial Department offered courses in shorthand, typing, commercial arithmetic, spelling, civics, bookkeeping, and public speaking; agriculture was taught as a science course. All in all, courses must have been vigorous and geared to students wishing to continue at the University of Texas or to enter the business world.[28]

The college administration comprised the president and a dean, Walter R. Glick, a history teacher. The faculty numbered ten at first and grew to 13 by 1930. It had far fewer Swedish members than did the student body, which had, on average, 75 percent or more Swedish surnames in the school's 26-year history.

There were glee and dramatic clubs and basketball, baseball, and football teams. Women could play tennis, baseball, volleyball, or basketball, although only intramurally.[29] They could also join the booster club, called the W Association, which supported the men's athletic events. The W Association's pithy slogan — "Though our arms may fail you, Wesleyan, our hearts

Dr. O.E. Olander (seated, center), Texas Wesleyan College, 1910's

never shall" — was, according to David Carlson, typical of the school's spirit at the time.[30] The Literary Society was really more of a debate club. They took up current events (the League of Nations, American self-sufficiency) and topical if still controversial ideas (the Theory of Evolution), but no specifically Swedish ones — Texas Wesleyan College was a more Americanized school than its Lutheran counterpart in Round Rock.

Social events were hosted and chaperoned by the president and his wife. One of the strict rules of the college stated that "Permission to girls to go automobile riding is given only occasionally and only when properly chaperoned!"[31]

The location of the school made it very attractive to its giant neighbor, the University of Texas. Largely as a result of that proximity, the land for which the Austin Businessmen's League had paid $6,300 in 1911 was worth more than $135,000 by 1931. O.E. Olander, then president emeritus, was still an active participant in the life of Texas Wesleyan, and he recommended that it would be in the best interests of the college to sell the school to the university and use the funds for other purposes. Although the school was breaking even financially, it was meeting stiff competition from other, non-Swedish Texas Methodist colleges. (The board had already discussed the possibility of a merger with Blinn College of Brenham.) Faced with the prospect of increasing competition, small enrollments, and an offer they could hardly refuse, the suggestion to sell was taken up and adopted on May 26, 1931. The agreement with the university was, however, that the college, at no additional cost, would continue to operate for another two years.

By 1935 more than 100 students were enrolled at Texas Wesleyan, with a graduating class of 60 more, even though the college had had its standing downgraded to an academy after a struggle with the Texas Women's College of Fort Worth, which wanted (and got) the name Texas Wesleyan College. Thus, in terms of actual enrollment, Texas Wesleyan, now called Texas Wesleyan Academy, was more "successful" than its Lutheran counterpart, Trinity College.

But by 1936 the generosity of the University of Texas finally came to an end. The academy had operated for an additional five years instead of the stipulated two, but by May 1936 the building and land were needed. An action on June 22 dispersed the school's furniture and fixtures. The educational history of Texas Wesleyan College/Academy was thereby ended.

Some of the remaining funds from the sale of the college were put into a scholarship fund for students of Swedish ancestry. This fund—the most enduring legacy of Texas Wesleyan College—ultimately became the Texas Wesleyan Foundation, which distributed a total of $59,000 in scholarships to more than 340 students before its funds (capital and interest) were exhausted in 1976.

The Academy Music School, operating out of a building on the old college campus, was finally closed in 1956, but the scholarship program continued under the old academy name until it became the Texas Wesleyan Foundation in 1961. An attempt was even made, and funded, to operate a Swedish summer school for six weeks in 1951, but the attempt does not seem to have been repeated.

The foundation, having finally exhausted the funds so arduously garnered over the years, dissolved itself officially in August 1976, after donating the last of the money to the Olander Room of the Memorial United (formerly Central) Methodist Church in downtown Austin, where Olander had served both as pastor and educator.

The final chapter of the story of Texas Wesleyan College/Academy concerns the fate of the main building after its acquisition by the University of Texas in 1936.

The building was renamed "Wesleyan Hall," and its brick façade was given a coat of white paint. For many years it served as an office annex to the growing School of Law to the east of the building. But finally, with the planned expansion of the law school and the proposed new construction, old Wesleyan Hall was condemned to the wrecker's ball. It was demolished in 1978 to the sorrow and consternation of many Swedish Texans. But David C. Carlson, a graduate of Texas Wesleyan College and the longest-serving trustee ever to serve on the board (from 1925 through 1976—an astonishing 51 years!) managed to secure the massive front doors and side panels from the main building before demolition commenced. Mr. Carlson (who was also instrumental in the numerous and often labyrinthine negotiations involving school funds in the 1930's and 1940's) had done more than anyone to preserve the history of this unique experiment in education by and for the Swedish Methodists of Texas.

20

Swedish-Texan Cultural Groups

Texas Swedish Pioneers Association

Toward the close of the 19th century Swedish Texans felt a need to celebrate their success in America by staging a reunion of all the earliest settlers still living. They realized that the unique contributions of Swedes to the Lone Star State specifically, and to Swedish America in general, might well go unrecorded if a central, secular organization to chronicle their collective efforts did not exist. Thus, from the beginning, the Texassvenskarnes Banbrytareförening (Texas Swedish Pioneers) was founded with an eye to the future, to record, recognize, and celebrate the achievements of the hardy pioneer generation.

The first milestone was the 1917 celebration of the 50th anniversary of the first mass immigration to Texas at the end of the Civil War, the 100 men, women, and children who emigrated from Forserum in Jönköpings län via Göteborg, Hull, Liverpool, New York, Galveston, and Houston to Palm Valley in the summer of 1867.[1]

The first actual reunion was held in Manor, in Abrams Park, as early as 1896.[2] For several years afterwards, thanks largely to J.O. Öjerholm and *Texas-Posten*, Midsummer celebrations, including an "old settlers'" reunion, were held in Austin. In 1900, for example, the *Austin Daily Tribune* reported on the

241

huge Midsummer celebration in Hort's Pasture. More than 1,000 people turned out on a warm Saturday night to hear speeches by Governor Sayers and Mayor McCall. The festivities were lit by colorful paper lanterns; a 50-foot *majstång* (Midsummer Pole) was raised; speeches were held in "the Scandinavian [*sic*] and Swedish tongues," and a mighty chorus joined in to sing "Du gamla, du fria," the Swedish national anthem. The party lasted until 2 o'clock on Sunday morning.[3]

But with time, participation — and the number of available participants — diminished. Finally Johannes Swenson of Palm Valley stepped in. The son of Johan i Långåsa was a "67er" himself, and he saw his generation dwindling rapidly. He sought out Anders Palm (a "48er," one of the earliest settlers) and S.A. Lundell of Decker (also one of the 1867 group), and together they formed an informal committee to plan and mount a memorial celebration.

The first was held in Nelson Park in Round Rock on Midsummer Day, 1912, on ground donated to the city by Andrew J. Nelson, an immigrant of 1854. Until 1967, when the installation of the Swedish Log Cabin in Austin's Zilker Park made it a more natural meeting place, the annual "banbrytarmöte" (Pioneer Meeting) was held on or near Midsummer in Round Rock's Swedish park or the Austin Municipal Auditorium.

Later, under the leadership of Johannes Swenson, Anders Palm, and S.A. Lundvall, celebrations became more and more successful, and by the 50th anniversary of the 1867 emigration, a large-scale event, complete with an anniversary booklet written and compiled by August Anderson, was arranged.[4]

It took place between 10 a.m. and 3 p.m. on June 22, 1917, in Nelson Park. The assembled crowd led the parade, singing "Vår Gud är oss en Väldig borg" ("A Mighty Fortress Is Our God"). Later they prayed and listened to the choir of 90 men's voices sing sentimental Swedish songs. Dr. Olander of Wesleyan Academy gave a speech in English; J.O. Öjerholm gave one in Swedish; "The Star-Spangled Banner" was sung; and everyone adjourned for lunch and entertainment by music students from Kimbro and Round Rock. In the afternoon Governor Ferguson gave a speech; Dr. Stamline presented a historical sketch of Swedish migration to Texas; the choirs sang the Swedish and American patriotic songs, and the meeting closed with a general singing of "America."[5]

From 1917 to the present, the Texas Swedish Pioneers have continued to meet annually, either in Round Rock or Austin, to commemorate the first mass migration into Texas. At the first meeting there were still eight living members of the party

John M. Öjerholm (front, center) *and members of the Southern Swedish Song Alliance, Round Rock, June 22, 1917*

of 25 emigrants who had left Barkeryd parish in 1848 and 34 from the 1867 group.

The celebration of the tercentenary of the founding of the New Sweden colony on the Delaware River in 1638 was also the 100th anniversary of S.M. Swenson's arrival in Texas in 1838, and Carl Widén of Austin planned "a big show" for July 9 and 10, 1938. The guest list was headed by Bishop Edward Rohde, the Bishop of Lund, Sweden, who conducted a Swedish Lutheran worship service. Rohde was on a state visit to the U.S. to commemorate the Delaware colony. Other dignitaries — consuls-general, ambassadorial delegates, city and state functionaries — flanked the bishop on the dais. The largest auditorium in Austin at that time — Gregory Gymnasium on the University of Texas campus — held a capacity crowd of nearly 6,000.

The first day began with a series of films from Stockholm and Hollywood depicting life in Sweden. Next morning Bishop Rohde celebrated a solemn Swedish *högmässa*, or morning service, and preached in Swedish — an organ had been installed especially for the event. A meeting in the afternoon recapitulated the high points of the history of the Swedish presence in Texas and the general accomplishments of Swedish Americans in the three centuries following the founding of New Sweden on the Delaware in 1638.

It was the largest assembly ever to gather to celebrate a Swedish-Texan event, and Mr. Widén, the efficient organizer, had every right to glow with pride. Every year since then, the same Midsummer Day celebration has taken place, albeit on a more modest scale.[6]

Two other organizations with purposes similar to those of the Texas Swedish Pioneers Association were founded in 1951.

Texas Swedish Cultural Foundation

The Texas Swedish Cultural Foundation, founded by the first Swedish consul-general in Houston, Gunnar Dryselius, grew out of a desire to help Swedish Texans discover (or rediscover) the land of their forefathers or, occasionally, to help a visiting Swede who wished to pursue research in Texas. Most of the more than 50 scholarships ranging from $500 to $2,000 have been awarded to scholars of all levels, from graduate student to full professor, who planned to work for a year in Sweden.[7]

The foundation itself comprises a number of Swedish-Texan trustees and the honorary Swedish consul in Houston. Usually scholarships are awarded annually, but, in some cases, more than one has been bestowed in a given year.

One of the more tangible efforts of the TSCF has been in funding the work of Ms. Siv Vedung, a Swedish librarian from Uppsala University, who came in 1983 to the University of Texas at Austin. Her job was to undertake a thorough evaluation of the Swante Palm Collection, donated to the university in 1897 and presently housed mainly in the Collections Deposit Library in Austin. The result of her year-long study was a monograph entitled "A Book Collector on the Texas Frontier. Swante Palm and His Swedish Library at The University of Texas at Austin." It is hoped that her recommendation to the university — that the

Palm Collection be reassembled and placed in a worthy environment — will soon be realized. If so, much of the credit will be due to the Texas Swedish Cultural Foundation.

The Linnéas of Texas

The Linnéas of Texas, an organization of women of Swedish heritage, was formed in 1951 to provide for the mutual enrichment of people from Texas and Sweden through education, literature, and art. Their accomplishments are numerous. They have contributed books and periodicals to Rice University, the University of Houston, Baylor College of Medicine, and the University of Texas at Austin. For many years the group's major project was the placing of books in the Houston public schools and city libraries.

Since 1979 their activities have focused on the University of Texas at Austin, where, through their prodigious fund-raising efforts, they have established the Linnéas of Texas Swedish Centennial Endowed Scholarship. Two undergraduate scholarships are awarded each spring to outstanding students enrolled in Scandinavian Studies. That department's growing national reputation owes a great deal to the women who have devoted so much effort every year to endow, and continue to add to, this fund, the first of its kind at the University of Texas.

For almost 40 years the Linnéas have preserved their Swedish heritage in the Houston area by remembering traditional Swedish holidays: they sponsor a Lucia pageant at Christmas and observe Midsummer every June. They have done much to preserve the ties between the Old World and the New, and to pass those traditions on to a new generation.

Gulf Coast Scandinavian Club

Since 1968 the Gulf Coast Scandinavian Club in Texas City has been actively promoting the study and enjoyment of various aspects of Scandinavian culture, such as foods, languages, music, and dancing.

The club was conceived at a Scandinavian Christmas celebration in 1967. Early the next year, under the leadership of Inga-Lisa Calissendorff, nearly 100 recent immigrants organized the educational club. They began publishing a newsletter with activities and news of interest to Gulf Coast Scandinavians.

In addition to their monthly meetings and their classes and lectures, the members celebrate Christmas in the Scandinavian way with lutfisk, *glögg*, roast pork, rice pudding, and the traditional dance around the Christmas tree. They sponsor a smörgåsbord each year and put on a "Bit of Scandinavia Festival" to raise money for a scholarship fund. Between 1968 and 1986 the Gulf Coast Scandinavian Club gave out scholarships in the amount of $15,000 to young people of Scandinavian ancestry.[8]

Gulf Coast Scandinavian Club folk dancers, Texas Folklife Festival, San Antonio, August 1980

Austin Scandinavian Club

The year 1985-1986 marked the sesquicentennial of the Austin Scandinavian Club: the women members commemorate their history as having begun with S.M. Swenson's arrival. In recent years they have become very active in preserving Swedish customs in the state capital—the city with the largest Swedish-American population in the state. They are also responsible for preserving much of the old Swedish-language liturgy in churches in the Central Texas area. During their Jubilee Year Swedish worship services were held in New Sweden, the Austin Evangelical Free Church, Palm Valley, and the old Gethsemane Church in Austin. They have also regularly celebrated Lucia Day in December and, with the Texas Swedish Pioneers, Banbrytaredagen (Pioneer Day) on or near every Midsummer.

Carl XVI Gustav Vasa Lodge (Dallas)

The only Texas lodge of the national fraternal Vasa Order of America was founded in February 1976 to coincide with the visit of its royal namesake, King Carl XVI Gustav, to Texas.

Some newly established Swedish organizations in Texas are the Swedish Club of Houston, a chapter of the Carl XVI Gustav Vasa Lodge in Austin, the Swedish American Chamber of Commerce in Houston, and the San Antonio Scandinavians.

The Swedish Log Cabin in Zilker Park, Austin — In 1965 in Zilker Park Carl T. Widén (longtime president of the Texas Swedish Pioneers Association) reassembled a small, square cabin built of stout, hand-hewn timbers cleverly plastered and neatly fitted together with half-dovetail notching. Acquired at his own expense, with the assistance of the Austin Park Board and the TSPA, the log cabin had first been located near the site of the present Montopoulous Bridge. Widén believed that it had been built by S.M. Swenson as a temporary residence while he was consolidating his land purchases in and around Austin about 1850; there are other versions of the cabin's origins, however, including a statement by Mrs. Carl Gustaf Palm that a Scot named Grumbles built it some time before her husband's family moved in in 1852.

Swenson's uncle Gustaf Palm and his family lived in it while Gustaf worked off his passage at Govalle. (See page 39 for photograph c. 1934.) Later the cabin was dismantled and moved to serve as a washhouse at Palm's city home in Austin at 14th Avenue and San Jacinto and eventually came into the possession of Louis Palm (Gustaf's great-nephew), who once again dismantled the old house and moved it to Round Rock between 1940 and 1947.

Carl Widén found it there and persuaded authorities to erect it in Nelson Park, but in May 1965 the park was to be rebuilt and the cabin was moved again, this time to Austin's Zilker Park. The interior was furnished with authentic pieces from Swedish families in Texas and in Sweden. (See Lena A. Palmquist's "Swedes," *America's Architectural Roots: Ethnic Groups that Built America*, pp. 154-55; David Stanley's "Vernacular Housing in an Immigrant Community— New Sweden, Texas (thesis), p. 61; "Swedish Pioneer Cabin: A Frontier Home of the 1840's" brochure, Texas Swedish Pioneers Association and Austin Parks and Recreation Department.)

248

Afterword

In the years between 1838 and 1918, some 5,000 Swedes left their homeland and immigrated to the plains and cities of Texas. The relatively small number of Swedes in the Lone Star State belied the vigor of the institutions, both religious and secular, which they established and stubbornly maintained for a century or more. Their religious diversity — 60 percent Lutheran, 37 percent Methodist, and a number of Evangelical Free Church, Baptist, and Mission Covenant congregations — could not disguise the fact of their ethnicity: every one of these early churches was built by and for *Swedes*. Their two colleges (Texas Wesleyan College/Academy for the Methodists and Trinity Lutheran College for the Lutherans) were established and maintained, for as long as maintenance was possible, by the Swedish community alone. Their newspapers may have been read in Rock Island, Illinois, or in Lindsborg, Kansas, but they were written by and for the Swedes of Texas. Their celebrations — Pioneer Day in Austin and Round Rock, for example — commemorated their *own* history, their independence, and their pride. Nowhere else could one find a blend of cultures so particularly, uniquely Texan: chili and lutfisk, spareribs and meatballs, iced tea and ostkaka. From Swedish chuck wagons on the Throckmorton ranch to Swedish cotton gins in Williamson County, Swedes adapted to the land and fused their customs with those of the New World around them. In that fusion, much — perhaps most — of what they brought with them from distant farms in Småland was lost. But much remained or at least has left its mark on a modern state where the early pioneers on their endless prairies would not have felt at home. Gradually the influx of new blood ceased, and the old men with their Old World accents and memories passed, one by one, into the shadows.

Now most traces of them have vanished, and they have become almost invisible save to the most dedicated of trackers. All but a handful of their colonies have disappeared, not even a roadside sign to mark the site of the former towns. Most of their country churches have long since vanished, their dwindling congregations either joining larger, urban "American" churches or quietly disbanding altogether.

But they *were* here, these hardy sons and daughters of Sweden, and their grandchildren have seen to it that their culture will be remembered. Only Minnesota has as many historical markers commemorating Swedish-American achievements. Nowhere in America did any group of Swedes as small as that in the Lone Star State ever even conceive of, much less write and publish, such a huge record of their lives and deeds as *Svenskarne i Texas*. And nowhere but Texas did so few try to build so much — and come so close to fulfilling their Texas-size dreams.

Johanna and John Edwin Rolf with their children and friends, New Sweden, 1900's

Notes

Chapter 1

[1] The years Almquist spent in America are best documented in Ruben G. Berg's *C.J.L. Almquist i landsflykten 1851-1866*. This passage is found on pp. 243-45. The unpublished essay in English is with Almquist's posthumous papers, now in the Royal Library in Stockholm.

[2] Ibid., p. 245.

[3] Carl Starkenberg, "Swenson den store" (typescript), p. 43.

[4] Johan Bolin, *En beskrifning öfver Nord-Amerikas Förenta Staterna* (Wexiö [Växjö], 1853), pp. 164-70.

[5] Ibid., p. 166.

Chapter 2

[1] See Lars Ljungmark, *Swedish Exodus*, p. 10. One of the most vexing questions addressed by the Uppsala Migration Project at Uppsala University in the 1960's was just how many Swedes — often mistakenly identified as Finns, Norwegians, or Danes, or not identified at all — actually emigrated. The figure of 1.25 million is now accepted. The massive volumes of the official Swedish investigation of the century of emigration, *Emigrationsutredningen*, have been shown to be consistently too conservative in estimating numbers of emigrants and re-migrants, that is, those who were emigrating for a second and even third time.

[2] Harald Runblom and Hans Norman, eds., *From Sweden to America: A History of the Migration*, provide a detailed demographic look at the whole problem of class representation in the emigration. See pp. 130-33.

[3] In 1988, the 350th Jubilee year since the founding of New Sweden, numerous articles chronicled the colony's short career and ignominious end. Many classic works were also reprinted. A good brief history of the whole era, down to the dawn of the 19th century, remains J.C. Clay, *Annals of the Swedes on the Delaware* (Chicago, 1938).

[4] Ulf Beijbom, *Amerika! Amerika!*, pp. 47-52.

[5] Franklin Scott, *Sweden: The Nation's History*, pp. 367-68.

Chapter 3

[1] Vilhelm Moberg, *The Emigrants* (New York: Warner Books, 1983), pp. 3-20: a detailed description of Småland by one who knew it best.

[2] *Historiskt-geografiskt lexikon öfver Sverige,* vol. I, pp. 139-40.

[3] *Barkeryds kyrka,* p. 6.

[4] Peter Wieselgren, *Ny Smålands beskrifning,* pp. 343-46.

[5] Josef Ryden, *Nässjö under järnvägsepoken,* pp. 33-35.

[6] Carl Martin Rosenquist, "Swedes of Texas" (1945), pp. 16-29; Magnus Mörner, "Swedish Migrants to Texas," pp. 49-73, especially pp. 55-57.

[7] Rosenquist, "Swedes of Texas" (1945), p. 21.

[8] Ibid.

[9] Rosenquist, "Swedes of Texas" (dissertation, 1930), p. 27.

[10] Jean T. Hanneford, "The Cultural Impact of European Settlement in Central Texas in the Nineteenth Century" (thesis), p. 71 and fig. 11, p. 69.

[11] Robert Ostergren, in his dissertation, "Rättvik to Isanti: A Community Transplanted," discusses a larger chain migration from Rättvik in the province of Dalarna, to Isanti County, Minnesota, in the 1880's.

[12] August Palm, 14 years old at the time of his own emigration in 1848, is credited with being the first Swede to raise cotton in Texas as well as the first Swede to build a cotton gin in Williamson County.

Chapter 4

[1] Rosenquist, "Swedes of Texas" (dissertation, 1930), pp. 111-12.

[2] Ibid., p. 115.

[3] See Chapter 3, above, "From Småland to Govalle;" Rosenquist, "Swedes of Texas" (dissertation, 1930), p. 125 and table, p. 126.

[4] Ibid., p. 126.

[5] Ibid., pp. 80-81.

[6] Ibid., p. 89.

[7] Ibid., pp. 79-80.

[8] Ibid., p. 98.

[9] Ibid., p. 94.

[10] Ibid., p. 127.

[11] Ibid., p. 190.

[12] Ibid., p. 196.

[13] Lilly Lorenzen, *Of Swedish Ways,* pp. 197-224.

[14] Folke Hedblom, "Bland bomullsplockare och cowboys i Texas," p. 109.

[15] *Texas-Posten,* January 7, 1982.

[16] *Austin Daily Tribune,* June 25, 1900.

[17] See Chapter 20, "Texas Swedish Pioneers Association," for a detailed account of the 50th anniversary of the Pioneer Days celebration and the centennial of the arrival of S.M. Swenson.

[18] Lena A. Palmquist, *America's Architectural Roots,* pp. 154-55.

[19] Rosenquist, "Swedes of Texas" (dissertation, 1930), p. 145.

[20] Ibid., p. 146.

[21] Palmquist, *America's Architectural Roots,* p. 155; David Stanley, "Vernacular Housing in an Immigrant Community" (thesis), p. 68. This seems confirmed in Linda Lavender, *Dog Trots and Mud Cats,* pp. 38-39. However, Henry Glassie, in *Patterns in the Material Folk Culture of the Eastern United States* (Philadelphia: University of Pennsylvania Press, 1960), pp. 82, 94-95, disagrees.

[22] Annie Branham, *Tales and Trails in the Lone Star Cactus State,* p. 70.

Chapter 5

[1] The material in this chapter is translated from the Bergman letters, collected, edited, and annotated by Otto Robert Landelius in *Amerikabreven* in 1957. See also H. Arnold Barton, *Letters from the Promised Land* (Minneapolis: University of Minnesota Press, 1974).

[2] Landelius, *Amerikabreven,* p. 22.

[3] Ibid., p. 110-11.

[4] Ibid., p. 115.

[5] Ibid., p. 116.

[6] Ibid., pp. 118-20.

[7] Ibid., p. 123.

[8] Ibid., pp. 126-28.

[9] Ibid., p. 139.

[10] Ibid., p. 107.

[11] Ibid., pp. 154-56.

[12] Ibid., p. 169-70.

[13] Ibid., p. 177.

[14] Ibid., pp. 180-82.

[15] Ibid., p. 187.

[16] Ibid., p. 194.

[17] Ibid., pp. 197, 202.

[18] Ernest Severin et al., *Svenskarne i Texas,* vol. I, p. 267.

[19] Landelius, *Amerikabreven,* p. 196.

[20] Ibid., pp. 209, 211.

[21] Ibid., p. 205.

[22] Ibid., p. 25.

Chapter 6

[1] Swenson belonged to the last generation of his family to use the old Scandinavian system of patronymics, still in use today in Iceland. Men simply added "son" to their fathers' Christian names, while women added "dotter." Thus, Sven (or "Swen," as it was more usually spelled a hundred years ago) the son of Israel became Sven Israelsson, and Sven the son of Sven became Sven Svensson.

Swen Magnus Swenson regularized his name in America, but often used the diminutive "Swante" (or "Svante") as did his uncle Swante Palm, who had gone so far as to take a family name instead of the patronymic "Andersson." His several brothers followed suit in Texas, and all became "Palms" eventually. Nils William Olsson seems finally to have sorted out this problem as well as that of the "Swen" vs. "Swante" confusion; see *Swedish Pioneer Historical Quarterly* 13 (January 1962): 19-20.

[2] The material on Swenson and Palm in this and the following chapter is drawn from a number of sources listed in the Bibliography. The facts about Swenson's early career are based on Carl Starkenberg's unpublished biography of Swenson entitled "Swenson den store: Barkerydspojken som blev grundaren av svenskheten i Texas." The manuscript is now in the Archives of Emigrantinstitutet (The House of Emigrants), Växjö, Sweden.

[3] Letter, S.M. Swenson to Baron Carl Nordenskiöld, April 1, 1840, reprinted in Albin Widén, *När svensk-amerika grundades*, pp. 15-17.

[4] Ibid., p. 15.

[5] Ibid., p. 17.

[6] Ibid.

[7] August Anderson, *Hyphenated*, p. 128.

[8] Henry Goddard Leach, "Svante Magnus Swenson," p. 20.

[9] Gail Swenson, "S.M. Swenson and the Development of the S.M.S. Ranches" (thesis), p. 60; Carl Widén's figures for Swenson's land holdings were 100,000 acres: "Texas Swedish Pioneers and the Confederacy," *Swedish Pioneer Historical Quarterly* 12 (1961), p. 101.

[10] G. Swenson, p. 55.

[11] Jeanette Dyer Davis, "*Hyphenated* Refuted" (typescript), p. 2.

[12] Rosenquist, "Swedes of Texas" (dissertation, 1930), p. 13; Otto Landelius, *Swedish Place-Names in North America*, pp. 217-18.

[13] Letter, S.M. Swenson to R.A. Taylor, December 29, 1862. From Swenson-Palm Letterbook.

[14] Leach, "S.M. Swenson," pp. 20-22.

[15] C. Widén, "Texas Swedish Pioneers," p. 104.

[16] Contract between S.M. Swenson and E.M. Renie dated May 5, 1854, and renewed until August 1, 1855. Austin/Travis County Collection, Austin Public Library.

[17] Leach, "Two Eminent Swantes in Texas," p. 35.

[18] Rosenquist, "Swedes of Texas" (dissertation, 1930), p. 18.

[19] C. Widén, "Texas Swedish Pioneers," p. 103.

[20] Contract and letter of April 1, 1861, Swante Palm Papers, Barker Texas History Center Archives, Austin.

[21] Anderson, pp. 202-205; Mary Clark confirms this, *Swenson Saga*, pp. 85-86.

[22] Ibid, p. 63.

[23] Davis, p. 3.

[24] Clark, pp. 83-88.

[25] G. Swenson, p. 61.

[26] Ralph A. Wooster, "Foreigners in the Principal Towns of Ante-Bellum Texas," p. 218.

[27] Clark, p. 90.

[28] Ibid., pp. 82-90.

Chapter 7

[1] See note 1 for Chapter 6.

[2] Severin et al., vol. I, pp. 167-68.

[3] Starkenberg, pp. 29-31. Palm is unequivocally named as the editor of *Calmar-Posten*, not *Barometern*, in Bernhard Lundstedt, *Sveriges periodiska litteratur*, item 583, p. 171.

[4] Ibid., p. 30.

[5] Thomas F. McKinney and Samuel M. Williams formed a partnership in 1834 which became the McKinney Williams and Co. trading firm. It was the largest mercantile establishment in early Texas. The partners personally financed much of the Texas Revolution, functioning, in essence, as the only bank in the republic. Later McKinney and Williams were authorized to issue banknotes and so established the first legal bank in Texas. At the time Swenson contacted them, they had moved to Galveston; ultimately, they came to own nearly one-fifth of that city. Walter Prescott Webb and H. Bailey Carroll, eds., *Handbook of Texas*, vol. 2, p. 118.

[6] Letter, S.M. Swenson to McKinney and Williams, March 1844.

[7] "Mina första steg . . . ," autobiographical sketch, Swante Palm Papers and *A Swedish Miscellany*. The entire manuscript has been translated by L.E. Scott as "A Renaissance Gentleman Arrives in Texas: Swante Palm's Account of His Voyage from Sweden to the Lone Star Republic in 1844," *Swedish-American Historical Quarterly*, July 1983, pp. 178-93.

[8] Ibid., p. 187.

[9] Ibid.

[10] Gullbrandsson's destiny has long been the subject of misunderstanding. The editors of *Svenskarne i Texas*, acting in good faith, recorded the fact that Conrad Gullbrandsson "died shortly after his arrival in Texas and he is probably the first Swede to be buried in the Lone Star State" (p. 178). In fact, Gullbrandsson stayed less than a year in Texas. As Palm wrote to Swenson in 1846, "G. left Texas and took the steamboat up the Mississippi in order to try his luck at business or the like. The fall before we arrived here, he had been sick in Ohio (pronounced "Ohayo") and upon his departure from here, he got sick again. Nevertheless, he travelled nearly 1400 English miles north up that river to a town Cincinnati (in the aforementioned state Ohio), in the neighborhood of which he stayed for a while with a country-dwelling Swede. He had been under a doctor's care in Cincinnati and was better when he left for the country, but soon became sick again at the Swedish residence, where he died on June 6, after a year's visit in the U.S. He was buried in Cincinnati in a nearby cemetery. The remains of this good and hopeful young man now repose far from home, family, and friends." See Nils William Olsson, *Swedish Passenger Arrivals in New York*, p. 60, and also *Swedish Passenger Arrivals in U.S. Ports (except New York)*, p. 92. Olsson was himself also misled for a time, but finally located Palm's letter in the Fredrik Roos Papers at the Barker Texas History Center Archives, Austin (NWO to LES, April 1983).

[11] Rosenquist, "Swedes of Texas" (1945), p. 18.

[12] Letter, S.M. Swenson to Nordenskiöld in A. Widén, p. 17.

[13] Harry Ransom, "Swante Palm and His Books," *American Swedish Historical Museum Yearbook*, 1949, pp. 28-36.

[14] Starkenberg, p. 40.

[15] Poem, "Haf mycken tack, wår kjäre Mr. Palm!" (by Henry Zacharias, 1879). "Ethnic Group" Collection, Railroad and Pioneer Museum, Temple, Texas.

[16] Severin et al., vol. I, p. 169.

[17] Bethany College President C.A. Swensson to Swante Palm, May 25, 1896, Swante Palm Papers, Barker Texas History Center Archives, Austin.

[18] Ibid.

[19] Unfortunately, it did not last long in one easily accessible spot or location, but rather was broken up into various subjects and dispersed throughout the general collection.

Then, in the early 1960's, the long-lost Gethsemane Lutheran volumes — some 2,500 of them — came to the University of Texas on permanent loan to "rejoin" their scattered brethren. At that juncture, an attempt was made to reconstitute the entire Palm collection in one spot. The 3,000 volumes in Swedish or other Scandinavian languages are now housed together in the university's Collections Deposit Library in Austin, while many of the English-language volumes are still part of the main collection. The many bibliographic rarities which Palm collected so assiduously are now part of the Humanities Research Center's rare book collection.

The Gethsemane volumes have also been placed in the Collections Deposit Library, but are not considered part of the Palm Library (i.e., of the 10,000-volume library originally given to the university). They are presently uncataloged and make up the bulk of Palm's rather comprehensive collection of theological writings. A recent study of the Scandinavian portion of the Palm collection by Siv Vedung has reinforced earlier conclusions about his taste, his collecting habits, and his interests. See Alfred Rogers, "Swante Palm" (thesis), p. 20, and Siv Vedung, "A Book Collector on the Texas Frontier" (thesis).

[20] The bust was executed after Palm's death. The university's Alumni Association was the actual sponsor.

[21] "Minnesruna—Swante Palm," *Texas-Posten*, June 29, 1899.

[22] "Notabelt dödsfall," *Svenska-Amerikanaren*, Chicago, July 4, 1899.

Chapter 8

[1] Webb and Carroll, vol. 2, p. 445.

[2] Allan Kastrup, *Swedish Heritage in America*, p. 159.

[3] Nels Hokanson, *Swedish Immigrants in Lincoln's Time*, p. 135.

[4] Olsson, *Arrivals in New York*, p. 59, and *Arrivals in U.S. Ports*, p. 92. August Anderson, *Ett Femtio-års Minne*, p. 3, also lists him among the immigrants of 1848, but this is clearly erroneous.

[5] Hokanson, p. 136.

[6] "Swen Pärson" was Palm's pseudonym, but editor Hasselquist makes it clear that he knew the author to be the same voice of the Texas Swedes who had defended slavery in the August 1855 number of the paper, that is, Swante Palm. *Hemlandet*, July 24, 1866.

[7] Ibid.; Hokanson, p. 135, found von Wolfcrona listed as "Adolph Wolferson" in an unidentified military source.

[8] The material that follows is drawn from Roos af Hjelmsäter's diary, ''Min dagbok från år 1850, när jag för tredje gången lämnade mitt fädernesland," preserved in the file entitled *A Swedish Miscellany*, Barker Texas History Center Archives, Austin. It has been edited and translated by N.W. Olsson as "The Diary of an Early Swede with a Texas Connection," pp. 1-18. See also further notes on Roos by L.E. Scott and Erik Wiken in the same journal, vol. 4 (1984): 123-25.

[9] Letter from "Swen Pärson," *Hemlandet*, August 16, 1866. (The first of Palm's three letters, which had mentioned the fact that Roos af Hjelmsäter was known as Hamilton in Texas, had appeared in *Hemlandet*, August 27, 1857.)

[10] Ibid.

[11] Swante Palm Papers, Barker Texas History Center Archives, Austin.

Chapter 9

[1] Clara Stearns Scarbrough, *Land of Good Water*, pp. 428, 449.

Chapter 10

[1] *Hemlandet*, June 7, 1855.

[2] Ibid., June 14, 1855.

[3] Rosenquist, "Swedes of Texas" (dissertation, 1930), p. 256.

[4] Ibid., p. 255.

[5] Ibid., p. 256.

[6] Ibid., p. 257.

[7] See Folke Hedblom's version, for example, in "Bland bomullsplockare och cowboys i Texas," p. 108.

[8] Scarbrough, p. 171.

[9] Ibid., p. 111.

[10] Mörner, p. 61.

[11] *Texas-Posten*, August 11, 1898.

[12] Webb and Carroll, vol. 1, p. 351.

[13] Helge Nelson, "The Swedish Stock in Texas," p. 302.

[14] This is the story reported by Hasselquist in the introduction to a letter by an anonymous Swede, formerly of Texas, in the June 21, 1865, issue of *Hemlandet*.

[15] Hokanson, pp. 70-71.

[16] Ella Lonn, *Foreigners in the Confederacy*, p. 39.

[17] See Chapter 3.

[18] Carl T. Widén, "Texas Swedish Pioneers," pp. 105-106.

[19] Severin et al., vol. I, p. 339. In the records of Palm Valley Lutheran Church, Nelson's death is described as follows: "died the 18th of May 1866, most cowardly shot to death by farmer Joh. Karlsson in front of his home" (p. 39).

[20] Rufus A. Palm Jr., "The Arrival of the Palms in Texas" (typescript), p. 10.

[21] C. Widén, "Texas Swedish Pioneers," p. 108.

[22] Severin et al., vol. I, p. 327.

[23] Ibid., pp. 179-80; Palm Valley Lutheran Church, Round Rock, *Minutes*, 1874-1944, p. 69. Microfilm in Swenson Swedish Immigration Research Center, Rock Island, Illinois.

[24] Severin et al., vol. I, p. 176.

[25] Ibid., p. 978.

[26] Hokanson, pp. 137, 141.

Chapter 11

[1] Lars Ljungmark, *Den stora invandringen* (Stockholm: Sveriges Radio, 1965), p. 178.

[2] Ljungmark, *Swedish Exodus*, p. 31.

[3] Beijbom, pp. 82-110.

[4] Johannes Swenson, in Severin et al., vol. I, pp. 153-58. (Translated by Carl Widén as "A Journey from Sweden to Texas—90 Years Ago," *Swedish Pioneer Historical Quarterly* 13, pp. 128-35.

[5] Widén's version adds a paragraph extolling the exploits of Texas Swedes.

[6] Nelson, "Swedish Stock," p. 302.

[7] Ibid.

[8] *Daily Austin Republican*, June 14, 1866, p. 3.

[9] Ibid., October 26, 1866, p. 3.

[10] "H.P.J — —n," *Svenska-Amerikanaren*, p. 1.

[11] Ibid.

[12] *Jönköpingsbladet*, December 1, 1868, p. 1.

[13] Ticket Book, Swante Palm Papers. Swante's nephew, August B. Palm, was also an immigrant agent in partnership with cousin Johan in Barkeryd. Palm even had his own recruiter in Sweden, Carl Lundgren, who signed up and led to Austin a party of 150 emigrants from Småland in 1870: being a Palm seemed to imply a predeliction for the job of immigrant agent.

[14] Emigrant poster for American Emigrant Co., Eugene Nelson Papers.

Chapter 12

[1] For a fuller account of the early Swedish Lutheran church in America, see Eric Norelius, *De svenska lutherska församlingarnes . . .* , vol. I, pp. 114-223.

[2] *Protokoll* (Minutes), Congregational Records, Gethsemane Evangelical Lutheran Church, Austin, pp. 2-4 (December 12, 1868).

[3] *Historik* (Historical Sketch), Gethsemane Evangelical Lutheran Church, Austin, p. 3. See also Severin et al., vol. I, p. 48.

[4] *Historik*, p. 3.

[5] Gethsemane *Minnesalbum (40th Anniversary Booklet)*, p. 19.

[6] Gethsemane Dedication Program, p. 4.

[7] Severin et al., vol. I, pp. 53-55.

[8] Ibid., pp. 55-56.

[9] J.A. Stamline, "Mina minnen."

[10] Mrs. Luther G. Lundgren, *A Century on the New Sweden Prairie*, p. 13.

[11] *Texas-Posten*, May 15, 1924.

[12] Lundgren, pp. 37, 38, 51-52.

[13] C.G. Wallenius and E.D. Olson, "A Short History of Swedish Methodism in America," reprinted from Erik G. Westman and E. Gustav Johnson, eds., *The Swedish Element in America*, vols. I-IV.

[14] C.C. Charnquist, *Sjelfbiografiska anteckningar*, pp. 300-302.

[15] Ibid., p. 302.

[16] Memorial United Methodist Church, Austin, Texas, *Forsamlings Historik 1873-1923 [?] (Congregational History)*, p. 2. Microfilm in Swenson Swedish Immigration Research Center, Rock Island, Illinois.

[17] Ibid.

[18] Charnquist, *Sjelfbiografiska . . .* , p. 301.

[19] Ibid., p. 302.

[20] Viktor Witting, *Minnen från mitt lif som sjöman. . .*, pp. 91-98.

[21] Memorial United Methodist, *Forsamlings. . .*, p. 2.

[22] Severin et al., vol. I, pp. 88-90.

[23] Decker United Methodist Church, Program, Marker Dedication, October 21, 1973.

[24] *Swedish Evangelical Free Church of America, Golden Jubilee. Reminiscences . . . 1884-1934*, pp. 27-33.

[25] *Minnesskrift, utg. med anledning af Sv. Evangeliska Frikyrkans i Amerikas 30-års-jubileum*, pp. 6-8.

[26] Ibid., p. 10.

[27] Swedish Evangelical Free Church, p. 181.

[28] Severin et al., vol. I, pp. 117-24; Swedish Evangelical Free Church, pp. 177-87.

[29] Plaque pictured in *Austin American Statesman*, August 9, 1977, p. 11.

[30] Martin A. Lind, ed., *Fiftieth Anniversary Booklet, Kimbro Evangelical Free Church*, p. 3.

[31] Ibid., "Orchestra History."

[32] Ibid.; Gustaf F. Johnson, *Brinnande Hjärtan*, pp. 9-13. Johnson was born in Nässjö, just east of Barkeryd, in 1873 and, at the age of ten, immigrated with his parents to Texas. He was converted to Methodism in Decker in 1891 and began his spectacular career as an evangelist in that denomination. He soon crossed over to become a minister in the Free Church, in which capacity he dedicated the Free Church in Kimbro. Shortly thereafter, he was called to the Free Church in Rockford, Illinois, one of the largest in the country. Having tried Methodism and the Free Church, he then joined the Swedish Mission Covenant Church and ended his career as pastor of the Mission Covenant Tabernacle in Minneapolis, one of the largest in *that* denomination in the whole country. He always had a soft spot in his heart for Texas, site of his (first?) conversion. He died in Minneapolis in 1959.

[33] Severin et al., vol. I, pp. 124-26.

Chapter 13

[1] *Texas Almanac for 1986-1987*, p. 66.

[2] *Texas-Posten*, September 20, 1900.

[3] *Augustana*, October 4, 1900.

[4] Ibid., October 18, 1900.

[5] *Minutes*, Zion Lutheran Church, Galveston, p. 88.

[6] Lutheran Church in America, *Yearbook*, 1986, p. 356.

[7] Severin et al., vol. I, pp. 92-93.

[8] Ibid.

[9] Ibid., vol. II, p. 1132.

[10] Ibid., p. 1134.

[11] Ibid., p. 1135.

Chapter 14

[1] *Texas-Posten*, June 24, 1924; Severin et al., vol. I, pp. 183-84.

[2] Ibid., pp. 274-75.

[3] Plaque, Old Lundberg Bakery, Austin, 1966.

[4] *Austin American Statesman*, March 26, 1876; Old Lundberg Bakery Brochure, Heritage Society of Austin.

[5] List of Families on Swedish Hill, Travis County Collection, Austin Public Library.

[6] Severin et al., vol. I, p. 97.

[7] Ibid., p. 98.

[8] *Svenska metodist-episkopalförsamlingens i Georgetown, Texas, 25-årsfest*, October 28-November 1, 1908, pp. 1-10, 31-40.

[9] Ibid., p. 40; Severin et al., vol. I, p. 487; vol. II, 1179.

[10] Severin et al., vol. I, p. 332.

[11] Ibid.

[12] Everett Lloyd, "The Nelson Brothers of Round Rock," pp. 9-11.

[13] I have listed some of the typical businesses from advertisements placed in the various catalogues of Trinity College, Round Rock, between 1906 and 1922.

[14] Severin et al., vol. II, p. 1032.

[15] Landelius, *Amerikabreven*, pp. 162-63.

[16] Severin et al., vol. II, p. 1038.

[17] Ibid., p. 995.

[18] Landelius, *Amerikabreven*, pp. 169-70.

[19] Ibid., p. 78.

[20] Severin et al., vol. I, p. 77.

[21] Ibid., p. 78.

[22] "I helgedomens tjänst. Altartaflor af Olof Grafström," advertising brochure (Rock Island: Augustana Book Concern), p. 21.

[23] Ibid.

[24] Correspondence, Mrs. E.P. Rodeen to Ms. S. Maurer, April 1984.

[25] Lund Lutheran Church, *Sixtieth Anniversary Booklet*, p. 11-13.

[26] *Texas-Posten*, September 25, 1981.

[27] Lund Lutheran Church, p. 15.

[28] Ibid.

[29] Clark, p. 103.

[30] Gail Swenson, p. 98.

[31] Clark, pp. 17, 131.

[32] Severin et al., vol. II, p. 639.

[33] Ibid.

[34] Clark, p. 134.

[35] Ibid., p. 135.

[36] Ibid., p. 136.

[37] Ibid., p. 172.

[38] Severin et al., vol. II, pp. 682-84.

[39] Bethel Lutheran Church, *Seventeenth Anniversary Booklet*, p. 6.

[40] Ibid., p. 12.

[41] Ibid., p. 13.

[42] Bethel Lutheran Church, *Minutes*, 1906-1965, p. 89. Microfilm in Swenson Swedish Immigration Research Center, Rock Island, Illinois.

[43] Bethel Lutheran Church, *Seventeenth Anniversary Booklet*, pp. 22-23.

[44] Ibid., p. 13.

[45] Clark, p. 149.

[46] Ibid., pp. 185-89.

[47] Ibid., p. 194.

Chapter 15

[1] Otto Landelius, *Swedish Place-Names in North America*, pp. 218-19; Severin et al., vol. II, p. 1043; Rosalie Swenson, "History of Kimbro 1877 to 1980," typescript, p. 1.

[2] B.H. Rupar, "Olivia, A Consolidated History of the Swedish Settlements in Calhoun County, Texas," (n.p., n.d.), pp. 1-5; *Korsbaneret* (1949), pp. 183-84.

[3] Landelius, *Swedish Place-Names*, p. 218; Biographical Introduction to a typescript of Nelson Chester's diary of his years at sea, which corrects a number of Landelius's errors, Swenson Swedish Immigration Research Center, Rock Island, Illinois.

[4] Landelius, *Swedish Place-Names*, p. 220.

[5] Ibid., p. 221.

[6] Ibid.

[7] Ibid., p. 220; Severin et al., vol. II, p. 1162.

[8] Landelius, *Swedish Place-Names*, p. 220.

[9] Ibid.; Severin et al., vol. I, p. 84.

[10] Ibid., pp. 95-97; Evangelical Covenant Church, Stockholm [Lyford], Texas, "Historical Highlights . . ." [1957?]. *Minutes*, 1913-1957. Microfilm in Swenson Swedish Immigration Research Center, Rock Island, Illinois.

[11] Webb and Carroll, vol. I, p. 149, and vol. II, p. 695.

Chapter 16

[1] Folke Hedblom, "Swedish Speech and Popular Traditions in America," p. 137.

[2] Hedblom, "Bland bomullsplockare och cowboys," pp. 101-102.

[3] Folke Hedblom, "Bland smålänningar i Texas och Kansas," *Natio Smolandica* XXIX, p. 32.

[4] Hedblom, "Bland bomullsplockare och cowboys," p. 113.

[5] Carl M. Rosenquist, "Linguistic Changes in the Acculturation of the Swedes of Texas," *Sociology and Social Research* XVI (1931-1932), p. 223.

[6] Sture Ureland, "Report on Texas Swedish Research," *Svenska landsmål och svenskst folkliv* (1971), p. 30.

[7] Ibid., p. 31.

[8] Ibid., p. 30.

[9] Ibid., pp. 42-50, 64.

[10] Rosenquist, "Linguistic Changes," p. 226.

[11] "SVEA Nytt" has appeared semiannually since April 1980.

[12] An example of the new Swedish literature — so different from the largely religious works popular in the heyday of *Texas-Posten* — appeared in the September 1981 number of "SVEA Nytt." It is a short poem by Berit Greechie entitled "Sydstatsommaren 1981" ("Summer in the South, 1981"), which deals with the startling new Texas environment encountered for the first time by a typical northern European. In many ways, Greechie's reactions to the alien fauna of Texas parallel those of her predecessors a hundred years earlier, but they could not take time to put their feelings into verse:

På sommaren i sydstaterna
leker man kurregömma med
kackelackorna
och dansar klapparedanser
med myggen, feta
och fulla av blod.

Mindre små kräk kilar och slinker
omkring utan namn.
Ingen bryr sig om deras
latinska legitimation.
Nej, bara fåglar och svamp
är tillräckligt vackra
för att slå upp i
uppslagsboken.

Periplaneta americana
låter väl fint
och vackra är dom visst
i sina bruna mahoganyfärg
när på kvicka små ben
med nålvassa taggar
dom gör blixtsnabba lopp
uppför väggen.

Myggen dansar i grannens gårdsljus
små, små gråa tussar
i natten.

(In the summer, in the South,
you play hide-and-seek with
the cockroaches
and you dance slapping dances
with mosquitoes, fat
and full of blood.

Smaller creatures scratch and slink
around, nameless.
No one cares about their
Latin identification.
No, only birds and mushrooms
are beautiful enough
to bother looking them up
in the encyclopedia.

Periplaneta americana
certainly sounds grand,
and they are rather elegant
in their brown mahogany color
when, on swift tiny legs
with needle-sharp claws,
they make lightning-quick dashes
up the wall.

The mosquitoes dance in the
neighbor's backyard lights,
small, small gray cotton balls
in the night.)

Chapter 17

[1] Only one issue of this unique newspaper is known to exist, that in the Royal Library in Stockholm. This particular passage is from *Södra Vecko-Posten*'s "profnummer," or trial edition, February 9, 1881.

[2] Viktor Witting, *Minnen från mitt lif som sjöman,*, pp. 91-98.

[3] Ibid., pp. 95-98.

[4] Ibid., p. 93.

[5] *Södra Vecko-Posten*, February 9, 1881.

[6] Ibid.

[7] Ibid., April 14, 1881.

[8] Ibid., May 29, 1881.

[9] Ibid., July 6, 1881.

[10] Witting published these volumes in Austin between October of 1880 and October of 1881.

[11] *Texas-Posten*, June 14, 1981.

[12] Ibid., Fiftieth Anniversary Number, May 30, 1946.

[13] Severin et al., vol. I, pp. 236-37.

[14] *Texas-Posten*, reprint of first editorial of April 1896, Fiftieth Anniversary Number, May 30, 1946.

[15] Severin et al., vol. I, pp. 236-37.

[16] *Texas-Posten*, July 5, 1928.

[17] Ibid., banner after 1949.

[18] T. J. Westerberg, "En hälsning från Chicago," *Texas-Posten*, May 30, 1946.

[19] Lissa Bengtsson, "30," *Texas-Posten*, February 5, 1981.

[20] David Samuelson, *Texas-Posten*, January 14, 1982.

[21] *Texas-Bladet*, Editorial, September 11, 1907.

[22] Ibid., May 18, 1908.

[23] Its existence is documented by Alfred Söderström, *Blixtar på tidnings-horisonten*, p. 43.

[24] *Texas-Posten*, May 30, 1946.

[25] E. Walfred Erickson, *Swedish-American Periodicals*, p. 105. Ernst Skarstedt's *Våra Pennfäktare*, 1897, and *Pennfäktare*, 1930, are invaluable sources for biographies of otherwise obscure Swedish-American writers and journalists.

Chapter 18

[1] Recently, however, two brief pamphlets, both by Charnquist and both printed in Manda, have surfaced at the Garrett Theological Seminary in Evanston, Illinois. See bibliography.

[2] Severin et al., vol. I, p. 272.

[3] The material here summarized has been taken from Wiel-Öjerholm's "Sjelfbiografi" (Autobiography) in *Vildblomster*, pp. 193-214.

[4] "Kan han förgäta?" *Prärieblomman* 4 (1904), pp. 273, 275. In the same issue, J.A. Enander discussed the work of the Texas Relief Committee and Wiel-Öjerholm's contributions, pp. 142-44.

[5] "Vid Mathilde Wiel-Öjerholm's bår," *Vildblomster*, pp. 176-78.

[6] Wiel-Öjerholm, "New York," *Vildblomster*, p. 150.

[7] "Hemlängtan," *Vildblomster*, pp. 79-80.

[8] Severin et al., vol. I, p. 452.

[9] Typescript, Barker Texas History Center Archives, Austin.

[10] August Anderson, *Ett Femtio-års Minne 1867-1917*.

[11] T.C. Richardson, "The Sage of Cedar Bayou," pp. 329-39.

[12] A book-length study of Sjolander's life and work has recently been published: Barbro Persson McCree, *John Sjolander, Poet of Cedar Bayou*.

[13] Barbro Persson McCree, "John Peter Sjolander, Cedar Bayou, Texas," p. 241.

[14] Richardson, p. 331.

[15] *National Encyclopedia of American Biography* (NAB), vol. 13, p. 1390.

[16] Richardson, p. 332.

[17] NAB, vol. 13, p. 1390.

[18] McCree, *John Sjolander, Poet*, p. 247.

[19] John Peter Sjolander, *Salt of the Earth and Sea*, p. 36.

[20] *Svenska Tribunen-Nyheter*, October 15, 1919.

[21] Sjolander, p. 83.

[22] This is Barbro McCree's statement in *John Sjolander, Poet*, p. 60.

[23] Sjolander, p. 96.

Chapter 19

[1] Robert W. Solberg, *Lutheran Higher Education in North America*, pp. 179-80.

[2] Alfred Scott, "Trinity College, Round Rock, Texas," p. 96.

[3] H.C. Alden, "The Evangelical-Lutheran Trinity College of Round Rock, Texas" (thesis), p. 17.

[4] Kansas Conference, Augustana Synod, *Referat* [Summary and Annual Meeting] (Rock Island: Augustana Book Concern, 1904), p. 16.

[5] Alfred Scott, *Trinity College*, p. 100; Alden, p. 25; Severin et al., vol. I, pp. 134 ff.

[6] Ibid., p. 137.

[7] Alden, p. 46; *Texas-Posten*, January 25, 1906.

[8] Trinity College, *Catalogue for 1906*, pp. 3, 16.

[9] Ibid., p. 4.

[10] Ibid., pp. 9-10.

[11] Ibid., p. 11.

[12] Alden, p. 77; *Catalogue*, pp. 11-15.

[13] *Catalogue*, p. 13.

[14] On *Väktaren*, see Alden, p. 101.

[15] *Catalogue for 1910*, p. 6; *Catalogue for 1911*, p. 11.

[16] Alden, p. 98.

[17] *Väktaren*, January 13, 1913, p. 2.

[18] Alden, pp. 107-33.

[19] Ibid., pp. 116-20.

[20] Lutheran Augustana Synod, *Minutes of the Sixth Annual Convention*, Texas Conference, pp. 30-31.

[21] Ibid., pp. 13-14.

[22] *Texas-Posten*, June 13, 1929.

[23] *Texas Inner Mission News*, vol. 2, no. 7, June-July 1931, p. 2.

[24] *Texas-Posten*, June 13, 1929.

[25] Lutheran Augustana Synod, *Minutes*, p. 14.

[26] Texas State Historical Marker, Trinity Lutheran Home, Round Rock, 1972. The text reads as follows:

Trinity Lutheran College

Founded by the Lutheran Augustana Synod in 1904, Synod representatives, seeking a location, selected Round Rock because of the offer of a well, fourteen city lots and freight concessions on building materials hauled by International and Great Northern Railroad. Cornerstone was laid on July 13, 1905, for a three story native stone school building.

With Dr. J.A. Stamline serving as president, first session opened on October 2, 1906. There were four faculty members, 48 academic students, and 11 enrolled in the Music Department. Total enrollment rose to 96 the first year. Successive presidents were Alfred Andersson, 1909-1914; Theodore Seashore 1914-1921; Dr. J.A. Stamline and Oscar Nelson ad interim 1921-1923, and Harry A. Alden, 1923-1929.

Despite such recognition as state accreditation (achieved 1920) the school failed financially. In 1929, it merged with the Evangelical Lutheran College which was founded in 1891 at Brenham, moved to Seguin in 1912, and with this merger became Texas Lutheran College. On the vacated Round Rock campus, the Lutheran Welfare Society on October 9, 1929, opened Trinity Lutheran Home to care for children and aged persons. In 1972, only one of the former college buildings still survives.

[27] Material for this chapter has been freely adapted from David Carlson's excellent history, "Texas Wesleyan College," published in nine weekly installments from September 18 to November 20, 1980, in *Texas-Posten*. Mr. Carlson is a genuine Texas Wesleyan "insider:" he was graduated from the college and served as a member of its board for more than 50 years. He also served on that board's successor, the Texas Wesleyan Foundation, until its dissolution. Other sources for the history of the college include the Texas Wesleyan College Papers, Barker Texas History Center, Austin, and T. J. Westerberg's articles in *Vinterrosor* (1921, pp. 59-63; 1913, pp. 104-13).

[28] Texas Wesleyan College, *Twenty-Fifth Anniversary Yearbook and Catalogue*, Austin, pp. 20-22.

[29] Carlson, *Texas-Posten*, October 9, 1980, p. 18.

[30] Ibid.

[31] Texas Wesleyan College, *Twenty-Fifth Anniversary Yearbook*, p. 16.

Chapter 20

[1] Anderson, *Ett Femtio-års Minne*, pp. 14-15.

[2] Ibid.

[3] *Austin Daily Tribune*, June 25, 1900.

[4] Anderson, *Ett Femtio-års Minne*, p. 15; Severin et al., vol. I, pp. 142-44.

[5] Anderson, *Ett Femtio-års Minne*, "Program," p. 30; *Texas-Posten*, June 28, 1917.

[6] Phil Hewitt, Interview with Carl Widén, July 12, 1977, pp. 16-20.

[7] Van Lindhe, "Texas-Swedish Cultural Foundation," pp. 8, 28.

[8] In the summer of 1986 the folk dancers of the Gulf Coast Scandinavian Club were invited to perform at the *hembygdsgård* (open air museum) in Barkeryd, Småland. They were, in fact, the only folk dancers who performed there on "Texasdagen" (Texas Day). All the dancers wore traditional folk costumes and also performed (with appropriate Texas headgear) several American square dances. The tour was covered by "SVEA Nytt."

Bibliography

Anderson, August [Q-r-]. *Hyphenated: or The Life Story of S.M. Swenson.* Austin: n.p., 1916.

_____, ed. *Ett Femtio-års Minne 1867-1917. Minneskrift för 50-årsminnet af Banbrytarföreningen.* Austin: *Texas-Posten,* 1917.

"Ammälan." *Texas-Posten,* vol. 1, no. 1 (April 18, 1896), Austin.

Augustana Evangelical Lutheran Church. *Minnesskrift med anledning af Augustana-synodens femtioåriga tillvaro.* Rock Island, Ill.: Augustana Book Concern, 1910.

Austin American, March 11, 1915.

Austin American-Statesman, November 30, 1972; June 11 and August 9, 1977.

Austin Daily Tribune, June 25, 1900.

Austin Weekly Statesman, October 22, 1872.

Barclay, Margaret. "Swen M. Swenson, the First Swede in Texas." *The Will to Succeed: Stories of Swedish Pioneers.* New York: Bonniers, 1948.

Barkeryds kyrka. Historik, beskrivning, och Inventarieförteckning. Forserum: Strandbergs tryckeri, 1972.

Beijbom, Ulf. *Amerika! Amerika! En bok om utvandringen.* Stockholm: Natur och kultur, 1977.

Bengtsson, Lissa. "30." *Texas-Posten,* February 5, 1981.

Benson, Adolph, and Naboth Hedin. *Americans from Sweden.* Philadelphia and New York: A.B. Lippincott, 1950.

Berg, Ruben G. *C.J.L. Almquist i landsflykten 1851-1866.* Stockholm: A.B. Bonniers, 1928.

Bethel Lutheran Church [Ericksdahl Community], Avoca, Texas. *Seventieth Anniversary Booklet, 1906-1976.* Avoca: Bethel Lutheran Church Historical Society, 1975.

Bethlehem Evangelical Lutheran Church, Elgin, Texas (Lund). *70th Anniversary History,* 1967.

Bethlehem Lutheran Church, Manor/Lund, Texas. *Sixtieth Anniversary Booklet, 1897-1957.*

Branham, Annie. *Tales and Trails from the Lone Star Cactus State.* New York: Greenwich Book Publishers, 1959.

Capitol Bakery in Austin, advertisement. *Texas-Posten*, May 16, 1907.

Carlson, David C. "Texas Wesleyan College." *Texas Posten*, September 18, 25; October 9, 16, 23, 30; November 6, 13, 20, 1980.

Charnquist, C[arl]. *Bihang Till "Morgonstjernan," En Samling Kärnfriska Evangeliska Sånger, Till Väckelse och Uppbyggelse.* Utgifna af C. Charnquist. Manda, Texas, 1901.

————, ed. and trans. *Den Ljufwa Rösten, En samling af P.P. Bliss, Ira D. Sankeys Evangeliska sånger no. 1 and 2, sjunga wid de Stora Wäckelsemötena hållna af MOODY OCH SANKEY i Europa och Amerika, jemte ett urval sånger af andra författare.* Austin: Eugen von Boedman, 1877.

————, ed. and trans. *Den Ljufwa Rösten, andra samlingen.* Austin: Eugen von Boedman, 1877.

————, *Hvad är sanning? Tvenne frågor Besvarade. 1. Till Tvifvel På Dess Inspiration? 2. Eller komma Sådana Tvifvel Från Annat Håll?* Tillegnad Den Swänska Ungdomen af C. Charnquist. Manda, Texas, 1902.

————, *Minnen och Sjelfbiografiska anteckningar.* Manda, Texas: C.C. och P.H. Charnquist förlag, 1900.

————, *Sjelvbiografiska anteckningar.* Memorial United Methodist Church, Austin. *Minutes 1879-1906.* Microfilm in Swenson Swedish Immigration Research Center, Rock Island, Ill.

Clark, Mary Whately. *The Swenson Saga and the SMS Ranches.* Austin: Jenkins Publishing Co., 1976.

Daily Austin Republican, June 14, 1866; October 26, 1868; December 28, 1870.

Decker United Methodist Church. *Program,* Dedication of Texas Historical Marker, Decker, Texas, October 21, 1973.

Edblom, Carl P. Letter in *Augustana*, May 12, 1892, pp. 298-99.

Enander, J.A. "Svensk-amerikanska insamlingar för nödlidande i norra Sverige [winter of 1902-1903]." *Prärieblomman* 4 (1904): 118-60.

Erickson, E. Walfred. *Swedish-American Periodicals: A Selective and Descriptive Bibliography.* New York: Arno Press, 1979.

Evangelical Free Church. *Minnesskrift utgifva med anledning af svenska evangeliska frikyrkans i Amerika 30-årsjubileum 1914.* Chicago: Holmberg Publishing Co., 1914.

Evans, Mayne. "Sir Swante Palm's Legacy to Texas." *American Scandinavian Review,* Spring 1949, pp. 41-45.

First Lutheran Church, El Campo, Texas. *75th Anniversary Commemorative Booklet.* n.p., n.d.

Flodman, Johnny. ". . . och Texas är Barkeryd." *Svenska Dagbladet,* July 21, 1981.

Frantz, Joe B. *Texas: A Bicentennial History.* New York: W.W. Norton and Co., 1976.

Friend, Lerena. *Sam Houston: The Great Designer.* Austin: University of Texas Press, 1954.

Fritiofsson, Bengt. "Barkeryd är Texas." *Svenska Dagbladet*, July 26, 1981.

Fromen, Ethel. "John Peter Sjolander 1851-1939, 'The Sage of Cedar Bayou.'" *Yearbook of the American Swedish Museum* (1960): 63-66.

Gethsemane Evangelical Lutheran Church, Austin, Texas. *Dedication Program of New Church*, March 1-2, 1963.

Golden Jubilee. Reminiscences of Our Work Under God. Swedish Evangelical Free Church of the U.S.A., 1884-1934. n.p., n.d.

Haterius, C.J.E. Letter in *Augustana*, March 10, 1892, p. 156.

Hagberg, F.L. "Texas Wesleyan College." *Vinterrosor* 23 (1929): 157-59.

Hedberg, Lydia Persson ("Bergslagsmor"). "En Resa till Texas." *Reseminnen från USA*. Skövde: Isakssonska boktryckeri AB, 1925.

Hedblom, Folke. "Bland bomullsplockare och cowboys i Texas." *Svensk-Amerika berättar*. Malmö: Gidlunds, 1982.

———, "Place Names in Immigrant Communities: Concerning the Giving of Swedish Place Names in America." *Swedish Pioneer Historical Quarterly*, October 1972, pp. 246-61.

———, "Svenska personnamn i Amerika. En aktuell forskningsuppgift." *Studia Anthroponymica Scandinavica* (Tidskrift för nordisk personnamnforskning) 2 (1984): 87-105.

———, "Swedish Speech and Popular Tradition in America: A Report from the Uppsala Tape Recording Expedition 1964." *Swedish Pioneer Historical Quarterly*, July 1965, pp. 137-54.

"Hem i Texas! En svensk koloni i Texas." Advertisement for Salina colony in North Texas on Wichita Valley Railroad, F.M. Hamilton, agent. *Augustana*, April 7, 1897, p. 224.

Historiskt-geografiskt lexikon öfver Sverige, vol. I. Stockholm: Johan Beckman, 1859.

Hokanson, Nels. *Swedish Immigrants in Lincoln's Time*. New York and London: Harper and Bros., 1942.

Hutto Evangelical Lutheran Church, Hutto, Texas, 50th and 75th Anniversary Congregational Histories (1952, 1967), 90th Anniversary Memorial Booklet, and Dedication of Memorial Windows (1979).

Johnson, Gustaf F. *Brinnande Hjärtan*. Minneapolis: Veckobladets tryckeri, [1922].

Jönköpingsbladet, November 1868, no. 143, p. 3.

["J-n, H.P."] *Svenska-Amerikanaren*, Chicago, September 4, 1867.

Kastrup, Allan. *The Swedish Heritage in America*. St. Paul, Minn.: Swedish Council of America, 1975.

Kimbro Evangelical Free Church, Kimbro (Elgin) Texas. *Fiftieth Anniversary Booklet*, 1947.

Klint, Alex. "Verser (insändt) författade och sjungna vid frikyrkans tältmöten i Kimbro, Decker, och Brushy, Texas, 1923." *Texas-Posten*, August 16, 1923.

LaFollette, W.T. "Peter Swenson: Oil, Orchards and Idealism." *Scandinavia*, Grand Forks, N.D., May 1924, pp. 14-17.

Landelius, Otto Robert, ed. *Amerikabreven*. Stockholm: Natur och kultur, 1957.

Landelius, Otto. "Texas." *Swedish Place-Names in North America*. Carbondale and Edwardsville: Southern Illinois University Press, 1985.

Lavender, Linda. *Dog Trots and Mud Cats: The Texas Log House*. Denton: North Texas State University, 1979.

Leach, Henry Goddard. "Svante Magnus Swenson." *American Swedish Monthly*, August 1955, pp. 8-9, 20, 22, 29.

_____. "Two Eminent Swantes in Texas." *Yearbook of the American Swedish Museum* (1958): 28-36.

Liljegren, N.M., et al. *Svenska metodismen i Amerika*. Chicago: Svenska M.E. Bokhandels-Föreningens Förlag, 1895.

Lind, Martin A., ed. *Fiftieth Anniversary Booklet*, Kimbro (Texas) Evangelical Free Church, n.d.

Lindhe, Van. "Texas-Swedish Cultural Foundation." *American Swedish Monthly* 46 (February 1952): 8, 28.

Lindquist, Emory. *Bethany in Kansas, The History of a College*. Lindsborg, Kans.: Bethany College, 1975.

Ljungmark, Lars. *Swedish Exodus*. Carbondale, Ill.: Southern Illinois University Press, 1979.

Lloyd, Everett. "The Nelson Brothers of Round Rock." *Swedish-American Trade Journal*, January 1930, pp. 9-11.

Lonn, Ella. *Foreigners in the Confederacy*. Gloucester, Mass.: Peter Smith, 1965.

Lorenzen, Lilly. *Of Swedish Ways*. Minneapolis: Dillon Press, 1964.

Lundgren, Mrs. Luther G. "A Century on the New Sweden Prairie." Elgin: Powell's Printing, 1976.

Lundquist, M.L. *One Family of God, A Brief History of the Texas Conference of the Augustana Lutheran Church*. Rock Island, Ill.: Augustana Book Concern, 1962.

Lundstedt, Bernhard. *Sveriges periodiska litteratur, En bibliografi*, vol. III. Periodisk litteratur tryckt i landsorten 1813-1899. Stockholm: Bokförlaget Rediviva, 1902; facsimile ed. 1967, p. 171, item 583.

Lutherska Texas Skolkonferensen. *Referat*. Trettonde årsmöte [13th annual meeting], 1919.

McCree, Barbro Persson. *John Sjolander. Poet of Cedar Bayou*. Austin: Eakins Press, 1987.

_____. "John Peter Sjolander, Cedar Bayou, Texas." *Swedish-American Historical Quarterly*, October 1985, pp. 239-51.

"Meddelande från Dundee, Texas, 1 Maj 1892." *Augustana*, May 19, 1892, p. 316.

Melin, N.A., ed. *Texas Missionsblad. Månadlig Tidskrift för Evangelisk Luthersk Kyrka och Mission* no. 1, (November 14, 1908); nos. 5-7 (March 19, April

24, May 29, 1909). Austin: Evangelical Lutheran Church and Mission, 1908-1909.

Minnesalbum, utg. med anledning af Sv. Ev. Lutherska Gethsemane församlingen i Austins 40-års fest. Austin, November 5-7, 1915.

Minnesskrift, utg. med anledning af Sv. Evangeliska Frikyrkans i Amerikas 30-års-jubileum. Minneapolis: 1915.

Mörner, Magnus. "The Swedish Migrants to Texas." *Swedish-American Historical Quarterly*, April 1987, pp. 49-74.

Munson, Kay. "The Saga of Some Swedish Texans." *American Swedish Monthly*, October 1962, pp. 10-11.

_____. "Texas Pioneer — Carl T. Widén." *American Swedish Monthly*, April 1961, pp. 32-33.

Nelson, Helge. "Svenskar och svenskbygder i Texas." *Svensk geografisk årsbok för 1939.* Lund: Sydsvenska geografiska sällskapet, 1940.

_____. "The Swedish Stock in Texas." *The Swedes and Swedish Settlements in North America*, vol. 1, Skrifter utfivna av Kungl. Humanistiska Veten-skapssamfundet i Lund, no. 37. Lund: Gleerups, 1943.

New Sweden Lutheran Church, New Sweden, Texas. *Ett minnesalbum 1876-1916.*

Norelius, Eric. *De svenska lutherska församlingarnes och svenskarnes historia i Amerika*, vol. I. Rock Island, Ill.: Augustana Book Concern, 1896-1906.

Öjerholm, J.M. "Den svenska banbrytaredagen i Texas." *Vinterrosor* 23 (1929): 114-18

Olson, Karl A. *By One Spirit.* Chicago: Covenant Press, 1962.

Olsson, Nils William. "The Diary of an Early Swede with a Texas Connec-tion." *Swedish-American Genealogist* 3, no. 1 (March 1983): 1-18.

_____. *Swedish Passenger Arrivals in New York 1820-1850.* Chicago: Swedish Pioneer Historical Society, 1967.

_____. *Swedish Passenger Arrivals in U.S. Ports 1820-1850 (except New York).* St. Paul, Minn.: North Central Publishing Co., 1979.

Owens, James Mulkey. *Travis County in Stone, Bronze and Aluminum.* Austin: Aus-Tex Duplicator, 1972.

Palm, Swante. Letter in *Hemlandet*, August 28, 1855. (Dated Austin, July 9, 1855.) Translated in *Yearbook of the Swedish-American Historical Society* (1923): 67-70.

Palmquist, Lena A. "Swedes." *America's Architectural Roots: Ethnic Groups that Built America.* New York: Preservation Press, 1986.

_____. *Building Traditions Among Swedish Settlers in Rural Minnesota.* Stockholm and Växjö: Nordiska museet and Emigrantinstitutet, 1983.

"Pärson, Swen" [Swante Palm]. *Hemlandet*, August 27, 1857.

_____. "Erinringar om Swenskar i Texas." I. "En Grefwe Posse i Texas." II. "Adolph von Wolfkrona," *Hemlandet*, July 24, 1866, p. 2.

_____. "Erinringar om Swenskar i Texas. III. Johan Fredrik R--- af H--- samt Julius H---." *Hemlandet*, August 19, 1866, pp. 5-6.

273

"Plan of Subdivision of Wolf Point Ranch, situated in Calhoun County, Texas, lately purchased and opened to settlers by Rev. C.J.E. Haterius." *Augustana*, May 19, 1892, p. 320.

Ransom, Harry. "The Booklore of Swante Palm." *Library Chronicle of The University of Texas* IV (Summer 1952): 102-11.

_____, ed. *Notes of a Texas Book Collector, 1859-1899: Selections from the Marginalia of Swante Palm*. Austin: Texas Book Club, 1950 [1953].

_____. "A Renaissance Gentleman in Texas: Notes on the Life and Library of Swante Palm." *Southwestern Historical Quarterly*, January 1950, pp. 225-338.

Richardson, T.C. "The Sage of Cedar Bayou." *Southwestern Historical Quarterly* 48 (July 1944-April 1945): 329-39.

Rosenquist, Carl Martin. "The Swedes of Texas." *American Swedish Historical Museum Yearbook* (1945).

Runblom, Harald, and Hans Norman, eds. *From Sweden to America. A History of the Migration.* Minneapolis and Uppsala: University of Minnesota Press/Acta Universitatis Upsaliensis, 1976.

Runeby, Nils. *Den nya världen och den gamla: Amerikabild och emigrationsuppfattning i Sverige 1820-1860.* Studia Historica Uppsalients XXX. Uppsala: Almkvist and Wiksell, 1969.

Rupar, B.H. *Olivia, A Consolidated history of the Swedish settlements in Calhoun County, Texas.* n.p., n.d.

Ryden, Josef. *Nässjö under järnvägsepoken.* Stockholm: Liber förlag, 1979.

Sanningens och Fridens Baner. Georgetown, Texas, November 1908-1911.

Scarbrough, Clara Stearns. *Land of Good Water: A Williamson County History.* Georgetown: Williamson County Sun Publishers, 1973.

Schön, Anders. "Mathilde Wiel-Öjerholm." *Prärieblomman* 4 (1904): 273, 275.

_____. "Swante Palm." *Prärieblomman* 1 (1900): 181-89.

Scott, Alfred L. "Presidenten för Trinity College i Round Rock." *Texas-Posten*, April 19, 1906.

_____. "Trinity College, Round Rock, Texas." *Korsbaneret. Kristlig Kalender för 1907.* Rock Island, Ill.: Augustana Book Concern, 1908, pp. 95-102.

Scott, Franklin D. *Sweden: The Nation's History.* Minneapolis: University of Minnesota Press, 1977.

Scott, L[arry].E. "En liten Vägvisare." "SVEA Nytt" 2 (September 1981): 6-10.

_____. "Johan Fredrik Roos." *Swedish-American Genealogist* 4 (September 1984): 123-25.

_____, ed. and trans. "The 'Renaissance Gentleman' Arrives in Texas: Swante Palm's Account of His Voyage from Sweden to the Lone Star Republic in 1844." *The Swedish-American Historical Quarterly* (July 1983), pp. 177-93.

Severin, Ernest, publ., Dr. Alf. L. Scott, Pastor T.J. Westerberg, and J.M. Öjerholm, contrib. eds. *Svenskarne i Texas i ord och bild (The Swedes of Texas in Words and Pictures), 1838-1918.* Austin: E.L. Steck, [1919?].

"Sir Swante Palm: An Appreciation and a Plea." *The Alcalde* 21 (February 1933): 106-107.

Sjolander, John Peter. *Salt of the Earth and Sea.* Dallas: P.L. Turner Co., 1928.

Skandinavien. "Lagar och stadgar för brandstodsföreningen *Skandinavien* i Jones County, Texas." Rock Island, Ill.: Augustana Book Concern, 1908.

Skarstedt, Ernst. *Pennfäktare. Svensk-Amerikanska författare och tidningsmän.* [Revised version of *Våra Pennfäktare,* 1897]. Stockholm: Publicistklubben, 1930.

Söderström, Alfred. *Blixtar på tidnings-horisonten.* Warroad, N.Y.: Alfred Söderström, [1910].

Södra Vecko-Posten, Austin, Texas, February 1881 to July 1881.

Solberg, Robert W. *Lutheran Higher Education in North America.* Minneapolis: Augsburg Publishing House, 1985.

Stamline, J.A. "Mina minnen." Fortieth Anniversary Booklet, New Sweden Lutheran Church, New Sweden, Texas, 1916.

_____. "De första skandinaverna i Texas." *Prärieblomman* 3 (1903): 170-80.

Sundbärg, Gustaf, ed. *Emigrationsutredningen.* Supplement XX, *Svenskarna i utlandet.* Stockholm: P.A. Norstedt & söner, 1911. Tables 15 and 16, pp. 115-16.

"SVEA Nytt." Houston, Texas, April 1980-September 1987.

Swedish Evangelical Free Church of the U.S.A. *Golden Jubilee: Reminiscences of Our Work Under God 1884-1934.* n.p., n.d.

Swedish Methodist Episcopal Church in Manda, Texas. *Sändebudet,* October 25, 1910, p. 3.

Swedish Methodist Episcopal Church. *Southern Swedish Mission Conference Official Journal.* Third Annual Session, December 4-7, 1927.

_____. Southern Swedish Mission Conference. *Journal.* Tenth Annual Session, 1921.

Swenson, Johannes. "A Journey from Sweden to Texas — 90 Years Ago." Trans. Carl T. Widén. *Swedish Pioneer Historical Quarterly,* October 1957, pp. 128-35.

Texas Bladet. Elgin, Austin, and Georgetown, Texas, 1900-1909.

Texas Conference, Lutheran Augustana Synod. *Minutes of the Sixth Annual Convention,* March 21-25, 1928. Rock Island, Ill.: Augustana Book Concern, 1928.

Texas Inner Mission News, Round Rock, vol. 2, no. 7 (June/July 1931); no. 8 (September 1931); vol. 3, no. 14 (August/September 1932); no. 17 (February/March 1933); vol. 4, no. 19 (June/July 1933).

Texas-Posten, Austin, April 1896-January 1982.

Texas-Posten, Austin, May 1946 (*Fiftieth Anniversary Number*).

Texas Swedish Pioneers Association. *130th Anniversary Program.* Municipal Auditorium, Austin, Texas, June 23, 1968. Other programs for 1969, 1970, 1971, and 1977.

_____. *Swedish Pioneer Cabin: A Pioneer Home of the 1840's.* Austin: Texas Parks and Recreation Department, 1972 [?].

Texas Wesleyan College. *Yearbook and Catalogue,* 1930-1931. Austin: 1930.

Trinity College. *Catalogue and Announcements for 1906-1931.* Round Rock: 1905-1930.

Ureland, Sture. "Preliminary Report on Texas Swedish Research." *The Nordic Languages and Modern Linguistics,* ed. Hreinn Benediktsson. Reykjavik, 1970, pp. 540-50.

_____. "Report on Texas-Swedish Research." *Svenska landsmål och svenskt folkliv,* 1971, pp. 28-74.

Wallenius, C.G. "Texas Wesleyan College och några ord om dess grund-läggare. *Sändebudet,* September 27, 1928, p. 2.

Webb, Walter Prescott, and H. Bailey Carroll, eds. *The Handbook of Texas,* 2 vols. Austin: Texas State Historical Association, 1952.

West, Eliot. "S.M. Swenson: The Lone Star Swede." *American Swedish Monthly,* September 1966, pp. 26-27.

Westerberg, T.J. "Kyrkoinvigning i Hutto, Tex., söndagen den 28 maj, 1911." *Sändebudet* 50 (June 27, 1911): 9.

_____. "Minnesruna öfver Pastor Carl Charnquist." *Sändebudet* 49 (November 1, 1910): 3.

_____. "Svenska metodismen i Texas." *Vinterrosor* 19 (1921): 59-63.

_____. "Texas Wesleyan College." *Vinterrosor* 11 (1913): 104-13.

Westin, Gunnar, et al., eds. "Witting, Viktor." *Svenska folkrörelser,* vol. II. Stockholm: Lindfors bokförlag AB, 1937.

Wheeler, Kenneth. *To Wear a City's Crown: Beginning of Urban Growth in Texas, 1836-1865.* Cambridge: Harvard University Press, 1968.

Widén, Albin. *När svensk-amerika grundades.* Borås: Vasa Order of Amerika District Lodges nos. 19 and 20 for Northern and Southern Sweden, 1961.

Widén, Carl T. "The Swedes in Texas." *Swedish-American Trade Journal* 18 (July 1924): 180-83.

_____. "Dr. Johan August Udden 1859-1932." *Yearbook of the American Swedish Historical Foundation* (1962): 50-52.

_____. "From Småland to Palm Valley in Texas." *Swedish Pioneer Historical Quarterly,* July 1967, pp. 128-31.

_____. "Swedish Pioneer Mutual Aid Societies in Texas." *Swedish Pioneer Historical Quarterly,* April 1965, pp. 100-103.

_____. "Texas Swedish Pioneers and the Confederacy." *Swedish Pioneer Historical Quarterly,* July 1961, pp. 100-107.

Wiel-Öjerholm, Mathilde. "Hvem är lycklig?" *Prärieblomman. Kalendar för 1902,* pp. 204-206. Rock Island, Ill.: Augustana Book Concern, 1903.

_____. *Vildblomster. Sagor och poem.* Austin: Texas-Postens tryckeri, 1911.

Wieselgren, Peter. *Ny Smålands beskrifning, inskränt till Wexiö stift.* Part III. Wexiö: Kungl. Gymnasii Jubelstipendiefonden och Centrala Nykterhetsföreningen, 1846.

Wiken, Erik. "Johan Fredrik Roos." *Swedish-American Genealogist,* September 1984, pp. 122-23.

Wilson Ranch Nyheter, Austin, September 1913.

Witting, Viktor. *Minnen från mitt lif som sjöman, immigrant och predikant samt en historisk afhandling af Metodismens Uppkomst, Utveckling, Utbredning bland Svenskarne i Amerika och i Sverige från dess början, 1845, till dess organiserande i konferenser, 1876 i Sverige och 1877 i Amerika.* 2nd rev., exp. ed., pp. 91-98. Worcester, Mass.: Burbank, 1904.

_____, ed. *Stilla stunder. Christligt månadsmagasin för härd och hem.* Austin: n.p., 1881.

Wooster, Ralph A. "Foreigners in the Principal Towns of Ante-Bellum Texas." *Southwestern Historical Quarterly,* October 1962, p. 218.

_____. "Wealthy Texans, 1860." *Southwestern Historical Quarterly,* October 1967, p. 178.

"Yorick." "Missnöje med kung drev till emigration." *Svenska Dagbladet,* November 2, 1964.

Zeeck, B. "Tomhänt eksjöbo förste svenske nybyggaren i Texas." *Smålands folkblad,* April 4, 1970.

Ziegler, Jesse. *Waves of the Gulf.* San Antonio: Naylor Co., 1938.

Manuscript Sources

A Swedish Miscellany, 1737-1849. Barker Texas History Center Archives, Austin.

[Johan] Fredrik Roos [af Hjelmsäter], papers, 1826-1874. Barker Texas History Center Archives, Austin.

Swen Magnus Swenson Papers, 1843, 1858-1896. Barker Texas History Center Archives, Austin.

S.M. Swenson to McKinney and Williams (Galveston), March 14, 1839. S.M. Swenson Papers, Barker Texas History Center Archives, Austin.

In the Swante Palm Papers, Barker Texas History Center Archives, Austin:

Letter from Swante Palm to his brothers Anders and Johannes, undated [1846?].

Swante Palm to his parents ["Wördade Föräldrar!"], May 1846.

S.M. Swenson to his brother Johan ("i Långåsa") August 15, 1862 [Austin].

Swante Palm to Col. Allston, October 29, 1864.

"Till C. Gullbrandson och Sv. Palm vid deras afresa från Calmar till New York, af *en wän.*" Anonymous poem ["Dagen är Kommen!"].

C.F. Peterson to Swante Palm, May 15, 1896.

T.E. Nelson Family Papers, 1851-1952. Barker Texas History Center Archives, Austin.

Eugene Nelson Family Papers, 1853-1884. Barker Texas History Center Archives, Austin.

Swenson-Palm Letter Book, 1863-1873. Barker Texas History Center Archives, Austin.

Gethsemane Lutheran Church, Austin. Minutes of organizational meeting (Austin, December 12, 1868), pp. 1-5. (Microfilm in Swenson Swedish Immigration Research Center, Rock Island, Ill.).

"Haf mycken tack, wår kjäre Mr. Palm." Poem signed Henrik Zacharias, 1879. "Ethnic Group" Collection, Railroad and Pioneer Museum Archives, Temple.

Gustaf Berglund to Olof Olsson [President of Augustana College], December 19, 1894. Olsson Papers, Augustana Archives, Rock Island, Ill.

Letter from G.N. Swan to Jakob Bonggren, December 22, 1932. G.N. Swan Papers, Swenson Swedish Immigration Research Center, Augustana College, Rock Island, Ill.

Alden, H.C. "The Evangelical-Lutheran Trinity College of Round Rock, Texas." M.A. thesis, The University of Texas, 1925.

Cogswell, George, and Larry Scott. Captions from 1976 exhibits **Swante Palm and His Library** and **Scandinavians in Texas**. Manuscript. Austin: Barker Texas History Center, 1976.

Davis, Jeanette Dyer. *"Hyphenated* Refuted." Typescript, J.D. Davis Papers, Barker Texas History Center Archives, Austin.

Hanneford, Jean T. "The Cultural Impact of European Settlement in Central Texas in the Nineteenth Century." M.A. thesis, The University of Texas, 1970.

Ostergren, Robert C. "Rättvik to Isanti: A Community Transplanted." Dissertation, University of Minnesota, 1976.

Palm, Rufus A. "The Arrival of the Palms in Texas." Typescript, n.d. Barker Texas History Center, Austin.

Rogers, Alfred E. "Swante Palm: With Notes on the Library of a 19th Century Texas Book Collector." M.A. thesis, The University of Texas at Austin, 1966.

Rosenquist, Carl Martin. "The Swedes of Texas." Dissertation, University of Chicago, 1930.

Stanley, David. "Vernacular Housing in an Immigrant Community—New Sweden, Texas." M.A. thesis, The University of Texas at Austin, 1972.

Starkenberg, Carl. "Swenson den store: Barkerydspojken som blev grundaren av svenskheten i Texas." Typescript. Archives, Emigrantinstitutet, Växjö, Sweden.

Swenson, Gail. *S.M. Swenson and the Development of the S.M.S. Ranches*. M.A. thesis, The University of Texas at Austin, 1960.

Swenson, Rosalie. *History of Kimbro 1877-1980*. Unpublished typescript.

Vedung, Siv. "A Bibliomaniac on the Texas Frontier: Swante Palm and His Swedish Library at The University of Texas at Austin." M.A. thesis, The University of Texas at Austin, 1983.

Letter, Robert B. Wheatley to Henderson Shuffler, July 10, 1968. The University of Texas Institute of Texan Cultures at San Antonio.

Photo Credits

Index

284

Acknowledgments

Neither the originator of this project, Dr. John L. Davis, nor its author had any idea how frustratingly long it would take to bring *The Swedish Texans* to completion. But John and his able successor as Director of Research and Collections at the Institute of Texan Cultures, Dr. James McNutt, have proven paradigms of patience, and I proffer my deepest gratitude. At least one person had to be thanked posthumously—Carl T. Widén, the *nestor* of the Swedes of Texas, who died in 1986 at the age of 101.

To do research on the Swedes of Texas while half a continent away would have been impossible without the resources of the Swenson Swedish Immigration Research Center at Augustana College. To all who aided me—archivist Kermit Westerberg, researcher Vickie Oliver, director and friend Dag Blanck— my thanks go beyond words.

To the staffs of the Royal Library and Museum of Scandinavian Antiquities (Nordiska museet) in Stockholm, who answered questions and performed prodigious feats of research and always within the confines of my limited time, *ett stort tack på avstånd.* And, closer to home, my regards to the kind staff at the Eugene C. Barker Texas History Center Archives.

To all my friends and sources in Swedish Texas—including, but by no means limited to, Keith Olander, (now, like myself, an exile), Carl Gronberg, James Christiansen, Joseph Wilson, my old Swedish-language class at Gethsemane Lutheran Church, and, despite everything, the Scandinavian section of the Department of Germanic Languages at The University of Texas at Austin—thank you for sharing your experiences with me. I only hope I've done them justice.

Finally, to all the individuals and organizations that supported *The Swedish Texans* financially—the Linnéas of Texas,

SVEA of Texas, Gulf Coast Scandinavian Club, Texas Swedish Cultural Foundation, Houston Endowment, Inc.—thanks for *your* patience: I trust you will find it worth the wait.

Larry E. Scott
Rock Island, Illinois
February 12, 1991